Sea-dog Tall T

Copyright © 2020 Paul Whittall

The moral right of Paul Whittall to be identified as the Editor of this work has been asserted in accordance with the Copyright, Designs and Patents Act of 1988.

All rights reserved.

Introduction: Sea-dog Tall Tales

Towards the end of March 2020 the severity the Covid-9 Pandemic was being realised. Lockdowns were starting to happen in many countries affecting many different businesses and leisure activities. Sea Anglers were hit hard in not being allowed to visit their favourite angling locations because of limitations on travel and Charter Boat skippers were in serious trouble as they were ordered to stay 'tied up' in many ports.

Restrictions were eased during the July to October 2020 period with people flooding in to seaside towns and beaches...often far in excess of the usual Summer Visitor numbers. There was a genuine fear from 'locals' that the virus would re-emerge with even greater rapidity once the enormous crowds of people had returned to their own counties and the weather started to change for the worse.

And now, at the end of October 2020, numbers are rapidly escalating and severe restrictions are to be again imposed from early November to December 2020. And who knows what is then going to happen.

As a reaction to the first restrictions back in March, one of the UK's best known Charter Angling Skippers, Mr Roger Bayzand, started writing some of his sea going memoirs on his Facebook page. And, being the sort of energetic and multi-talented man he is, Roger started sending messages to other skippers urging them to do the same.

Roger, retired in Australia, contacted me as one of those who ought to 'get writing' and I in turn turned to Weymouth Charter Skipper and new owner of my old boat *Offshore Rebel*, Jamie Pullin. Jamie is clever on computers and was able to call on the assistance of Weymouth's resident Web-Site Wizard, Mr Dave Gibson for any necessary assistance.

Thus the *Sea-dog Tall Tales* Facebook Page was created with Welsh angler Tyrone Covell revealing that he had an amazingly talented Father-in-Law, sadly now deceased, who painted the most amazing seascapes and ships including the painting of The Lifeboat Crewman that graces the cover of this new book.

Once the *Sea-dog Tall Tales* 'page' was established, invitations to our angling customers and friends were sent out and within two weeks over 1000 people had 'joined' the group. Stories and Tall Tales began to flood in along with some amazing photographs and memories. Many said that the page was providing some much needed Good Cheer and humour during this miserable period when we couldn't go to sea.

I was one of those who submitted stories and was very surprised to read so many very kind comments and requests for a book to be written. I was 'Locked Down' in Phuket in Thailand. It was a pretty draconian lockdown with regular visits to my house by police, medical teams and security guards. I asked one of the policeman what would happen to me, or anyone, if we were caught driving outside of our 'estate' without a valid reason for doing so.

It was explained to me that there were four stages: Firstly a verbal warning would be given, secondly a Fine issued, thirdly a visit to Jail would be incurred and finally I would be shot. He did say this with a grin...but then Thai people do tend to smile quite a lot.

The warning was clear...better to stay in my house and take the opportunity to write a book. This took many hours, mainly because I am so hopeless on a computer and in order for the book to be published a whole lot of time consuming 'Formatting' needed to be undertaken to meet the Publisher's requirements.

But I did it and learned from my many mistakes...so much so that the thought of doing it all again was not so daunting. And I also had a great deal of practical support from an old college friend who I discovered had already written and published 8 novels and was busy working on his ninth! Thanks to Mr Joe Taylor, I was able to fumble my way through the intricacies of meeting the Amazon Publishing requirements and my book *From Army Brat to Seadog* appeared in print.

I wanted right from the start to donate any money that the book made to the RNLI as I know that is an Institution that many of us Seafarers hold dear and are keen to support.

Many *Sea-dog Tall Tales* were sent in and so the idea of collating a number of them into another book seemed a good idea. My thanks to so many of you that have gone out of your way to submit a story or two and given your permission to include them in the book. Many of us are not good on computers. I have just spent a couple of days encouraging one of our contributors who told me it took him nearly five hours to write his short piece because of his fear of computers. Well, I understand that fear and it is all the more creditable that this *Sea-dog* in question stuck at it, describing it as a very stressful few hours constantly fearing he would press the 'wrong key' and lose everything he'd struggled to do. I'm sure many more have been in this situation and so I am very appreciative of how much effort has gone into the stories that have been submitted and now appear in this latest book.

As before, any 'profit' from sales will go to the RNLI and so I urge you all to Google *Amazon* and type in the new book title of **Sea-dog Tall Tales** (same title as the Facebook page) and buy the new book to support each other and the Lifeboat but also to impress your family, friends and loved ones with the fact that you are now in print as an Author!! So, Well Done everyone and I hope many people receive this book as a cheering Christmas Present!

Thank You again, to each of you who has contributed to the book and I look forward to further stories appearing on the *Sea-dog Tall Tales* Facebook page this Autumn and Winter. It has been my great privilege to re-read and edit these stories and I can assure you they have provided me with a very worthwhile activity during what is now my third session of lockdown, this time in an *Alternate State Quarantine* Hotel in Bangkok where we have been allowed outside into the Hotel Garden for a total of just three times for 45 minutes on each occasion in 16 long days!!

Ahhh....to be back out at sea and all this Covid-9 nonsense to go away!

Keep Safe, All.

Paul Whittall (Editor)

About William Coughlan's Cover Painting   by Tyrone Covell

The cover picture of this book Sea-dog Tall Tales is by gifted amateur marine painter, Billy Coughlan. This and other paintings for us to enjoy were submitted by Billy's son-in-law, Tyrone Covell. Sadly, Billy did not live to see the planned Exhibition of his lifetime's work dying just two days before it opened.

Tyrone writes:

Here is one of the many paintings by my late Father-in-Law, William J. Coughlan who specialised in maritime painting. Billy was ex-merchant Navy and a Welsh Guard who travelled all around the world, passing the equator numerous times.

He put so much effort into his paintings and was a self-taught artist. His paintings hang around Newport in various pubs and residential homes. He also had one hanging in the office of the Jamaican Government.

I own two of Billy's paintings of ships, one of which my Grandfather was captured on during the war, and the other of the ship my Great Grandfather went down on and died which was the Countess Evelyn. When they tried to recover the bodies only two were found. One was my Great Grandfather and the other one was a small girl that should never have been on the vessel.
Billy was a very modest man who disliked attention and in his 80th year he finally agreed to having an exhibition of his paintings. Unfortunately during the planning of it, Bill became ill and two days prior to its opening he passed away.

His work can be seen on YouTube if you type in .... 'A brilliant legacy, Newport artist Bill Coughlan' as well as on the Facebook page Sea-dog Tall Tales. He was a man of immense talent indeed and we are honoured that Tyrone has allowed the use of Billy's Lifeboat Man painting for the cover of this collection of tales.

"I know Billy would be delighted that his Lifeboat man painting graces the front cover of the Seadog Tall Tales and I am proud to give permission for it to be so used".
Tyrone Covell

Contributors in First Name Alphabetical Order

FIRST WAVE

Adrian Davies……Trust Your Captain

Andy Smith………..Rhubarb, Rhubard, Rhubard

Austen Rogers…..Sharing Information

Bill Smith……………Recollections

Bob Morrison…….Rescue

Chris Cole………….Don't Eat with Ivan!

Chris Ponsford…..At Sea with Pat Carlin

Cliff Williams Section

Tall Tale 1….My First Crewing Job; Tragedy and a near Escape.

Tall Tale 2….Late Night Rover and Needles Cod

Tall Tale 3…The Rougher the Better for Me

Clive Hodges………..Wrassing with Ivan

Colin Etherington…Remembering Dad

Colin Penny………….G is for George the Seagull

Colin Seales………….England CIPS World Championships

Cully Hussard……….Memories

SECOND WAVE

Dave Godwin

Tall Tale 1…My Old Boat

Tall Tale 2…The Outrageous Cost of Lead

Derek Norman…The Wonders of Whelks

Don Carter……… Skipper Chris Savage

Duncan Mackinnon Section

Tall Tale 1...A Long Trip Home

Tall Tale 2...Keeping a Sharp Look-Out

Tall Tale 3...The Launch of the Triton

The Geordie Dickson Section

Tall Tale 1...First Voyage of Artilleryman I

Tall Tale 2...My First Trip to Guernsey

Tall Tale 3...The Final Trip on Artilleryman 2

Tall Tale 4...Drug Running Part 1

Tall Tale 5...Drug Smuggling Part 2

Tall Tale 6...Facing The Court and Risking Losing Everything

Tall Tale 7...Difficulties of Chartering to the Scilly Isles.

THIRD WAVE

Howard James....Fishing with Skipper Chris Caines

Ian Bagley............One in a Million Drift

James Orpwood...Sundance Adventure

The John Hamer Section

Tall Tale 1...Angling for Fun

Tall Tale 2...The Lessons of Walton Pier

Tall Tale 3...Troublesome Tope

Tall Tale 4...Happier times North of the Border...but no fish

Tall Tale 5...Boat Fishing

Tall Tale 6...The 'Pleasures' of Night Fishing

Tall Tale 7...Another Learning Curve

John Krupa........The Jumper Lure

John Taylor........Memories of Ivan

Les Jones...........A Lesson Learnt

Lyle Stantiford...First Proper Rough Weather Lifeboat Shout

FOURTH WAVE

Malcolm Nightingale...Bassing with Stuart Arnold

Martin Sharp...............Big Game Fishing from a Tanker

The Mick Sands Section

Tall Tale 1 .... Mick's Epic Voyage; The Volunteer

Tall Tale 2...................Preparing Eisvogel

Tall Tale 3...................Azores to France

Nick Crouch...............Toed Off

Nigel McLoughlin......Inkgate and the Things it Taught Me

The Paul Maris Section

Tall Tale 1...Beware the Drop Off

Tall Tale 2...Cod Galore

Tall Tale 3...Maris, you're dead!

Tall Tale 4...Televised Conger Comp.

Tall Tale 5...First Involvement with Game Fishing

Paul Muffett........Bananas

Paul Thompson...Tall Tale 1...An Original Tall Tale

Paul Whittall........The Outstanding Seamanship of Skipper Chris Tett

The Phil Reed Section

Tall Tale 1...Whales and Tigers

Tall Tale 2...A Thresher in the Boat

Tall Tale 3...Alderney; Old and New

FIFTH WAVE

Raymond Crowe.....Wait for the Fat Lady to Sing!

Ric Pitkethly............'Our' Sea Monster

Richard Hinton.........Fishing with Geordie

Robert McQuillan...Stay in the Boat

The Roger Bayzand Section

Tall Tale 1...To Sea at Last

Tall Tale 2...Getting Started as a Charter Skipper

Tall Tale 3...We need a Bigger Boat

Tall Tale 4...Pirates of the Caribbean

Tall Tale 5...Crewing on the Lymington Lifeboat

Tall Tales 6...We need a Tackle Company!

Tall Tales 7...Moving to Australia

SIXTH WAVE

The Scott Belbin Section...Watery Reflections Tall Tales...1 to 8

BE CAREFUL, SEA-DOGS…..THE SEVENTH WAVE

Simon Dando…The Shooting Party

The Stephan Baker Section

Tall Tale 1…Recollections of the famous *Mistress*

Tall Tale 2…Stand-in Crews

Tall Tale 3…Final Thoughts on my Plymouth Trips

Steve Black…..The Sexiest Boat in Weymouth

Steve Harder…Bonwey and the famous Shambles turbot

The Steve Porter Section

Tall Tale 1…Trying to do the Impossible

Tall Tale 2…Tomatoes

Tall Tale 3…A Series of Unfortunate Events

Steve Woodward…The Fraught Delivery Voyage of *Seawolf*

EIGHTH WAVE

Tom Bettle...The Dangers of Bananas On-board

Trevor Small

Tall Tale 1...Boating is Not for Everyone

Tall Tale 2...Heroes

Tyrone Covell...See *Introduction Section* about the Cover Painting

Zac Cairns……..2020 Shark Encounter

FIRST WAVE

Adrian Davies

Trust Your Captain.

Ed. *Adrian is a very well-known local figure in Weymouth. His fossil hunting expeditions are inspirational to many of his Facebook 'followers' and his deep knowledge of the Dorset shoreline unsurpassable. He is also a very keen angler!*

Arms aching after a 20 minutes' fight and this amber jack got crunched by a bull shark just as I was abut to land it. Seeing as I had chartered the boat out of Cancun, Mexico, on my own I wanted to catch the bugger responsible.
The crew and skipper were 'Game On!!'
I'm a man of my word. Tackle, spears, gaffs and slings all of a sudden appeared and I was strapped in the fighting chair.
The fighting gear and leader were immense and within thirty seconds the hefty rod arched over to a point where me and both deck hands had to keep it from snapping over the back of the boat.
Knowing and studying big game fishing for years, I did not struggle too much as long before a trip I worked out to conserve the power and energy needed.
40 minutes into the fight and I had it beat as I was making constant line.
I could see the wire-cable leader emerging from the sea when the skipper came out and had a look over the back of the boat and instructed the hands to cut the line? WTF ?
Hence I'm alive! Trust your captain!

Andy Smith

Rhubarb, Rhubarb, Rhubarb.

Ed. *From Portsmouth and living in Brighton, Andy is an experienced EFSA member and has travelled the world in search of fish.*

This incident happened about twenty years ago when the tope fishing was pretty good out of Langstone Harbour. Having said that the tope could still be pretty finicky and my club, Worthing Deep Sea Anglers, were always looking for the perfect bait and bait presentation. We had been looking forward to the trip for several months and there were long discussions on the best rigs and bait for the job.
One of our members at the time was an England International and had recently won the EFSA European Light Line title. I shall not name him but he does not fish anymore and is now a serious yachtie, I believe. Anyway he told the rest of the club in no uncertain terms that there was only one great bait for tope and that was freshwater eel sections. There was some scepticism amongst the club members but he said, "I will show you".
The day of our trip arrived and it was a beautiful one, flat calm and sunny. Our England International's first words of the day were, "I have got the frozen eel sections and you will see". We got to the mark and anchored up. He brought out his Waitrose carrier bag, not Tescos, Sainsburys or ASDA for him, and carefully laid it on the bench seat. A crowd had gathered as he slowly and carefully unwrapped 2lb of frozen rhubarb! He did a double take and turned the rhubarb over several times before admitting to himself that these were not his beloved eel sections.
The jokes then started. "Do you have to whip it on the hook?"
"Do the tope prefer custard or ice cream with the rhubarb?"

I have never seen our man so quiet and for some reason he never fished with us again. The moral of this story is simple, make sure to check the bait in your freezer before putting it in your cool box!

Austen Rogers

Sharing Information

Ed. *Austen, from Plymouth, is at home on the river as he is at sea being a keen 'all round' angler.*

Good afternoon, gents. Are there any skippers, ex skippers or anglers on here who have heard of/fished at an area/mark called Hurd Deep?
When I lived in Plymouth back in the early 90's I used to hear stories of this place and the huge fish you could find there.
Apparently it was a place that could only be fished when the weather was flat calm and on the smallest of neap tides due to its location and depth.
Even now it has always been in the back of my mind and I always wanted to fish there but the weather was never perfect for such a trip.

Ed. *The Hurd Deep runs NE to SW and starts 7 miles to the NE of Alderney running for approximately 18 miles to the south west. It is believed to be a river valley...hence its V-shaped sides as opposed to U-shaped glacial trough sides. During the Ice-age, 10,000 years ago, someone in Alderney could look northwards across a rocky and ice-strew wilderness and see the water glinting in the river fed from what is now the Pyrenees Mountains. Reaching depths of 180 metres, there are a number of popular wrecks in the 130 metre range which produce pollack and ling, sometimes cod, and conger at anchor. At anchor? Yes...a few of us have anchored here using at least two coils (440 metres) of anchor warp along with an anchor in the 35kg to 40kg range and often with an additional 25 kg weigh to stop the rope 'lifting' in big swells.*

A snippet of interesting information came back to this question from Roger Bayzand currently in Australia.

The Baden (believed to be one of the wrecks regularly fished in the Hurd Deeps to the north of Alderney in 127 metres depth) and Nurnberg were German WW1 warships that had been scuttled at Scapa Flow where the German fleet were being held after surrender. Both were salvaged and used as targets by the Royal Navy to test armour piercing shells, after these tests they were used as target practice until they sunk. I read the RN report of the sinking of the Nurnberg which stated the ships carpenter on the towing vessel stood by with his axe to sever the towline when she eventually floundered!

Bill Smith

Recollections

Ed. *A lifetime sea angler with many memories collected along the way of places, boats, fish and sometimes even a storm!*

Having just read a request for us punters to add to the thread, I decide to give it a try. You may regret that request, Sir! This 'brain dump' starts out up north but eventually features some great Weymouth memories.

I grew up in the North West and began my fishing obsession at about 9 or 10 years old. With a few pals I discovered that we could walk out across the sands and gullies on Formby beach, between Liverpool and Southport, to fish the Formby Channel at low water, armed with an old 6 foot Tank Aerial rod and second hand Scarborough reel. The target was mainly flatties back then with the occasional whiting or codling in winter but my family took a real liking to eating dabs. It was about a mile or so across the sands and I'm sure my parents would have been horrified to discover how many times we managed to escape the quicksand and rapidly filling back gullies just to get that 'one more' cast in before we left. And my dad never really forgave me for 're-engineering' his garden spade with a hacksaw in order to make it more effective for digging up the black lugworm we used for bait.

I eventually saved up enough to buy a 7ft solid glass 'sea' rod from Woolworths and a Penn Seaboy (I think it was called) reel which proved perfect for the overnight sessions on Southport Pier. Those sessions actually resulted in me seeing my first ever rod caught bass……sadly by my mate and not by me though. From then on there was no stepping back.

So, in the 70s, together with three mates, we bought a 17.5ft open fibreglass boat with a cuddy on the front that we teamed up with a 10hp mercury outboard and a trailer. The Mercury was eventually replaced with a 20hp Yamaha. We launched the boat from its trailer through the surf (weather permitting) and had a good few years of enjoyable fishing out into the approaches to both Liverpool and Preston catching some decent fish at times including bass and cod although primarily mackerel, doggies and thornbacks.

We also towed this boat to other locations to fish, with regular trips to Rossall near Blackpool and Trefor on the North Wales Coast. This resulted in a lot more species such as tope and gurnard being added to the list whilst learning more about seamanship in the process. We even towed the boat all the way to Gairloch on the far northwest coast of Scotland where we had an awesome couple of weeks' fishing which included my mate landing a common skate of 80lb which we somehow managed to get on board and attempted weighing before returning it. Amazingly, he was using my old 7ft solid glass rod and a Scarborough reel at the time! And to this day I'm convinced that we caught more than one British Record dab as they were well over 2lb but our scales packed in and we never thought any more about it at the time.

Following this period, unfortunately personal relationships intervened and I pretty much gave up fishing due to a lack of interest in it from the other parties although I did manage to catch a few sharks from a Red Sea beach whilst working in the Middle East for a couple of years.

Relationships all safely out of the way and now living in the South East, I once more got back into fishing in the very early 1990s and was invited to join the High Wycombe Sea Angling Club which is now long since disbanded. The club organised regular charter trips and I had the pleasure of fishing in many different locations with some top class skippers. These included Bob Cox out of Bradwell, Roger Bayzand out of Lymington and a number of top skippers out of Weymouth, first of whom (if I recall correctly) was Lionel Hellier in a solid old wooden boat called Just Mary that chugged along. I recall having to lift the cable for the boat to pass under as we entered and left Portland Harbour on our way to the Bill but maybe my memory is playing tricks. Sorry Roger, but my Lymington memories are very sketchy, other than doing some boat-casting near the Needles and being surprised when a decent looking Blue Shark followed up an unexpectedly hooked gurnard. But I do remember we all thought it was a cracking day.

It was at this time that I had a number of excellent wrecking trips on board *Offshore Rebel II*, resulting in some great catches of pollack, ling, bass and cod plus a few decent conger too.

The summit of those trips on *Offshore Rebel II* was my first ever Alderney trip, which turned out to be an absolute classic, although memory is a bit clouded these days and I unfortunately have no photos to back it up. We started off quite successfully fishing a few wrecks on the way across and we had a plan to try and anchor up on the Hurd's Deep at low tide to try for conger as we were all kitted out with wire line outfits. Amazingly, skipper Paul did manage to get us on anchor there but after only ten minutes or so the flow defeated us so a few drifts had to then suffice instead. But this did result in some awesome ling being brought aboard. I was not long since recovered from having had a spinal fusion at the base of my neck and I had taken my surgical neck collar with me just in case but I do recall having to get it out of the storage and put it on after hauling up some ling doubles from 300+ foot. We then set off for Alderney and what turned into one of the most memorable experiences I have ever had afloat.

Not too long after having got underway, a thunderstorm struck us; one with unbelievable force, the power of the rain alone completely flattening the sea. But unfortunately the lightning took out every electric/electronic device on the boat and in the middle of almost zero visibility! Us punters were all crowding in or very close to the wheelhouse when Paul, with amazing speed, whipped out charts and rules, etc. from previously hidden depths and started to plot our position and route. The visibility didn't improve and we could barely see beyond the bow, so as soon as the lightning stopped some of us tried to act as extra pairs of eyes out on deck. Luckily we neither saw nor heard any other craft. Then, after an hour or so, we came out of the cloud and found ourselves almost perfectly lined up on the approach to Alderney Harbour.

Congratulations, Paul Whittall on what was one of the top pieces of seamanship that I will ever likely be witness to which was made even more special over the years when I have seen and learned so much more about those dangerous waters.

My recall of the rest of that trip is somewhat limited, possibly alcohol induced, but I do recall walking up from the harbour on our arrival and doing some sort of deal for a box of pollack, which gained us all fresh fish and chips on the way. We had some brilliant fishing that week for bass, pollack, cod and ling and we even challenged Paul to a fishing competition whilst drifting in the Alderney Race. No surprise, he beat us all hands down, catching roughly two fish to our combined one. I also remember an interesting day when a local fisherman in his own small boat led us through some interesting narrow rocky channels to what were new locations for Paul and we all had to man the rails looking out for rocks below the surface and yelling out to Paul if we spotted any. I also learned how to feather for launce outside the harbour on that trip, all such great fun.

Unfortunately for some reason since those days in the early 1990s, I have not managed to fish again with Paul (I really must correct this), but have had many quality trips on Peace & Plenty with Tetty, wrecking, bassing and turboting on The Shambles and some more memorable Alderney trips. These were then followed on *Peace and Plenty* with Jamie Pullin also taking us on some top quality trips. I aim to follow this up on *Offshore Rebel IV* now under the ownership Jamie but so far have not managed it for various reasons although we have got a trip booked in August and which may not take place due to the corona virus restrictions at Alderney.

These days my main focus is fly fishing, including salt water fly fishing around the globe for the likes of bonefish, permit, tarpon and GTs... but I won't bore you all any further with that lot.

Hope my ramblings aren't too boring and at least it has helped me pass a couple of hours.

Paul Whittall *Well...that's a very informative and entertaining series of recollections....and, because of that storm episode, it is one I remember very well.*

Bob Morrison

Rescue

Ed. Bob is a man of immense modesty yet enormous experience of the sea as (now retired) Captain of a 43,000 ton, 223 metre Ocean Going Container ship. He is one of those talented anglers that you just know will catch fish when he steps aboard a charter boat...no matter where he is taken or the conditions he fishes in.

Here is a little story and remind sports fishermen just how lucky they are.....here are the bones of a story from far flung places.
I picked up three Central American fishermen cast adrift with no provisions far out to sea in the Pacific and took them to New Zealand for repatriation.
They had been long lining for pelagics off Ecuador and Colombia. On their second night out they were boarded by seven heavily armed pirates and had their two outboards and 15 drums of fuel stolen. They were left adrift with their ice (for storing fish) and little else.
No oars, sails, radio, flares - nothing. There was no organised search for them.

They drifted some 500 miles over a couple of weeks until we spotted them and took them on board. The skiff was left at sea. A nice find for someone one day.....maybe.
Some fishing trip!

This is the official ship's report.

'Attacked by pirates, three South American fishermen were left drifting for two weeks in the Pacific Ocean. They were rescued by the Container Ship *Maersk Batur* in a challenging operation. On June 1, 2015, the three fishermen set out from their hometown of Cabo de San Lorenzo. The trio had done the trip a few times before and their skiff was carrying enough fuel, water and food for the return journey to Malpelo. Two days into their journey, disaster struck. Late in the evening on June 3 the group was attacked by a gang of heavily armed pirates who callously robbed them of both outboard motors and all fuel supplies.
Left with no means to navigate or communicate, it was a hopeless situation as the skiff drifted farther and farther into the vast expanse of the Pacific Ocean. In the days that followed, they tried to ration their limited provisions. They kept fishing and eating their catch but with no rain to replenish their lifesaving water supplies, they knew that time was running out.
12 days had passed since the pirate attack and the skiff had drifted nearly 570 nautical miles in open sea. On June 15, the *Maersk Batur* was just north of the Galapagos Islands, having departed Balboa, Panama two days earlier for its southbound voyage to Auckland. At 11.10 a.m. Captain Robert Morrison received a call from the bridge; the officer on watch had spotted a small boat apparently in difficulty with the crew waving with arms and flags. Fortunately, the officer on the bridge took the time to study the situation closely and, realising that all did not appear well, he initiated an immediate rescue operation. All officers and crew reacted swiftly and efficiently to carry out the delicate and precise manoeuvring required to position the 223 metre vessel safely alongside the small boat. The exhausted men below helped secure their skiff with the ropes and lines thrown to them and after less than an hour they were able to climb up the ladder to safety.
Safely on board the *Maersk Batur*, the exhausted men were grateful to receive a good meal and plenty of rest. They were able to contact their families and give them the good news that they would be returning home safe and sound. When the vessel arrived in Auckland on June 30, local Maersk Line staff were able to meet the three men before their flight back to Ecuador'.

Chris Cole

Don't Eat with Ivan!

Ed. Chris from Southampton lists many of the well-known anglers on the Seadog page as friends going back to the days of the great Roger Bayzand. Chris is an angler with Big Game fishing experience as well as a regular on the Channel Island trips.

I met Ivan in the harbour lights in Alderney one evening and we decided to order the very famous sea food platter to share. This mountain of food duly arrived in the dining room and placed by Rowie on the table between us. Ivan could crack crab claws with one hand while devouring everything else in sight with the other hand; truly impressive! I didn't stand a chance. Only Tim Lambert is close in terms of consumption!
 I was in there with *Smuggler* skipper, Mr Colin Dukes once. Three of us all fancied crab claws for starters he said, "leave it with me." He had a quiet word behind the bar and a while later the BIGGEST clay box I've ever seen was placed (with difficulty) on the table with what looked like the combined day's from all the potters in Braye Harbour that day! But...we finished it all and even I managed to grab some.

Chris Ponsford

At Sea with Pat Carlin

Ed. Chris is a keen sea angler who has fished with many of the South Coast skippers for years and is also an excellent freshwater angler. Among his many talents, Chris is a superb photographer...especially of Steam Trains, a passion he shared with the late, great Chris Caines.

Back when Patrick Carlin had his original offshore 105, myself and members of the Veals Wrecking crew had some epic trips. We would meet at Jeremy Salisbury VMO Fish House in Nailsea the night before and all sleep there, having enjoyed a great social evening before rising very early to drive to Weymouth. We usually got a breakfast at a cafe on the quay before meeting Pat.
 I always remember the smell of the newly fired up diesel engine but we would soon be heading out to fresh smells of the sea and fresh breeze in the air.
 Most would be on deck tackling up in keen anticipation of a great day ahead, myself and Nafe Cox usually in the wheelhouse talking old sea dog talk with Pat, our always affable skipper.
The steam out usually allowed plenty of time to settle down and get into the day. Trips become a blur after all these years and plenty of different faces joined us but sport was usually first class especially for bass which were caught on live sandeels picked up from a store by the Weymouth Pleasure Pier for our drift fishing sessions over the offshore wrecks and in the Portland Race. Days were long but fantastic.
 Lifetime friendships were made and loads of great fish were caught, photos taken and stories told in later years.

The Cliff Williams Section

My first crewing job; tragedy and a near escape.

Ed. *Cliff, from the Isle of Wight, is a man with a great sense of dry humour. He is man who has spent his life close to the sea and a fantastic angler.*

I was lucky enough to grow up near the sea, only about one mile away in Freshwater a village on the Western end of the Isle of Wight. I started fishing at eight years old, firstly from the local piers and shore. From the age of ten, I started going boat fishing out of Yarmouth on the odd mackerel trip and then general bottom fishing, joining Western Wight Angling Club at eleven years old and regularly fishing both boat and shore competitions.

At thirteen years old I was working every Saturday at the local Mac Fisheries in the village. My duties included icing the slabs, bringing the boxes of fish in from the walk-in fridge, serving customers and bleaching the slabs and floors clean each afternoon as we closed. It was handy for bait to go fishing on a Saturday evening or a boat trip on the Sunday along with the wages of about £1.00.

My dad ran a taxi business and was very often dropping or collecting fares from the taxi rank at Yarmouth Quay, often talking to the local charter skippers and harbour staff. He was also a retained firefighter at the local station. One evening he asked me if I still wanted to crew on a charter boat? "Yes," was the immediate answer. I finished at Mac Fisheries on the Saturday evening ready to start my dream job the following Saturday morning at 7.30 sharp.

The boat I would be crewing on was a Mitchell Mark 1 which was brand new and fitted with a Ford Mermaid diesel engine. The boat was owned by a chap called Bob Johnson. He was a former RAF fighter pilot, joining before the start of World War 2 and retiring in the late 1950's. He was very well spoken and still maintained a fine RAF handlebars style moustache. He had asked my dad if I would be interested as he knew I was keen to crew and learn as much as I could.

I was really looking forward to stowing away buffs, re-coiling the anchor rope and catching bait for the anglers. Making the tea and cleaning the boat at the end of the each day would be the down side but all part of the job. I went to bed on the Friday night looking forward to my first day as a crewman. The Saturday morning dawned and I overslept, excellent start for a new job.

My dad had already been taking fares to the ferry. He came home to collect me. He shouted upstairs. I rapidly dressed, grabbed my sandwiches and wet gear and went out of the front door. As we both got into the car, dad's fire bleeper went off. He rightly made the decision that the fire call was more important than me getting to work. From our house to Freshwater fire station was about a mile. We landed on the station forecourt; the dropped kerb was a bit high so the cars bounced to a stop.

There were men jumping out of cars, running up the street and within a minute the fire engine was off up Tennyson Road, blue lights and two tones on. I went into the Watch Room and Derek Smith asked what I was doing there. I explained what had happened and he said once we get a stop message I will take you to the harbour. He then looked at the message from Brigade Control to see what the shout was. The message read, 'Boat explosion. Yarmouth harbour. Persons in water'. We put the VHF radio on so we could hear the radio traffic between the crews and control (highly illegal but every station did it). After a period of time we heard the 'stop message' from Yarmouth Quay; it was: 'Stop for MFV Sea Angler. One boat severely damaged by explosion and fire. One casualty rescued from harbour, transferred to hospital with severe burns'. It then went on to give the equipment used to extinguish the fire.

Within seconds the station phone rang. I turned down the radio knowing this was Control with the official stop message. Derek wrote down the message and then put the details into the station duty

log book. Turning to me he said that we can shut the station doors and take you to Yarmouth. I replied, "I won't be working today. The boat that exploded was the one I was working on."
Even at thirteen years old I could see the relief on his face that I was safe. He promptly phoned my mum to tell her I was at the fire station not Yarmouth.

How did a brand new boat explode? Bob Johnson had moved the boat off its mooring on to the fuel berth; this at the time was on the main quay wall next to the crane. The fuel berth also had a marine engineering workshop attached and a small office. It was run by Robbie Lakeman and his wife, Delphi. They had run the business for a number of years. Delphi ran the fuel pumps while Robbie tinkered in the workshop.

Bob's old boat was fitted with a petrol engine. The new Mitchell was fitted with a diesel engine. Delphi had passed Bob the 4 star petrol pump nozzle, as she would have done for many years, not the diesel nozzle. He didn't realise the error. Unfortunately he had also lost his sense of smell during his time in the RAF so couldn't smell the petrol. He filled the tank almost to the top, refitted the filler cap and paid for the fuel. He went back on board and turned the ignition to start the engine. The boat exploded and the force of the explosion blew him out of the boat across the harbour. He and his clothes were on fire. Passers-by and harbour staff rescued him from the water. *Sea Angler* was moved along the quay wall away from the fuel berth.

Any boat fitted with an inboard petrol engine will have a fuel tank vent pipe that vents to the outside atmosphere. At the time an inboard diesel engine fuel tank vent pipe could vent into the boat's bilges as it was not considered an explosive mixture. The fumes from the incorrect fuel filled the bilges with highly explosive petrol fumes, and when the key was turned in the ignition, a spark ignited the high volume of fumes and resulted in a major explosion.

Within a year Bob Johnson was running *Sea Angler* which had been repaired. He was still recovering from the severe burns. Many people said at the time he never fully recovered. He ran *Sea Angler* for a few more years and sold it to Derek Toms, another Yarmouth charter skipper.

After my failed first attempt, I started crewing for Trevor Haward on his boat *Telstar* later the same year. It was hard work and great fun. I learnt a lot about boats, angling and people.
I also continued to fish on *Telstar* and later *Santa Maria* for many years and can tell some more Sea-Dog tales!

Tall Tale 2

Late Night Rover and Needles Cod

One of the good things about growing up on the Isle of Wight was the amazing shore and boat fishing. It still is a great place to live and the fishing while changing a lot is still excellent.
After leaving school I became an apprentice marine engineer working for a small Company in Yarmouth called West Marine. Unfortunately this was just at the time that VAT was increased on all leisure activities and most of the work we did fell into the leisure category. Work dried up and the Company went under. I was in luck and went on continue my apprenticeship as a motor mechanic with a local garage. At the end of my apprenticeship I was made redundant which was quite common in those days to save paying a full wage. I started doing some contract work in London. I was also repairing my dad's fleet of taxis and minibuses in the workshops behind our house; a bit of spare cash was earned carrying out work on friends' cars.

I regularly fished with Trevor Haward on his charter boat *Telstar* and had done so for many years along with two years crewing from the age of 13. He owned an old Rover P6. It was sat on Yarmouth Quay every day he was out fishing so the salt atmosphere had had its way. This was compounded by the Quay being flooded with sea water when an Atlantic storm combined with big spring tides.

It was the 21st of December when Trevor rang me to say his Rover needed an MOT on the 24th of December. There was a very big BUT coming. He said the rear brake callipers were seized. On a Rover P6 this was a major problem as the callipers worked both the foot and handbrake and were mounted inboard on either side of the differential. Luckily he also had a donor car. He said he would remove the callipers off the donor and rebuild them. We agreed to strip and repair the car on the following evening of the 22nd.

At about 7pm I arrived at Trevor's house to find him rebuilding the first donor calliper. I jacked up the car to be repaired and started trying to undo all the bolts. Everything was seized solid. Luckily we had Plus Gas and WD-40 along with a blow lamp if needed. About 2 hours later everything was stripped. The rear discs were past it so were both callipers. Luckily both callipers and the pair of discs from the donor car were in reasonable condition. With both callipers overhauled, the discs cleaned and lock tabs salvaged we were good to start rebuilding. By 1am we were ready for a road test out to Compton Bay and back. Everything went well. We got back and shut the garage doors.

Trevor said, "I will pick you up at 7.30 in the morning".

" Why?" I asked.

"We are out on a trip,"

he said. Talk about short notice. It was now nearly 2am. I had no gear ready. Bait was all in the deep freeze and no sandwiches or flask were made. I got home, grabbed two x 5lb boxes of squid out of the deep freeze, then sorted out my two rods and reels along with my tackle box. The deep freeze and my gear were in the workshop so I didn't disturb the whole household.

The following morning I was up at 6.30am, made sandwiches and had a flask sorted out plus my wet gear readied. On going outside it was apparent we had a heavy frost. I checked the squid. Both boxes had started to thaw. I chucked them in a bucket and grabbed my gear. At 7.45 Trevor appeared so we loaded and were away. On the boat that day were 3three other anglers, all very experienced and knew how to catch cod.

We left the quay at about 8.30. It was cold with a light mist but the sun was rising. It looked like it was going to be a lovely sunny winter's day. Most of us put boxes of squid on the engine cover before leaving harbour. I checked my box about 20 minutes later but it was frozen solid again. Everyone else had exactly the same results. We had a butane or propane gas bottle for the cooker and a blow lamp attachment on board. With the cooker disconnected and the blow lamp fitted we could gently defrost the squid. No , that didn't work either because it was so cold the gas would not light or if it did it was only for a couple of seconds. Boxes of squid then went into buckets of freezing cold sea water.

We anchored the 13/4 mile gulley South of Scratchells Bay at around 9.30. It was a lovely sunny day and the bait was still near frozen solid. Between 5 of us we had over 45lb of squid and it was basically useless. In the end we used a luke warm kettle of water to get the first box defrosting which was used by us all to start fishing.

It was one of those days that you couldn't believe. From the start we had bites. The first cod was about 22lb and landed within 25 minutes of us anchoring. As many people will know the Needles Cod Fishery in the 1960's 70's and 80's was renowned for its large average size of fish, not so much for its numbers, with the average size was probably between 18 and 22lbs. You were considered unlucky to catch one below 15lbs at that time.

We fished for about 4.5 to 5 hours. We would have fished longer but ran out of bait. We had used roughly 10lb of squid per hour, or 2lbs per angler an hour. The net result was 27 Cod between five of us, the smallest about 16lbs and the biggest just over 26lbs. I caught six cod between 17 and 24lbs and had four whiting between 3 lb and 4lbs each as well. Trevor managed seven cod including the largest and smallest of the day. Along with the other 14 cod we also caught five congers up to 50lbs, a pollack of 14lbs and some good size whiting between 2.5lbs and 4.5lbs and we didn't see a single dogfish or pout all day. We did though have 2two anglers dragged from the cabin down to the stern by large "unstoppable" fish. Both Trevor Haward and George Bernowicz were top class anglers and in their opinion the bites were from a cod. I saw George's bite. It was without doubt a "Cod" style bite. He gave the fish line twice in between good bites but the fish then just swam off dragging George down the deck while he was trying to reset the drag.

By 3pm we were pulling anchor. As soon as we were motoring in, Trevor asked me to take the helm while he cleaned his fish. Less than 10 minutes later he was sound asleep in the corner between the wheel house and anchor rope locker. We woke him up as we passed Fort Victoria about 10 minutes from Yarmouth.

He asked, "Did I doze off??"

We unloaded on the quay and put the boat on the mooring. There were quite a few people on the quay wall many enjoying the winter sun and also commenting on the number of cod. One big mouthed man - who judging by the accent been born near the sound of Bow Bells - insisted five of us hadn't caught this amount of fish; we must have had an f---ing net!

To this day it remains my best Cod fishing trip off of the Needles. During the 1981/82 Cod Season I caught 38 Cod from the Needles area. *Telstar* had over 780 in the same season and the biggest caught was 40lbs+. All the cod would have been caught bottom fishing at anchor, many in strong tides with anglers using all-roller rods, narrow spooled reels like the Penn Super Mariner and wire line with up to 2lbs of lead.

And...on Christmas Eve the Rover passed its MOT!

Tall Tale 3
The Rougher the Better for Me!

I remember fishing the Weymouth two day Species Hunt Competition one year. The first day had seen reasonable sea and weather. Myself and a few others from the Isle of Wight stayed at one of the caravan sites at the top of Weymouth Bay. On Day Two, we woke up to a howling South to South East gale and torrential rain. Driving down into Weymouth we could regularly see big waves crashing over the harbour wall and water going 20 to 30 feet high. We all walked into the *Sailors Return* for breakfast. Andrew Selby and Chris Caines were sat talking. We asked where we would be fishing today and the answer was Portland Harbour.

The common reaction was, "You're having a f--king laugh."

"Why?" was the question from both Andy and Chris.

We explained about the waves breaking over the harbour walls but they were both convinced we were over exaggerating the conditions.

Everybody went to their boats and the skippers prepared to leave the moorings. I was on *Tiger Lily* the Offshore 105 owned by Chris Caines. As we left the mooring, he asked me into the cabin.

He said, "Is it really that bad?"

I said, "Yes!"

Chris winked and said that he'd hang back and let someone else be a guinea pig.

Pat Carlin had just left his mooring and his boat *Cara Cara* was bigger than the 105. He went down the harbour towards the entrance. As both boats got towards the Nothe Fort we could all see waves breaking over the harbour wall and Chris straight away decided to turn around.

He said, "F--k that; we will fish on the mooring!"

Pat couldn't safely turn Cara Cara around in the entrance so he was forced to go out of the harbour to get enough room to manoeuvre. Alan Bravery commented later it was the first time in about 50 years of fishing he had been scared on a boat.

We all went back to the moorings and tied up, there was then a skippers' meeting to agree rules and times for a competition. On *Tiger Lily* the boat draw went ahead. I had position 8 up under the cabin port side with the boat moored facing up the harbour which was good in two ways as there was plenty of room to cast about and the cabin roof gave me a bit of protection from the driving rain. I also remember Andy Smith, Billy Short, Dick Barnes and Neil Powdrill being on board, I think we started fishing at 9am, fishing to the same rules but we would be stopping fishing at 2pm or 3pm. At the start, I cast as far as I could up the harbour. I was using a Conoflex Sensortip rod and a small Daiwa fixed spool reel. Within seconds the rod was bouncing. I finished baiting up my spare trace, I picked up my rod and lifted into the weight, all hell broke loose. I asked Chris Caines for the net and he came out with a little prawn net and asked if it was big enough.

Billy said, "I don't think so looking at his rod. We need the proper net," which caused a serious problem as it was still down below and buried by spare gear. Both Chris and his crewman were trying to untangle the net from spare rods etc. The net finally appeared and Chris netted a treble shot of bass for me.

Billy was really impressed. His comment was, "For f--k 's sake, Cliff".

The bass were not huge but two were well in size and a schoolie. This was a great start and around 40 points on the board. From then on, I caught fish regularly including more bass, pollack, ballan and corkwing wrasse, gobies, blennies, small pout and pin whiting.

Billy Short at position 7 and Dick Barnes at position 6 were also catching fish but positions 1, 2, and 3 were hampered very badly because of the quay wall. At around midday, I reeled in some more whiting and called them for Chris to mark down. He informed me that was my 10th whiting!

There was a loud comment from either Andy or Neil, "I f--king hate you, number 8."

About 20 minutes later Billy said he had nearly run out of ragworm. I replied there was another 2lb in the back of my van and did he want some?

"Yes," was the quick reply. I asked Chris if it was ok to go ashore for some ragworm and he confirmed it was OK. I made a quick dash up to the van and was back with about 3/4lb of good quality Isle of Wight ragworm. Billy was now smiling for probably the first time that day, then caught a good number of fish on his free worms. A bit later a local boatmen came down the quay selling live fresh prawns.

Chris asked if we wanted some and yes was the answer from nearly everyone.

A quick change of trace and a few casts later, bass number 10 came over the gunwale for me. We finished fishing and the score sheet was added up. I had won the boat by a reasonable margin. Again Mr Smith or Mr Powdrill shouted out, "I still f--king hate you, number 8".

To this day it is the only competition I have fished all day on the boat mooring. It's also the only one where I have been ashore to get bait or had someone walking along selling bait.

It will be interesting to see how the two Andys and Billy remember the day.

Andy Smith. *I remember it well! I have tried to erase it from my memory but failed miserably.*

Clive Hodges.

Wrassing with Ivan

Ed. *An experienced and enthusiastic freshwater angler, just having achieved a PB 10lb 9oz zander, Clive from Bognor Regis is just as much at home fishing from boats for bass, wrasse as he is from the shore describing himself as a 'Big Bait and Wait' Autumn angler.*

Ivan was the 'go-to-skipper' for the *Really Wrecked Club*'s annual wrasse fishing trip. He would take great pleasure in showing us how to 'prepare' the big hardbacks that were used. After two years of enduring sore hands for a couple of weeks after those trips some of us started to use gloves to protect our delicate pinkies. Those of us that did got enormous stick from the big man but were smug b*st*rds at the end of the trip compared to the others.
 Our club's best ballan wrasse weighed in at an impressive 7lb 12oz and was returned by Stevie Newham. We tried to estimate the number of ballans caught on those trips and we reckon they averaged 4lb to 5lb on each trip

Colin Etherington

Remembering Dad

Ed. *Colin, Freshwater Angling Magazine contributor and author, recalls a poignant moment.*

I found this in my late father's loft. It was old and shabby but I decided to have it reframed. It's the story of his 19lb 2oz personal best cod caught off the beach at Newhaven in very rough conditions in 1972. The picture hung for years in the fishing tackle shop where my father had bought his tackle. I'm aged four in the picture stood alongside him and I still have his Sea Streak reels … such fond memories of an awesome angler!
 RIP and God Rest Your Soul x

Colin Penny

G is for George the Sea-gull.

Ed.   *Colin has been skippering the Flamer series of Weymouth based charter boats for ever. Prior to that he served his apprenticeship as crew to a true Gentleman of the Sea, Sam Flowler, on the original* Flamer. *Colin, a staunch supporter and fund raiser for the RNLI throughout his years of chartering, is well known for his Shambles Banks trips and Specimen Hunts.*

G is for George the Sea Gull. For those of you who did not come out on the various *Flamers* that George has frequented, I will tell you the story.
 George first started to visit me on the original *Flamer* in the late 1990's and I gradually enticed him to come and feed out of my hand. When I changed boats to the *Flamer II,* which was a different type of vessel and was yellow and white not black and white like my previous boat, George still came to visit. I joked to the customers that George must be able to read or did he just recognize me?

He still visited when I changed to the *Flamer III* and he would find me in a range of about 4 miles in any direction from Portland.

One particular year another Sea Gull came to visit and this one also fed out of my hand and I named it Georgette. Now I recognized George because he had a distinct walk and his feathers stuck up on the top of his head. Georgette, however, had a dab of yellow paint on her breast.

One particular day I had a bunch of holiday makers on the boat who thought the skipper must have been bonkers as I talked to the two Sea Gulls by name and feed them. Georgette was only around for one Summer. she could have been a girlfriend of George or may have been one of his family? George only came to visit me during the months of March up to and including October. I think he went to live on a Council tip in the winter months. I would feed George a varied diet of mackerel strips and sand eels. If I gave him a squid head he would run away. I also liked to have some fun by throwing him bits of ginger nut biscuits, cheese and curried baked beans which he would catch in his beak and swallow.

George was a visitor on various *Flamers* for 7 years. I remember going off on one of my five day West Country Trips to Dartmouth and when I returned...No George! So I guessed he had died. I am not sure how long Sea Gulls live for.

Anyway about three years later I had a guy who was a Vet on the boat and I told him the story about George which included me feeding him curried baked beans. He informed me that Sea Gulls can only shit and cannot fart.

So did poor old George die of Old age or Natural Gas?

Colin Searles

England CIPS World Championships.

Ed. Anyone fishing next to Colin will soon realise that this is a man who fished at a level way higher than us mere mortals. Representing England for many years, Colin is a superb and highly competitive angler. If you are fishing next to him...keep quiet and observe. You will learn more in an hour of watching him than a lifetime than a lifetime discovering on your own!

One of my best memories and not a million years ago took place in 2014. During the the CIPS World Boat Angling Championships being held out of Weymouth, England against very tough opposition. On day two I was drawn on *Offshore Rebel* along with multi world champions from Italy amongst other super stars. I held my own and even drew blood when necessary but received great mental strength from Mr. Paul Whittall.

After a hint from crewess, Jai, "Colin" check out cabin" I looked forward and saw Mr. Paul holding up an A4 sign saying, "C'mon Colin..... C'mon England!"

This was 'not allowed' but was greatly received...... I will never forget it and we won the gold and were crowned..... World Champions!!

Comments from the adoring crowd.

Horst Schneider, EFSA President.   *Super Heroes !!!!*

Paul Hart, EFSA Superstar.   *Inspirational stuff, . Always a great day out with Mr Whittall. Even when the fishing was slow, the banter was always first class.*

Trevor Hare, lifelong supporter of charter fishing.......*A legend in his own time.*

Paul Whittall, mad skipper. *Yus!!! C'mon, Colin!!! Engerrrland!!!*

Cully Hussard

Memories

Ed's note. *Cully was for many years the crew on Lloyd Saunder's* Saltwind of Dart *based in Dartmouth. Cully, an excellent and enthusiastic angler ever since a young lad has gone on to work on various commercial boats and has forged a great friendship over the years with Clem Carter, skipper of Weymouth based Wild Frontier, as well as retaining a strong bond with the great Lloyd Saunders.*

All these old pictures and stories (referring to the Sea-dog Tall Tales Facebook page) are a great insight for many of us to look back through history and remember some amazing times.
I grew up in a small village in Devon on the River Dart called Dittisham, locally known as Ditsum.
I was sold at a very early age at anything to do with fish.
I started working on a charter boat age 12 called *Saltwind of Dart*. Many of you will know of Lloyd Saunders I'm sure so will realise that I had a good training right from the off.
I first met Clem Carter in 1998, I think. We struck up a great friendship for life from the first time we met and soon I was invited on his first charter boat on a Channel Island trip to do a bit of helping out and of course a bit of angling.
That first ever trip was amazing and on the last evening we stayed on a bit longer as was often the way with Clembo as he was as keen as any of us if the fish were biting. It was a perfect flat calm evening and with the sun setting, I caught a massive brill of nearly 11 pound which was my reward that special day!
As time went on, I managed to talk a few of my friends to book once a year, normally springtime to chase flatties.
We had plenty of good laughs and we always caught plenty of fish!

God, it would be lovely to be there now!

SECOND WAVE

Dave Godwin

One Liners and Tall Tales

Ed. *Dave from Southend, ace lead guitarist, shore angler and skipper reveals one of his many one-liners.*

Tall Tale 1

My Old Boat

Whilst making a long trek back up the River Thames one afternoon we passed by the wreck of the SS *Richard Montgomery,* an American Liberty ship built during WWII
As I was accompanied into the wheelhouse by a customer with a "How does that work? What this switch for?" and other landlubberly questions, I brought into play my masterly, one line comment. "That's my old boat."
He took the bait. "What happened?"
"It sunk."
"Was you on it?"
"It didn't get there by itself."
"What did you do?"
"Swam to Kent and called my wife to pick me up."

The story promptly circulated the boat.

Tall Tale 2

The Outrageous Cost of Lead

Whilst fishing out of the wheelhouse one day, I snagged up a cast and snapped off.
After the usual swearing, I tackled up and cast back out.
A short while later, I missed a bite and reeled in a bare hook with the weight I had just lost hanging on the hook!
The angler nearest to me was amazed and asked how I did it.
I explained that they cost about £1 each so I wasn't leaving it in the sea.
He swallowed the story and told everybody on the boat.

Derek Norman

The Wonders of Whelks

Ed. *Derek, from Chichester, an experienced wreck and inshore angler and particularly good at catching large cod!*

In these troubled times it can be nice to sit and reminisce.

A funny story just came to mind about one of the most awkward situations you can ever encounter on a small boat. Many years ago when the family was small and money was tight, a friend of mine had a boat which he towed to Lymington to launch. In truth he knew very little about fishing and even less about where to fish but I was so keen to go fishing, I would tag along whenever I could. Speaking to a local on the slipway one day, he advised us to join the local sea angling club so we both signed up with the Lymington Sea Angling club. My friend was also a keen golfer which meant his weekends were taken up chasing a ball of elastic round some fairway or another, thus the opportunities for fishing were quite few and far between. I was reading the club's newsletter one day and saw another member was looking for a reliable person to fish with on his small boat and as luck would have it, he was reasonably local to me. I made contact and we arranged a trip for the following weekend to get to meet each other and to hopefully plunder some monsters from around the famous Needles grounds.

I must confess I was at the time not a very experienced boat angler but I was very keen to learn and really excited about going. I told the wife I was going fishing on Sunday and she said it would be nice if we could perhaps take the little ones to the beach on Saturday. The car was duly loaded with buckets and spades and three excited toddlers and off we headed for Selsey. I will never forget the kids' excitement as we arrived at the seaside or mine when I spotted the fresh seafood stalls. In those days we really didn't have the proverbial pot to piddle in and living some 50 miles inland, seafood was a rarity in the house and to see bags of fresh boiled whelks still in their shells was my idea of heaven. I remember they were a pound a bag and I bought three bags to eat on the beach, not to mention a large tub to eat en-route.

The kids had a great time splashing about and building sandcastles whilst I sat looking at a flat calm sea, and with the aid of a cocktail stick, worked my way through all three bags of whelks. It was like I had died and gone to heaven, to be at the seaside with the family and gorging myself on my favourite seafood, I really couldn't see that life could get much better. As the afternoon wore on my attention turned to the following day's fishing trip and with the kids now clutching an ice cream each that was rapidly melting over them and my car seats, we strapped them in ready for the journey home. I glanced over at the seafood stall and saw the guy was about to close, I suddenly had this urge to buy another couple of bags of whelks to take home and quickly ran over and bought the last two bags he had. I remember the journey home, three happy ice cream covered faces looking back at me in my rear view mirror and my wife with her window open moaning about the smell of the bags of whelks that I kept dibbing into. I must admit, they didn't smell much better that night either and I later found myself sleeping alone as she disappeared downstairs with her duvet to sleep on the couch, uttering something that doubted my parentage as she left the room. I really had overdone it on the whelk front and as I lay in bed trying to sleep, my tummy was churning like a Hotpoint and making noises you would normally only hear in the woods.

The following morning saw me heading down the M3 with the windows open for most of the journey and I remember what a pleasant morning it was driving through the New Forest with the dawn just breaking. I pulled into the car park and saw my new found friend already there removing the carriage straps from the trailer and so after the usual pleasantries we slid the boat from the trailer with no problems and tied it to the pontoon whilst he parked the car etc. I thought this might be a good time to visit the little boy's room as things were still not feeling or sounding good Due South. I spent a good 10 minutes with my thumbs embedded in the side of my head and hoping after which things would settle down soon.

We boarded and untied and headed off down Lymington river towards the Solent. The curlews were singing their sweet tune from the marsh and bird life was everywhere, nature truly is wonderful, particularly this early in the morning before the rest of the world is awake.

The little Orkney chugged on effortlessly and we tackled up the rods before we reached the mouth of the river where my new found buddy then pushed the throttle forward and away we went. The boat was quickly up on the plane and skipping over a rippled surface which created a throbbing feel to the boat which to my horror started to wake up the temporary settled feeling in my stomach. I thought after my earlier visit to the can I was going to be ok but now things were not looking so hopeful as the cramps were starting again and I was beginning to break sweat. So picture the scene, two of us that had only just met, in a 16ft boat hammering up the Solent with the whole day ahead of us, and me now with an upset stomach, busting for a poot!

I said earlier I had not had a great deal of small boat experience at the time and was desperately thinking how was I going to deal with this, when suddenly I had a flash of inspiration, I figured as I was right at the stern, when he goes up the front to lower the anchor, I can quickly lower mine (so to speak) over the stern at the same time and relieve the pressure. I would have to time it well but figured if I could aim and fire as the anchor chain was going noisily through the bow rail, I could relieve the pressure and an embarrassing situation could be averted. I had already undone the top button and zip of my jeans in readiness as he slowed the boat down as we approached our mark, and for what seemed like ages, he fiddled and farted about (excuse the pun) before he was happy we were in exactly the right place.

The sweat was building on my brow and my fingers were in the loops of my waistband as I waited for him to go up the sharp end. Things were almost at that touch and go stage so you can imagine my horror when he dropped the anchor over the side of the boat. What happened to the good old days when skippers dropped the anchor from the bow? What the flip is an Alderney ring anyway? Aaaagh, I couldn't believe it, nature was about to take its course and my only hope of dealing with it without blotting my copybook or my pants for that matter, and my chance of future trips had just been dashed. I had no choice now but to come clean and admit my situation as time was definitely no longer on my side and I had no fingernails left to chew.

I put it as delicately as I could for a stranger on a small boat who was on his first and now most likely his last outing. Would you believe this guy didn't even have a bucket on board! The very best I could do was to go up the bow with a carrier bag and hope for the best, it was at this time I realised I actually needed three hands, one to hang on to the rail and the other two to hold on to the bag! All I can say is the conversation for the rest of the day was a bit strained and my boarding pass was never re-issued!

Don Carter

Skipper Chris Savage

Ed. *Don from Southampton recalls a memory with Chris Savage, brother of Lymington based Arthur Savage, one of the driest skippers ever and a very sad loss to our angling community.*

I remember taking out a guy from the pub on his first ever charter trip with my old mate Chris Savage on *Private Venture*. It was a cod trip to *The Needles*.
 We had all lectured the newcomer on how to fish for cod and how, if he should have a bite, to give it plenty of time, even to the extent of walking away from the rod. We also gave him the spot directly outside Chris' wheelhouse so he could be tutored.
 Chris was leaning against the bulkhead when the guy's rod gave an emphatic thump in time honoured cod style. Despite all the previous help and advice he had received, he immediately yanked the rod high in the air.
 Needless to say the cod had gone. Chris in a way only he could do, put a hand on the guy's shoulder and said, "Well done, Nipper, you saved that bait before he could get it."
 We all fell about laughing out loud.

Don Carter writes about Chris Savage….cutting up bait on his new boat!

Another little Chris Savage memory goes back to when Chris and Arty had just replaced the original steel *Private Venture* with a newly built glass beauty.
Out of the corner of his eye Chris spotted one of our regular crew, John Baddams, filleting fish on his new transom. Casually walking over he asked John what car he was driving. John replied, "It's the red Jaguar, Chris. You know it is".
Chris answered, "Just making sure. I don't want to gut my fish on the wrong bonnet when we land".
A 'Chris cutting comment' at his best; always got the point over.

Slightly more subtle than I suspect brother Arty's response would have been as I suspect that that would have been more along the lines of, "How well can you swim, John?"

Duncan Mackinnon

Tall Tale 1

A Long Trip Home.

Ed. *Duncan from Sunderland, a real traditional small boat lover, shares an experience.*

Well, there are some exciting tales and exotic venues on here! My small offering is thus:

Years ago I used to use a pal's coble, a 20ft Triton with a Kubota 2cylinder inboard engine; so no great speed there. Anyhow, a pal and I left Amble Harbour probably about 7am to catch a bit of the tide to help us on our way to Craster, about 10 miles and a two hour steam for us. By about 6pm we had around 70 fish. There were no monsters in the catch, just the general stamp of fish expected in this location. I said to my pal that it was time to head for home and pointed him in the direction of Coquet Island and told him to head for that and to watch out for boats, salmon nets and all the other propeller ensnaring flotsam we were likely to come across.

I duly set about dealing with the fish, facing the back of the boat. About 1930, I was more or less sorted and knew that we should be in the vicinity of Boulmer Buoy (there was a buoy there then) but I quickly realised something was wrong; very wrong! What I could see was the Island to the west of us, instead of it being to the east of us. The boy had gone badly off course and couldn't explain why. We then had a very long and scary trip back to harbour, although sea conditions were ideal but I was a very unseasoned sailor.

The street lights were on by the time we pulled into Amble Marina. Bear in mind at that time I was navigating with just a compass and a watch with only a radio for company... plus a plethora of life rings and life jackets that I kept noticing!

I found out years later the blighter had gone to sleep at the wheel!!!

Tall Tale 2

Keeping a Sharp Look-Out

Well, since I haven't been hoyed off yet for boring folks, here's another Tall Tale.

Myself and two pals were heading north from Amble yet again...we rarely went south... so I gave them the task of making safe passage northwards with the usual words of warning regarding nets and other boats etc etc. It is worth a mention at this point they are both jolly good talkers. My task was to tidy 'oot the wee cabin after the owner had been out. 'Tidy' was not his middle name, for sure.

I had been down there a canny while, when there's a hefty thud. I pops 'oot of the cabin to find they had run into the Boulmer Buoy which stuck out of the water about 6 foot clear. Suitably chastised, we proceeded onwards once we had had established from inside there was no damage.

Later external inspection showed a wee bit red pain on the hull.

We were very fortunate to get away with that one!

Tall Tale 3

The Launch of the Triton

Venue: Amble Boat Club.

High tide: Trailer backed up ready to roll down and float her off (it's a lovely launch point; not concrete but very firm ground).

Are we good to go????
Kicks choc away from jockey wheel and off she flies!

Who's on the boat?????????? O. M. G!!

Eventually gets someone aboard and there's still one strap holding the trailer which is now floating with the boat.

Fail to Prepare and *Prepare to Fail* was never truer than on that day.

The Geordie Dickson Section

Ed. Geordie Dickson. To many, Geordie was THE pioneer of Offshore wrecking and his exploits and the seas he ventured out in are the stuff of legends. There are many anglers 'out there' who will be able to recall the amazing fishing that Geordie offered travelling to unfished wrecks with distance no object. These 'Tales' are not about the actual fishing....I leave all that to Geordie's own forthcoming book and your own vivid memories...but more about the doggedness of the man facing the inevitable trials and tribulations that any kind of boat ownership brings. Also, as a charter skipper, there are unexpected obstacles to overcome particularly when visiting 'new' ports and especially new Islands such as the Scillies and the Channel Islands. Charter Boat owners inevitably and unexpectedly end up in confrontational positions not of their own making and it is up to each skipper how he deals with and overcomes the many obstacles that customers should never have to imagine.

There has been a lot of interest in Geordie's stories so I have selected a variety that relate to his Artilleryman 1, II and III charter vessels although there were other boats not mentioned here that Geordie skippered during his rather unsuccessful attempt at retirement!

And now...over to Geordie...

Tall Tale 1

First Voyage of Artilleryman I

The new boat was coming on fine. The wheelhouse had been fitted and the Ford engine was now on its bed. I still had to fit the electrics, radar and sounder but we were nearly there. Once the last few jobs were completed I took her to the mouth of the Creek give her a coat of antifoul, fit a new transducer and finish the rest of the painting.

I had 3weeks left to complete her before I was due to motor her up to Woolwich where she was going to be christened. I intended to call her *Artilleryman* and after I spoke to the Director of the Artillery's ASC, I was informed that the director would happily perform the christening. Just near Woolwich Ferry we have the Thames Police jetties so I rang them and asked if we could use their facilities for the Christening which they said we could. So that was everything organised. My Demob date was February 10th and that was the date we would perform everything.

The date soon came round and with many late nights and time off given by the display team I was nearly there. Only thing was I only had one side of the hull painted! I'd just have to make sure that the side not painted would be facing the Thames! Anyway, everything went well and a bottle was broken over her bows.

George Danby, one of the London Cadet Force adults, had said he would go with me to sail her to Plymouth and he arrived on time, so once we had finished and the visitors had left us we set sail for Yantlet where I still had some things to collect. We managed to get out of Yantlet before it dried out and made for Ramsgate where we intended to spend the night. We intended to spend the following day moving towards the Solent and it would depend on the weather whether we travelled through the night or pulled into a port. The weather was kind to us so we carried on through the night which saw us just entering the Solent around midday the following day.

Then it happened, the oil warning light came on and we got some scraping sounds coming from the engine. Checking, I found that the bilges were covered in oil. I discovered that the oil filter was loose hence the oil in the bilges. We topped up the engine again and managed to limp into Portsmouth and pull into a marina on the Gosport side. Further inspection told me that the engine would have to come out and undergo repairs.

The boatyard told me that I had two options. I could have the engine out and have it overhauled or they could fit a new unit using my marinised parts. Timewise, this would be the best option so I told them to fit the new unit. Being a Sunday they wouldn't start doing the change-over until Monday and said that with luck she would be ready to sail away the following Monday. George went back to London and I to Plymouth with the intention of meeting up again the following Saturday.

Getting back to the boat the following weekend George turned up complete with crutches and one leg in a plaster cast. I must give the man his due; he wasn't going to let a broken leg stop him helping me sail the boat round to Plymouth.

The boat was already repaired so we decided finish painting her. We slept on board that night and pushed off the following morning. We made a stopover at Mudiford and then spent the next 24 hours sailing to Weymouth. The engine was fine but we had to treat it gently only running at half throttle most of the time. In the morning I was talking to a local who had advised me to go round Portland Bill really close as if we went too far offshore we would have the Portland Race to contend with.. We rounded the Bill on a rising tide and I am sure at times we were going backwards. Eventually we got the ebb tide and were soon crossing West Bay but now we had a brisk westerly wind blowing which was making the weather uncomfortable. We reached Brixham that evening and tied up alongside a trawler who said he had been 'harbour bound' for a day because of the weather yet we didn't think it had been that bad and the boat had taken it in her stride once we got half way across the bay.

Left Brixham the following morning and pulled into Plymouth that evening. George stayed with us overnight and the following day I dropped him at the bus station where he caught his bus back to London.

Tall Tale 2

My First Trip to Guernsey.

Ed. *Nothing ever goes to plan. This Tale clearly shows the dogged determination that is part of Geordie's character. He is certainly a man prepared to meet and deal with rising problems head on.*

When I did my first trip over to the Islands it was to pick up the hull of *Artillerman 2* and tow it back to Plymouth.
 I had arranged for one of the lads who was running a 35 ft boat with twin engines to tow her back for me. That fell through on the very morning that we were due to leave and as the hull was being delivered to St Peter Port harbour that morning it was imperative that I got there that day or else there would be more storage fees to pay. With this in mind I decided to go over with Artilleryman 1 and tow it back with her. I was warned by many that my boat being only 27 feet long was a little small to be doing such a journey but I was determined that towing the new hull back was going to happen.
 So once I had filled up with diesel I pushed off, Informed Rame Head Coastguard of my intentions and that I would give them my position every 2two hours. I had received the forecast early that morning which was for light north westerlies which was confirmed by them.
 "Great someone is on my side," I thought.
 I didn't have an autopilot on Artilleryman I so it was a matter of me being on the wheel all of the time and if I wanted a cuppa I had to tie the wheel whilst I made one.
 Half way across the English Channel I found that though I was still getting Rame Head Coastguard but that they were not receiving me. That's when Amish the skipper of the Plymouth beamer helped out as he called me up and relayed all positions to Rame Head. I learnt one very good lesson there that if you were going to travel across the Channel to make sure that you have a VHF se- up which can keep you in touch. But that's another story which I will give you on a later date.
 We approached Guernsey from the west having looked at the chart and saw that if I kept here miles offshore I would be in deep water until I got to St Martin's point from where I had a clear run to the harbour
 Got in and found that my hull wasn't anywhere to be seen.
 I had a word with one of the harbour staff who informed me that Aquastar were only permitted to transport one boat each day down to the Harbour because it caused traffic problems and that they had taken that delivery with a trawler they had built.
 I rang Aqua Star and got hold of the manager who told me that my boat would be delivered the next morning. So I showered and went for a meal and eventually got into bed later Having come over on my own, I was soon deep in sleep.
 The next morning my hull arrived and everything was laid on to take her off the low loader with one of the dockside cranes when, on my inspection, I found that somewhere in transit the hull had been damaged and had pieces of gel coat missing from the bottom of the hull.

I had a word with the lorry driver who agreed to leave the boat away from the crane and take his cab away and said he would come back the next day.

I had a word with the crane driver and he said he would do the lift the following day so I now got the Aquastar foreman who had come down with the boat to take me up to the factory so I could voice my anger on the owner. I told him that before that boat was placed in the water I wanted all of the hull chips repaired. Over the next four hours he had a team of workers doing the repairs.

Once again had a word with the crane driver who said he would lift it in at 1630. So that's what happened and by 1700 I had the hull tied up alongside one of the jetties. It was too late to leave that day so off to bed early. The next morning I was up early intending on having an early start but on checking my engine I found that the header tank was empty of water. Further inspection showed me that there was corrosion around the inside stack which had corroded a hole into the casing. I took it off and went to a local machine shop who said the best they could do was a temporary repair in fibre glass.

So that was it. I got everything back on-board by midday was on my way stopping every now and then to check the header tank and found the repair was working.

I got into Plymouth at around 11 pm that evening and tied the two boats up and intended to move her round to Blagdon's yard the following morning where I was going to fit the new boat out.

Tall Tale 3

The Final Trip on Artilleryman 2

I had a party from Southampton booked me for what turned out to be the last trip out of Plymouth for *Artilleryman 2*.

We set off bright and early to an area of wrecks some 40 miles SW of Plymouth but then stopped short of them because of the increasing wind and decided to visit the small wreck I had found when a French trawler had come fast on it.

Some months before this I had fished it for 12 hours with a party from the Midlands and had taken into port a total of 7,500 gutted fish including cod, conger, turbot, pollock and ling as well as a couple of 30 lb coalfish. We reached the wreck and started catching pollock and ling but as time progressed the wind started picking up. We had a brisk Northerly increasing wind and I could see that we were going to have a choppy sea and heavy swell to contend with.

We managed to push into it at around 14 knots but even then the occasional wave hit us head on. When we reached the area southwest of the Eddystone Light we were hit by two large waves. Thank goodness I had put our canopy down which kept the party dry!

Shortly after Dale who was crewing for me said that we had water in the forward cabin. We checked the other holds out and found that we had water in the diesel tank bay and engine room. With the electric pumps and the hand pumps going we were still not coping so a Mayday was put out on Channel 16 which was answered by a trawler who was working in the area. Rame Head Coastguard scrambled a helicopter and the Plymouth Lifeboat to assist. The trawler got to us first and stood by us until the Helicopter arrived.

By then I had launched the life rafts and got the party into them, myself staying on board keeping in contact with the 'Copter crew who told me that I would be taken off first and then the members out of the life rafts but would I cut their rafts loose from the boat. I did this and was taken up into the chopper. They then cleared one of the rafts and had taken everyone out of the second one apart from my crew, Dale, and one remaining angler.

As they went to pick them up the downdraught turned the raft over tipping both of them into the water. The last thing I saw was the trawler taking them on board and the chopper then picking them up. Dale told me that the angler had kept him afloat as he had taken his lifejacket off as it got in his way when checking the anglers' lifejackets. He also admitted that he could not swim which surprised me.

We were landed on at Plymouth Hoe where an ambulance took us to the Naval Hospital at Stonehouse. We sat there waiting and as Dale and the angler were being kept in overnight decided that the rest of us would sign out and meet up at the Angling Club. When we got there I called the Coastguard and they told me that my boat was being towed in by the trawler with two members of the Lifeboat on-board who had transferred their large pump and were keeping *Artilleryman 11* afloat afloat.

Two hours later she was lifted ashore at Stonehouse creek and as the trawler skipper came ashore he said to me, "Hope you have good insurance as I am claiming Salvage."

"Charming," I thought. Over the years I have gone to the assistance of many boats at Plymouth including fishing boats and have never asked for anything. We live and learn.

Inspecting the hull I found that we had a hole under the diesel tank and damage round it which indicated that we had hit some large object. We heard later that a container ship had lost two containers whilst passing Plymouth and all Shipping had been informed. I wondered if our damage could have been caused by one of these?.

I gave my insurance their due. They didn't take long before informing me that they would be paying me the boat's value but would be giving the Trawler skipper the boat but he would have to pay all costs, which amounted to £40,000 including marina fees and lift out.

Tall Tale 4

Drug Running: Part 1

Before I sold *Artilleryman III*, she was in a boatyard which was visited by a couple of blokes who wanted to charter the boat. As I wasn't there at the time the yard owner told them that I would be back in the afternoon. They visited me here later that day and asked if they could look around the boat. I thought there was something not right when they wanted to look in every hold. Then they checked the fish rooms and I overheard one of them say, "That will hold plenty of gear."

Told him each one had a holding capacity of around 1500 lbs of fish including ice. They wanted to know how long it would take to get to Guernsey and I told him that to cross the Channel direct with no fishing would take about six and a half hours depending on the weather. It was then that I started to think this wasn't a fishing trip especially as they said they would want to go straight over and only do around one hour's fishing on the way back.

I told them they would have to ring me at home as I didn't have a list of my bookings on the boat. They told me that they would call down the following day to get more details as they would not be able to contact me as they would be out that evening yet one of them had been using a mobile phone whilst they were on the boat.

I was now sure that this was not a fishing trip but felt they were picking up drugs. So shit or bust I said to the main bloke, "This is drugs, isn't it and if so how much will I get paid?"

He told me that to me the first drop would be £1000 plus the cost of diesel meals and accommodation. Any future trips would be twice that amount.

After they went I went to Millbay Docks and rang Customs and told them I was parked in the ferry car perk and would await their arrival. Ten minutes later a plain clothes Customs Officer turned up and took my mobile number and said they would contact me. One of the people who wanted to use the boat, Martin, visited me in the morning and I told him that I couldn't see him then as I had to take my wife up to hospital to have a check-up but that I would be back in the afternoon so Martin confirmed he would come back around 4 pm.

I rang my contact and told him who said he would talk to me after the bloke had left.

Eventually I was rung and asked if I could meet at the transport cafe at Saltash. The following day I told Martin that I wouldn't be at the boat till the afternoon as I was taking the wife to Trago Mills. I turned up the following morning at the cafe and found there were three Customs Officers now involved; two men and one lady who seemed to be the senior. They told me that they had positioned an official within sighting distance and subsequently had the visitor to me followed and had taken his address from the details. So now they had two of the involved peoples' addresses. I told them Customs the 'smugglers' wanted to go with the boat the following weekend and I was told to have some reason to cancel them as Customs weren't ready.

I told the contact I had trouble with two of my injectors and was awaiting spares and he asked if we could do the following weekend.

"Couldn't see why not," I said but we will have to decide at the end of the week.

I looked at the forecast for the weekend and could see that the strong Easterlies were predicted and so told the party that once again we would have to cancel but would keep my eye on it. I informed Customs who were pleased because they were still not ready .

On the Monday I was contacted by Customs who said they wanted to plant a tracker on my boat and they were told that I would park my boat over on the Fish-Quay where they would have access to it. I told them to have one guy checking the boat's radar just in case someone got nosey. Anyway they had the job finished and I picked up the boat and took it back to its mooring. They were now ready so the coming weekend all being well we would be traveling to Guernsey.

On the Saturday morning, six blokes turned up with tackle which I wouldn't fish in a park pond with and we duly went on our way. Clearing the breakwater I then called Brixham Coastguard and told them we had eight people on-board and would be heading for Guernsey and the time of our arrival. The organiser of the trip was in the wheel house at the time and he wanted me to explain why I had told Coastguard and told him that if we didn't arrive at our destination on time they would put out a search for us. I had to do this by law and any infringement to it would entail a heavy fine. This seemed to do the trick and later when he came in and said there was a change of plan and that we were now going into Alderney. I said would have to inform Coastguard of our change of route and he said that was OK.

Got into Alderney and dropped off my passengers and went alongside a Customs Cutter which was alongside the jetty whilst two of our passengers were on board and were told by Customs that we couldn't park there as they were leaving shortly. So we then moved and parked alongside a trawler that had come in and asked him if we could lay there overnight.

"As long as someone is on-board," I was told.

We had a meal in the hotel and afterwards went for a walk on the pretence that we were looking to pick up some tobacco. I noticed that no matter where we went we had two minders close by watching every move we made. I had found out that the drugs were coming in from France on a yacht which the pub owner had got a lift on and once he had delivered the drugs would be flying back to the UK.

I had to inform Customs but how to not to give my passengers any indication of my main reason. I thought I will tell them I have to go into the Harbour Office to fill in the Customs Form and pay for a night's mooring. I then told them that I wanted them to fill in the form and that I couldn't care what they called themselves as long as it filled in the form.

It worked I had a bloke called Cagney and another called Thomas Thumb. Was expecting Micky Mouse but that didn't happen . I went into the Office and explained that I wanted to get a message to Customs and just then I heard the door open and a female voice said, "Will I do, Geordie?" It was the lass who interviewed me in the Cafe at Saltash.

She then listened to what I had to say and told me to be very careful. They now had everything sorted and would have someone at Exeter airport to pick up the pub owner when he landed.

Tall Tale 5

Drug Smuggling Part 2

It had just passed midday and I was told that my passengers were ready to leave and as we moved out of harbour I put up a Union Jack as an indication that the drugs were on board.

The main bloke came inside and said, "Why the flag?"

It told him that as we would be in French waters for a time we would have to fly it.

He asked, "Why didn't you fly it when we came in?"

I told him it didn't apply at night as the French Lookouts couldn't see it. I had got away with it again!

We did one drift over King Reef and caught a few fish on tackle belonging to the boat but then I was told to push off back to Plymouth. Still didn't know if they had picked up the drugs even though I thought they had as they had brought two large holdalls on board which they didn't have on the way over hence me raising the flag to indicate to the watcher that they now had the drugs on board.

I noticed that as we moved into Plymouth Sound that there was a lot of activity with what I thought were diving boats but eventually as we tied up these came along side us but not before two of the 'passengers' left the boat with the holdalls. Then merry hell broke out as two people jumped onto our boat and I told them to get off saying we haven't been cleared by customs yet.

I got the answer," We are customs and you are all under arrest."

As we were marched up the ramp and passed the large crowd which had formed outside the angling centre I heard a familiar voice say, "You can't arrest him. He is taking us fishing in the morning."

After which I was bundled into a car and taken along with the others to the local police station and placed into a cell.

Later I was told that they had picked up the two who had jumped ship when we got in at his house along with the two holdalls. Apparently when they jumped into a car one of the Customs ladies grabbed hold of the door and was dragged along the road but eventually let go.

They eventually let me out of the cell in the afternoon and told me that they would call and see me at home. The following day they told me everything which had happened and said we had caused a bit of a flap when they had found out we were going into Alderney which entailed them having to get someone into the port before we got there and also to inform the Customs Cutter to depart the harbour. Seems we got there just as this was happening.

I heard no more for a while until one day I was asked to meet at a Plymouth hotel which I did. I met two of the girls involved there and was told that the case against the group had been cancelled because the party had agreed to give information regarding the drugs trade in the west country and had moved address to Taunton. I noticed that there was a big drugs haul there some weeks later.

They asked me how much I had lost because of the incident and I told them £2000 which the girls said they would pay anyway. They handed me an envelope and told me to open it when I got home. Inside was £****.

I met two of the Customs blokes later in D.K. Sports and Dave said, " Here is the man!" at which the Customs said, "Well done." After that no more was said.

A couple of weeks later, one of my sons and I visited the car auctions at Taunton and I noticed the main bloke from the drugs bust and his minder were there. I told my son and we slowly moved away but were seen and approached. We were told that they were glad I was still about and they moved back giving me nasty looks. I wondered whether they would be waiting for us outside so I telephoned a contact number and told them what was happening and was told to stay at the auction for the next 30 minutes after which it would be free for us to leave. I did notice as we left that all the way back we had a car following us but left us as we moved into Plymouth. Then Lo and Behold, one day I was in the city centre with the wife and we saw the two people again but this time they crossed over the road and went on their ways.

I never saw them any more after that.

Tall Tale 6

Facing The Court and risking losing everything.

The catamaran was a very stable boat and took adverse weather in her stride although she didn't like head on seas when she would slam. To a certain amount this was cured by fitting two bulbous fittings to her bows but even this didn't cure it completely.

We also initially experienced a good deal of trouble with the outdrive propellers.

One day we were coming back from a trip and got a rattling noise coming from one of the engines. Inspection told us that it was coming from the universal joint so we came into port on one engine and stripped the part down and telephoned Lancing Marine who said they would post one to me by first class mail which I should get by the morning..

We got to sea a little later that day and just had to fish longer to keep the anglers happy.

Two months on and we had two more universal joints go on us and the last one entailed once again getting help from Plymouth lifeboat, this time coming back from Guernsey in an easterly swell. Once again one of the universal joints gave up but this time the whole outdrive leg came detached from the hull leaving a hole in the hull. The only thing stopping it falling off was the steering rod. This was quickly strapped up and my anglers were told to stand on the opposite bow to lift the damaged bow out of the water and once again I informed Coastguard and we were towed into harbour and beached.

I got my solicitor down who said I had a case and he said they would take Lancing Marine to Court for supplying equipment not suitable for the job it was bought for. We were fighting this case for two years having to travel to a Brighton court on quite a few occasions. On the final hearing the defence solicitor, Mr Bellamy, produced one of the rubber gaiters which protects the universal joint from water ingress and said it had been fitted upside down. I asked the judge if I could look at the item as I was the only person in the court who had not inspected it. When I looked at it I could not find any trace of antifouling anywhere on it and said to the court that when assembled I had painted the whole of the outdrive leg with anti-fouling and therefore why wasn't there some traces of the anti-fouling on the rubber gaiter. We were then dismissed and told to be in court the following day to hear the verdict. I sweated all night as I knew that if things went against me it would have meant losing my house and everything I owned.

Court Result.

We all turned up to hear the Judge's verdict at the Brighton court and I was more than a little worried that things could go against me. After all, if it did then I would have more problems to deal with. But thank goodness things turned out in my favour .
 The lady Judge also indicated that she also sailed boats as a pastime. She said that she had looked at all the evidence and could see that I had used qualified marine witnesses to back up my case whereas Lancing Marine had not had any qualified witnesses to back up their case relying on Mr Bellamy as their main witness.
 She also stated that his only qualifications was that he was a qualified painter and decorator. She therefore agreed with me that the goods were not sold as being suitable for their use.
It took around a week for the money to come through and the first thing I did was pay back Blythe Boat Builders, my solicitors and my legal aid bill and put the rest into my bank.
 What a relief after living under the shadow and fear of losing everything.
 I could now get back to the fishing.

Tall Tale 7

Difficulties of Chartering to The Scilly Isles.

Ed. *This is the sixth and final of Geordie's Tales. I sincerely hope that his book will be forthcoming as he has so much to tell. In the meantime, there are many stories and photo's on Geordie's own Facebook page to access. Geordie now lives in the Philippines where he is married to a very beautiful Filipino lady called Rachel since 2014.*

I started thinking of pastures anew and of the possibility of running trips out deep into the Western Approaches using The Isles of Scilly as a base. With this in mind we went to the Island and got a friend to pick us up from the airport and help to get around when we there. First place to visit was the Harbourmaster's Office. When we got there we explained what we wanted to do and was told there was no problem.

The HM indicated the Floating Moorings to use and told us to keep the steps at the jetty clear if not loading passengers as the Tripping Boats required to pick up and drop off there. He showed us where the fuel supply office where we were informed that fuel would be delivered in 50 gallon drums and syphoned down into the boat. Although this would be a very slow process we did at least have a supply.

On our first trip over there we pulled alongside and sent my passengers off to their bed and breakfast. During the evening a dinghy pulled up alongside of us and the chap on it said to me that it was to meet me again. I couldn't understand who he was but when he said I was one of the crew who was on the *Isles Of Scilly* yacht which lost a member over-board and "you found the body and towed the boat into Plymouth. I didn't thank you then but am doing so now".

The following morning I was alongside the Quay waiting for my anglers to come down and a voice shouted something down to me. I looked up and saw a short bloke dressed in Harbour Authorities dress looking down at us. I said, "Sorry. What did you say?"

"Well if you turned off those engines, maybe you would".

Switching them off he said in a stern voice, "Come up to my office now. I climbed up the tyres which were hanging down the wall and went into the office. It was like walking into the CO's office in the army. He was sat at a desk and on one side was another official and then on the other side was the bloke who Dave and I had visited to get the details for visiting the Islands.

He asked to see my licence and when I gave it to him he said, "This is no good. Where is your local licence?"

I told him that it was a Board of Trade licence which permitted me to work out 60 miles from a Safe Haven and the Isles of Scilly was indeed a designated Safe Haven. So I said why then why were we told when we came over on a recce that it would be ok by your assistant Harbour Master and pointed to the person concerned.

The other small bloke turned round and said, "I am the assistant Harbour Master .The person you spoke to was the assistant to the assistant Harbour Master. I nearly started out laughing but managed to keep my cool. "Now that we are here and my anglers have paid for five days B and B, what's going to happen now?" I enquired.

He told me that he would allow me to stay here this time but in future would have to have a local licence.

Back in Plymouth, I was spending a lot of time trying to get help with the Isles of Scilly problem but I was determined that I was going to fight the Isles of Scilly regarding taking anglers over there.

Mr Davison was my MP here in Plymouth and he was the main man in the Board of trade. I really thought he would help me and got a shock when I first rang his office in Plymouth and was told that to see him I would have to ring his secretary in London. I did that and told them what I wanted to see them for. Two days later had a message saying that Mr Davison could do nothing for me so I got back onto them and said I wanted to see Mr Davison the next time he was in Plymouth.

I received a message from them stating that he was not prepared to see me as he had said earlier he could do nothing for me. Wondered at the time whether it was because the Islands were Duchy of Cornwall property and he didn't want to question how they ran it. Maybe he was wanting a Knighthood and didn't want to upset the apple cart. Since then I have ever voted. Why bother? They give you a lot of crap when they are trying to get elected when really they couldn't care two hoots for the normal working man. (Davison retired after 10 years because he could get a very healthy pension).

Now I had to go somewhere else so I contacted The Professional Boatman's Association as I was a member. They told me that they did not take on individual problems and I told them to tell me that when all Councils stop other boats going into their harbours and tell that to the skippers who are running into France, Alderney and Guernsey and see how long you have an Association.

I cancelled my membership the following day and was told that there was another Association in the North of England who also fought for Boating Rights. So I got onto them and was told that they would love to take it up but I would have to join the Association. I did that the same day, paid my dues and sent them an e-mail informing them what I had done to date. I received an e-mail from them just over a week later telling me that they had been onto the Board of Trade and had managed to get them to have a meeting with the Duchy and Council on the Islands to see what they could do.

I was now on tender hooks wondering how it would turn out when I received a letter from the Council telling me that it had been agreed and that if I took a test I would be given a Local Licence and was advised to ring the licencing officer for more details. The day I was thinking of was when I had my French party fishing out of Falmouth so, if they agreed, we could fish the wrecks reroute, go into the Islands, have my test and then fish back to Falmouth. This they agreed to. I contacted the Council and they organised the test for 2pm on the day we would be working out of Falmouth.

I picked the French party up and fished the wrecks over and met the Tester on time. I had a feeling that I had met this man somewhere. He came on board, shook my hand and said, "How are you? It's been some years since we last met. Remember, I bought two diesel engines from you which you had taken out of an Aqua Star".

Then it came back to me. He had a good look around the boat's equipment and was very impressed and said we had as much equipment as the cargo ships carried when they came. He was very interested in my Offshore Navigator which ran on my laptop with GPS so I gave him the address where he could get the programme. I did a couple of runs along a couple of passages and he said "Ok, I am satisfied. Take me back. You have got your licence."

He told me that he would put the paper work in that afternoon and if I gave him the licence fee of £25 he would pay it in and maybe I would receive my licence by the weekend by post.

I did all that and told him that if he ever saw us in port to come and get some fish.
I received my Licence!

THIRD WAVE

Howard James

Fishing with Skipper Chris Caines

Ed. *Howard from Aylesbury is one of those fortunate enough to have fished with aboard Chris Caines' Tiger Lily and who captures Chris' instant charm and charisma perfectly.*

As a customer of the charter industry (albeit with a small insight into the whys-and-wherefores of what is after all a precarious occupation) there are the occasional moments of enlightenment. I was, as many of us are, used to boarding a vessel with the skipper firmly ensconced in his pulpit. After a short while they would emerge from said domain and bark, "Right then. Listen in, you lot; this is what's a'pning".
 Enter into the fray one Mr. Chris Caines, a skipper I had been recommended to by my last skipper who was inconsiderate enough to retire. I well remember my first trip on *Tiger Lily*. I had fished on many boats with many skippers on the south coast for a number of years. So as we all do I went aboard his domain with trepidation.
 When he stepped gracefully from his well-ordered wheel house (a place that everybody was welcome to visit at any time... which was the second revelation of the day by the way) and said in his quiet, soft, articulate way,
"Gentleman, if you'd care to listen..........I thought this is what we'd do today, if it's agreeable".
Hay ho!!! I was hooked, a strange thing for someone to say in this instance I think you'll agree? I will forever have an image of him in my mind. He had set on a perfect drift for plaice on the bank. The weather was perfect, the sun was shining and he was sat on the rope locker, mirrored sun glasses on, hand clasped over his ample frame with a smile of contentment emblazoned on his face.
 He looked at me and pointedly said, "I really must get a more stressful job" which is something I'm sure he'd done many times to many other customers. But the point is.....he could make EVERYBODY on board feel as though they had a right to be there

Trevor Small; *Skipper of Poole based charter dive boat Rocket. A good friend who is sadly missed. Chris Caines; a gentle giant with a heart of gold and boy did he make me laugh.* (Ed. Trevor was to meet a well-known, highly vocal, local boat builder who was going to assist him. Advice from Mr Caines came forth regarding said famous boat builder, known as The Honey Monster*). Chris told me, regarding the talented man who fitted out Tiger Lily; "Honey Monster is f***ing good at fitting out boats but before you see him, cut a banana in half & hammer the two remaining parts into each ear."*

Jones A Fish. *A fantastic man. A leader and true visionary of the charter industry. A pleasure to work for as a deckhand on many an Alderney trip. Extremely funny and liked a good laugh. Extremely hard to help get off a boat after a number of bottles of champagne and wine. There to help anybody, anytime. Taken way, way too early. RIP my friend.*

Roger Bayzand; *Skipper of Lymington based charter angling boat Sundance. Well said, Howard. I would love Chris to be here to share his tales with us. One I recall was us having dinner in the First and Last with our crews at adjacent tables. One of Chris's crew asked, "What time are we starting in the morning?" to which Chris replied, "11 o'clock. It's pointless going any earlier because you are all useless and won't catch anything."*
I nearly choked on my lobster bisque.

Ed. *Difficult to overstate just how much Chris did for our port in uniting skippers more than they ever had been before. It is thanks to him that the reputation Weymouth gained as a port where skippers* worked together and supported each other is all down to him. That fact that he is still so deeply missed by so many of us shows what an extraordinary man he was to us all. We were REALLY lucky to have him as part of our lives.

Ian Bagley

A One in a Million Drift!!

Ed. *Anyone who has fished with Ian will remember him with ease. Big. Loud. Full of fun. Enthusiastic. Loyal. Generous. And...a jolly fine angler; especially with turbot.*

I remember once I was out on Wrecking trip for cod in early 2001 aboard the *Rebel* of Weymouth and my mate Lee Woodfield was pirking for cod next to me when 'bang!!' a big cod caught him unawares and his nice brand new expensive Penn rod and reel was gone out of his hands in a flash, just like one of those yellow barrels did in the Jaws film.

Skipper Paul came out of his cosy office (half way from completing his crossword or cooking my sausages for me) to see what had happened and Lee said he can't fish for the rest of the day now as he did not bring another rod as in those days a 20-30 lbs Penn Waveblaster was all you needed for the day's fishing.... unlike some who have to bring along a caddie with them to carry all their rods!!

Paul then started the *Rebel* and went up tide a fair way to reset the drift and I started pirking again with Lee watching me. I had a weird bite, so I started to wind up and it all felt odd and not like a normal cod fight and I said to all on the *Rebel* that I reckon I got Lee's rod and a big cod on too.

Lee was on his knees praying I was right and with suspense I gently wound up till I saw a flash of long silver deep down and would you believe it, a Penn Waveblaster and reel was emerging from the depths but was being pulled down again by a very upset cod.

I finally managed got Lee's rod to the surface and he lent over the rail until he was virtually in the sea and it seemed that my pirk hooks had caught the very end eye of his new rod and he grabbed it and started winding his reel but the cod was gone. He turned to me and said thanks for losing his big cod, even though I just saved him about £350.00... that's bloody gratitude for you, eh!!

James Orpwood

Sundance Adventure

Ed. *Avid Highland walker, keen angler and now (26ᵗʰ October) author of his first book 'A Quest for Fulfiment', James from Aviemore, Scotland, recounts a tale aboard Roger Bayzand's famous Lymington based charter boat, Sundance.*

I have enjoyed becoming re-acquainted with some old (sorry, former!) fishing buddies through this group. Recently, a couple of us were musing over how diplomatic our skipper, Roger Bayzand, could be when anglers asked for advice such as what lure might work best and then completely ignoring that advice by going their own sweet way and then blaming everybody but themselves when they failed to catch! You know the sort.

Anyway, those of you seeing my recent posts on here will know what a huge amount of respect I have for Roger and how much I loved fishing on *Sundance I* and *Sundance II*, and hopefully always listening.

However ...on one occasion we were out on a mid-channel wreck from Lymington. It was early March, one of Roger's first trips of the new season, so a pollock-fest was very much the order of the day using jellyworms, redgills, shads and all that sort of thing. Anyway, after the obligatory question, "What's been catching recently skip?" this gentleman (a very good angler by the way) elected to fish a baited pirk, ignoring Roger's very informed advice.

Bang! The next thing we knew, the gentleman's rod was buckled under the weight of a good fish that dived and fought all the way to the top and soon, a 20 lb. 4 oz. coalfish was on the deck! This was quite a rarity for the Hampshire coast especially a good specimen at that being a potential new regional record at the time.

Poor Roger, it was difficult to convince the rest of us then that jellyworms were the way to go that day!

The John Hamer Section

Angling for Fun

Ed. *John has been a massive supporter of the Tall Tales Facebook page contributing a number of excellent stories. His contribution is grouped together here with 7 different tales. John should surely write his own book as he has a great style of writing on a range of angling experiences and adventures.*

Tall Tale 1

For about fifty five years I have been a keen sea angler, well let me explain 'keen'. I am not and never have been a Freezer filler nor a Medal hunter. I am one of those who enjoys the outdoors and the fellowship of other sea anglers. It is they who have provided the bulk of my stories.

It all started as an accident really. My mate Andy and I had been fresh water fishing for about three years and had been all over the place in search of good and easy fish to catch but we only had moderate success. Then one night duty we were gathered around the table in the mess room chatting about the fishing when another member of the relief suggested that we should try sea fishing as the fresh water game was too demanding on one's patience, tenacity and doggedness.

I omitted to state that we and I are all members of the Police Force as it was once called.

Andy was not too taken by the suggestion but I was and Derek, Colin and Pete were. Bernie who was the skipper on the relief had made the opening suggestion. He had also done a bit of sea fishing mainly from the shore, having relatives who lived near Canterbury in Kent.

During the following days we all talked more and more about the prospect of fishing in the sea and what would be the best way to go about it. The first priority was to decide on which area of the sport we were to concentrate on. Fishing from the shore was to be the choice. This made good sense as we lived in the north east of London and we had a large coastal area at our disposal. We decided on the Wash to Hastings which had plenty of water to fish at and there was bound to be plenty of fish to catch.

What did we need in the way of tackle? We set to and came up with all sorts of gear that each one of us thought would do the job. We had a lot to learn. Not even Bernie could help much because when pressed, he explained that the times he had been fishing he had been in the company of his relative and had used his tackle. The first venue to be fished by our intrepid band was Deal Pier in Kent, a well-known and famous location for sea anglers.

The day dawned dark and damp. It was in November and from the reports in the *Angling Times* we should be coming home with lots of whiting that were climbing up the anglers' lines. Bernie picked us up in his Hillman Minx Estate and Derek, Pete, Colin and I had a pleasant sleep all the way down to the seaside. On our arrival we unloaded the car and went to the local tackle shop and purchased the appropriate bait, that being large dried out black lug resembling chewing tobacco which were assured would do the job. Then onto the pier we sauntered.

Those who have fished this venue will now have to bear with me. We walked along the main arm of the structure which had yellow lines painted on the floor and the legend 'NO FISHING' all along its entire length. Therefore we were forced to go further and further along until we came to a 'T' shaped end and a lower deck that was crowded with anglers. A space for us was unavailable, at least for all five of us to fish together... so we had to split up. I spied a gap on one corner that was strangely empty and dragged Colin with me into it. As we were setting up we both discovered why this bit was unpopulated. We were both bending down over our gear with our backs to the sea when this huge wave broke over us and knocked us off our feet, tackle and bodies swilled around and then were dumped on the decking very wet and disorganised.

I later discovered that due to the strong southwest wind that was blowing the location we had chosen was a no-no. We also found out that the the pier was so crowded because all the boats for miles around had been forced to cancel so the boat anglers had also adjourned to the pier. The name of the game was now to watch the other anglers who we could see were able to go about the art of fishing from a pier in a gale of wind and maybe pick up a few pointers and boy did we need pointing. Derek was the only one of us with gear that was anywhere near being right for the job. He had secretly bought a Mitchell 624 multiplier reel and a Hardy *Long Bow* rod which was about 12 feet long and was tapered at both ends. It certainly looked the part and there was no other like it on the pier.

The stuff the rest of us had was a load of rubbish but thankfully none of it was ours as we had borrowed it from family and friends. We started to try and emulate the anglers who were casting leads fantastic distances. Our efforts were puny in comparison, all except for Pete that is as he was putting his leads out of sight but that was all he did as the line broke on every occasion. He was soon building an island of lead out in front of him and was christened by the other anglers as Ivor Krakoff. Fortunately the pier authorities allowed those who were short of tackle to have a pass out to the shop to buy more, I suspect the tackle dealer never had such a good day. Needless to say we did not set the world on fire on our first trip but we did learn a bit about what we were supposed to be doing. Advice was generously given by other anglers and gratefully received by us. One lesson was well learned by Colin which was not to turn your back on the sea in a gale of wind although later in this tale you find that I am a slow learner.

Gradually our equipment came together mainly by way of the *Angling Times* and *Anglers Mail* second hand sales column and were all fairly well sorted. I had found an Abu 484 and a Abu 7000 reel for £50 and the other bits and pieces were kept in a communal box. Deal remained our venue for the following winter and we got better at it and started to catch fish. Advice was always on hand from the resident angling club and although we never knew their names we are forever grateful. Who knows but for them our gear may have been put back into the 'Used' columns.

One trip to Deal remains vivid in my recollections. Andy had resisted all our attempts to let him to come with us but at last he relented and we picked him up one morning in January. it was freezing cold. We had sorted tackle for him but had told him to bring warm clothing. He threw a plastic bag into the back of my Saab 95 estate, climbed into back row of seats and promptly fell asleep. With others collected we made our way to Deal and upon our arrival woke Andy and dragged him out into the cruel winter cold. He was wearing a light sports jacket and slacks, V neck pullover and shirt and on his feet a pair of moccasins. He had no other clothing with him as the plastic bag contained his grub. We were not sure if he should come out onto the pier but he insisted he would be all right. It took only 20 minutes to convince him that this was not a good idea and a further 10 to convince us that we should do something about his fast approaching hypothermia.

So it was that we each in turn took him to the excellent café situated on the upper deck of the pier and injected him with hot meat pies and tea at about 30 minute intervals. I must admit that I at least was ready to take him when my turn came round. In fact I jumped the queue at least once and at one stage only one of our party tended the rods. That was the final appearance that Andy put in on the sea angling front and went back to his basket warming and to date remains so.
Shame really he has missed a lot of fun.

Chris Ponsford. *Cracking story, John. Guess we have all been there early doors. Poor old Andy, typical of so many folks' introduction to fishing and subsequent departure*

Tall Tale 2

The Lessons of Walton Pier

Having in the previous year learned the rudiments of casting a line with bait attached more than 50 yards, we then decided that we should broaden our horizons.

Every week we would scour the *Mail* and the *Times* to find out where the fish were being caught in our aforementioned area of operations. We then would choose the location on the strength of these reports having no regard to the tide tables or weather reports. All we did was to chase fish that had already been caught! It took us a long time to work that out but in the meantime we discovered some of the most beautiful and remote spots in the south east of England. We visited the right places at the wrong time but had a whale of a time doing it, like travelling to Shingle Street, unloading and going over the top and finding the tide right in casting straight out and losing gear hand over fist. As the tide receded we discovered why. We were hitting tank traps, large concrete blocks with lengths of railway line cast in them, remnants of the coastal defences set in 1940. We were able to retrieve our tackle as the tide went out and a lot of other gear not belonging to us. We had done one thing right, we had picked a big tide so the return of our tackle was a bonus but the object of the exercise still evaded us.

In our ignorance we still kept chasing 'the reports' and we were not showing much for our efforts. Newhaven was next on the list. We had been told to go east of the town to a beach near Seaford. We found a beach that was sheltered by a huge groin sticking out into the sea at right angles to the shore. The shingle was very steep and we great difficulty in getting up and down it. Other anglers were there and we copied what they were doing; we had quite a few fish codling and whiting. As the day wore on it went quiet and I went for walk along the shore and I found a broken fish box and an oar. I started to play around with these, taking it to the top of the shingle and sliding down to the water, great fun. As I came to the bottom on my third slalom, I spied a length of line half buried in the sand. This normally terminates in a set of tackle lost on a previous occasion. I abandoned my sledge and went to explore the fishing line. I had to move up and down the beach to avoid the waves, and then in a trough the line came up disclosing a swivel and weight. In my joy to recover this treasure, I turned my back on the sea for a second time. Yes, you've guessed it; it had me again. Thigh deep, rushing up the beach in front of me was SOLID GREEN WET COLD WATER.

In my haste to get out of it, I started to run up the beach. This was a bad move; only one foot in contact with terra firma and the sea coming back down the shingle had me off my feet and swimming in no time. Fortunately the next wave dumped me up the beach far enough to get a grip. I was left stranded but happy to be so and still had my prize in my hand. The lads dragged me up to the car where I was forced to strip to the bone and then wear a collection of clothing that was either spare or removed from them. I was in no position to argue. Our next outing was to Dungeness and yes you've guessed it, we chose a day when the weather was just right to be fishing on the opposite side of the Channel; it was a howling South-Wester. In spite of our best efforts, our tackle ended up back on the beach under our feet. Local knowledge was sought and we were introduced to the grapnel lead and the walk uptide prior to casting. This helped somewhat but we soon became unpopular with the locals as our gear was now affecting their fishing, being swept in but now collecting everyone on the down tide side of us. We were still unable to claim any sizeable fish and things were looking desperate and we were still chasing fish that had already been caught following the reports in the *Times* and *Mail*.

Other venues that we tried were more user-friendly. We decided to concentrate our efforts having fished the open beaches of Suffolk, Essex and Kent with not much to show for ourselves.

Following a council of war, we decided to choose a venue and fish it on a regular basis to the exclusion of all others despite what the reports in the press told us. Taking all the pros and cons into consideration we came out in favour of Walton Pier. We had taken the easy option in the eyes of the purists but as I stated in the opening, pleasure was our main pursuit. So began our real learning curve we each bought a season ticket for the pier. This allowed one on at any time night or day by means of an electronic lock, each ticket holder being responsible for the good order of the facility and to check on each other regarding proper use of the pier.

Have you ever noticed that when anglers get near water they have always got to be in it? The river angler with his swim so close to the edge his feet are in the water all day long; the game fisher up to his armpits in the stuff; the strand fisher same thing and pier anglers are no different. Walton Pier is about 800 yards long at right angles to the beach, fish are taken from the beach in good numbers but the pier angler has to be on the extreme end of any structure he finds himself upon. We followed the example set and struggled with our boxes and bags right to end and when we got there we found no place to fish, surprise surprise. However we set up our tackle and then watched the experts again. The distance some of these chaps get is unbelievable but we saw no fish. Eventually a gap appeared and we took it. The fishing was dismal and before long yours truly went for a walk-about.

There is not much option on a pier and being at the extreme end I could only go one way. Walton pier is used by the RNLI and they have a shed and a jetty just short of the end of the pier. Fishing is forbidden in this area. The Harwich side of the pier has a railway running the entire length, so fishing again was restricted to the Clacton side. From the shore to the end there are two shelters and these are favoured by the anglers who know the place and who fish it regularly. I stopped at the first shelter, that is the second coming from the shore, and there was a chap fishing here on his own. I stood and watched as he pulled whiting after whiting over the rail. His tackle was no better than ours and he was using the same bait as we had brought. I was unable to contain myself any longer and asked him how come he was catching when the lads at the end were fishless. He then gave me the best piece of info I was ever to receive in respect of fishing Walton Pier. He explained that he had fished this pier for about ten years and had learned its secret. He never went further up than here and sometimes not even this far, "No need to go out there, nor to cast away too far either". He told me that the best time was from high water down to two hours before low water, after that you can go home. I thanked him for his time and went back to join the others, not wishing to spoil the 'locals' fishing, I decided to leave the second shelter information under wraps for another time. On our next visit I let the cat out of the bag and stopped at the second shelter. The others who were behind me clattered into one another as they came to a sudden unexpected halt. "What's all this?" was the cry.

I told them that this was it for the day, as far as I was concerned. Colin was not impressed. He was looking out to sea I could see the yearning in his eyes. I told him to go if he must but this was my mark. Derek went on with Colin and that left Bernie and I to prove my point as I had not yet told them about the inside information I had been given. We tackled up and cast out a small strip of mackerel no further than fifty yards then turned away from the rods to get a sandwich and flask out of the bag. I turned round, cup in one hand and sandwich in the other, to see my rod doing a fandango. Bernie's was doing the same. Doesn't it always happen? You have a bite and the fish come on. Two cups of coffee went to waste in the grab for the rods but we both landed a fine whiting each which were about 2lbs and from that moment they kept coming. This was before the word conservation had entered the sea fishing vocabulary and before long we had run out of bait. Colin came down from the end and stated that Derek was packing up as the fishing was rubbish. We asked if they had bait left and let Colin in on the secret. He was gone in a flash and returned with Derek, panting for breath in his rush to get among the whiting. Following that day we never went beyond the second shelter and we had good fishing throughout the year with cod, bass, flatties - both dab and flounder and even, on one occasion, a smooth-hound and that was real fun getting that up to the deck.

Walton Pier was our mark for about three years and we had fun and learned a lot from our experiences and from other anglers who I find to be most free with information. We were developing into reasonably good anglers ourselves but we were unable to a man to cast a bait further than 80 yards even on a good day. That is when the third stage of this saga began.

Tall Tale 3

Troublesome Tope

At last the day had arrived, 16th May, 1999, and we were on our way; we being Mick, Steve, Mark, Pat, Don, brothers Andrew and Richard and myself John, the daddy of the party.
This fishing trip had been on the stocks since August 1998 and had only been confirmed in the new year by our skipper, Charlie Bartlett who runs *Miss Claudi*, a 34 foot Freeward, out of the picturesque port of Aberdyfi, Gwynedd, Wales.

We had met at 11am at the South Mimms services and had an uneventful journey up the M1, M6, M54, then to the last 50 or so miles through the beautiful countryside of Shropshire and the borders into Wales. We arrived at our Digs at about 4pm to be greeted by our landlady Cathy, who had the kettle on in no time flat. She was going to be OK as far as we were concerned. After settling into our rooms, Cathy moved her car from her space at the rear of the guest house and invited us to park there for the week. Following a walk around the village a drink and a meal, I checked with Charlie on the phone to ensure we would be on for tomorrow.

Monday 17th, following an excellent breakfast, we got our gear together and made for the jetty to embark. Charlie had already brought *Miss Claudia* from her mooring and was ready for us. The fishing tackle was stowed and Peter, the Mate, let go the ropes and off we went on our first day of a most memorable fishing holiday.

None of the lads had been here before. I had fished with Charlie before and therefore knew what we would be up against in the way of fish. I had told the stories of previous visits but they were taken with the proverbial pinch of salt by the lads who I must explain do most of our fishing in the Thames Estuary and are all familiar with uptide tackle and methods. The main difference here was in the numbers of fish and the fact that casting is not necessary. The tackle used was uniform throughout the 8 of us. We used weights in the 6oz to 8oz range, an uptide rod, ABU 7000 or similar reel, 18 lb line to a 50lb rubbing leader and a 250lb nylon biting piece, with swivels between each joint, terminating in an 8/0 O'Shaughnessy bronze hook. Weights varied depending on wind and tide and the position we were on the boat.

Following a run of about an hour the boat was positioned and the order given to commence fishing. Eight frozen mackerel made their way down to the bottom. The reason they were frozen is because fresh mackerel were not there to be caught. If they had been, I think the catch rate would have been even higher but the individually blast frozen ones were a very good standby bait and within 20 minutes Steve was into a fish. Two or three savage nods of the rod followed by a twenty yard run against the drag indicated that this was what we had come for. Charlie was at his shoulder giving advice and encouragement. The fish ran again. Steve lifted the rod, thumbed the spool and leant back into a very lively 25lb-ish tope, which after about ten minutes or so was boated by Charlie and Peter. Steve posed for photos and then it was returned. Seven baits were already in the water before Steve could get his breath back. Mick's bait was taken almost before it had hit the bottom, so again the lines were retrieved to allow him to play his fish as leaving lines in the water when there is a fish on is fatal. Mark had the next run and boated fish 3, 4 and 6. Pat had the 5th and 8th. I had the seventh and Richard boated number nine with Andy at number ten. Don failed to boat any but did have runs. In fact had we boated all the runs we would have had many more fish but such is the way of tope fishing and we were well satisfied with the day.

On Day Two, Tuesday 18th May, we were on board at 9am and out again over the bar. After a running time of about 45 minutes we reached an inshore mark. Charlie was working from his log book explaining that, "Big females show here, we will see if history repeats itself." Don was the first to experience a run and he boated a fine male tope of about 30lb.
"It is carrying war scars; been messing with the big females," announced Charlie.

Don's luck has definitely changed and during the day he boated numbers 1, 2, 8 and 11 all of which were male fish and were in fine fettle and full of fight. In fact tope number 11 had a go at Don and nearly had a piece of his thigh! Andy had tope 3, Steve had 4 and 12, Mick had 5 and 10, Mark 7,

Tall Tale 4

Happier times North of the Border ...but no fish....

Another trip to Scotland I recall was to Loch Goil. We did not stay there as we had hired a cruiser for the week. Pete, Don, Bill and I made up the crew. We intended cruising the Clyde Estuary and visiting old stomping grounds like Skelmorlie, Cumbrae and even further afield to Arran and Bute. The boat was 33 foot Broom. it was a beauty and had facilities for about eight people in comfort. As there were only the four of us we had the choice of berths, a luxury rarely afforded on boats. Don took the forward cabin, Bill took the aft cabin en-suite, and Pete and I took the saloon with Pete on starboard and myself, portside. It was the month of May and the night time temperatures were still quite low. I had not bothered to take my own sleeping bag as the others had done and was relying on the ones supplied which was a bad mistake.

We decided to remain at Loch Goilhead the first night and went into the village to buy provisions. Don did the buying as he was the Q.M. and cook for the week. All we did was get our fags and baccy. After a late meal we turned in and I soon found out that I had made a bad choice. The starboard bunk converted into a three quarter bed by using the back cushion of the port bunk. The port bunk remained a single but the occupant sleeper slid under what would have been the backrest therefore movement was restricted and turning over was out of the question. Due to my lack of foresight and the Scottish nights, I was freezing and spent nearly all the night awake not wishing or should I say daring to disturb the others who could be heard snoring their heads off. I was glad when morning broke and was obviously the first up and dressed. The quietness was deafening and upon sticking my head outdoors the scene was beautiful. The water of the loch was still without a ripple, the surrounding hills and mountains were reflected in it and the light was magical. I am not an artist but can appreciate beauty when I see it and this was perfection. It was a shame to start the engines and move for fear of destroying the moment.

Don was down in the galley doing his stuff and Peter cast off and thus started our adventure. As soon as we were under way, Bill had a lure trailing behind the good ship *Berg* and we slowly made our way down to Loch Goil and then out into the Clyde. Bacon butties and Coffee went down well. As we came abreast of Holy Loch and Faslane, the M.O.D. Police launch came over to us and requested us to speed up and clear the area. We did try to comply but the port engine did not want to play. Anything above tick-over, she cut out and would restart almost immediately but then would stop when more revs were applied so the Royal Navy had to wait for us to limp out of the way before they could go about their business.

Don, a diesel fitter by trade, and I by experience gained courtesy of the Blue Fox, decided between us that fuel starvation was the cause of the problem with the engine but seeing that we were on holiday and did not have any proper tools anyway, decided to contact the owners by radio. The *Berg* was fitted with VHF but the instructions were not to use it unless there was an emergency. In our view a radio call was warranted. However, we were unable to raise the owners but were acknowledge by the Kip Marina and invited in to use the telephone. By the time we had berthed, the Marina staff had been in touch with Lock Goil Cruisers and had been requested to look at the problem for them. We were boarded by a fitter who had with him a large adjustable spanner, a bent and equally large screw driver and a piece of rag. The floor boards were lifted and the engines exposed. He looked over the offending one and wiped it with his rag and asked Don to start it. It fired up immediately. He looked some more and having found no leaks his rag became redundant. He declared that we were fit for sea and requested that we take it for spin to prove him correct. We cleared the entrance of the Marina and he took the helm. He gunned the motors and was soon running on just one; his rag had failed him. We stopped all and he jumped down into the bay again this time he brought his spanner into play, Don nor I could watch, injector pipes and adjustables do not go together, well maybe once, but when the unions have been chewed they are rendered useless. Still who were we to argue. The engines were started again and again they failed. We returned to the berth in the Marina. The resident fitter left us muttering something about Fords and Lochgoil Cruisers.

From Lochgoilhead to Kip Marina by water is about an hour's running. By road it takes hours and it was by road that the owner's fitter came. He arrived in a steaming van that sighed with relief as he lifted out his tool kit. The box was almost the size of a steamer trunk, and he was barely able to lift it he left it on the jetty and made several journeys to it over the following three hours. Besides the tool box he was armed with fuel filters, seals, pipes, and even injectors. Don suggested that the fuel was not getting away from the tank and maybe if the pipe from the pump to the tank was cleared by compressed air the problem would be solved. As stated, three hours and four trial runs were needed to finally blow the offending object from the fuel delivery pipe. "I am on holiday," was Don's reply to the question, "Why didn't you fix it?"

Late afternoon saw us gently steaming down the Clyde towards Cumbrae, our first night's stopping place. We picked up a mooring off Millport and spent our second night in great comfort. I had stolen all the extra bedding from every nook and cranny on the boat. Next morning I went ashore using the inflatable, which was kept hanging on the stern in davits. The previous renters were very careful people. If the dinghy had been needed in an emergency an axe would have been required to release it. As it was Peter and I managed to undo the knotty problem but Don had cooked breakfast before we had it free. The reason for going ashore was to see if any bait in the shape of worms or shellfish were to be had but alas no and we decided to visit Fairlie to renew our search and for Bill to get to work with his garden fork. Peter and I stayed onboard, Don and Bill went ashore, Bill to dig and Don to get provisions. To cut a long story short, there was very little to show for Bill's efforts and Don left his Barbour in the mini cab and of course it was never handed in to the local Police station. I hope the driver of that cab gets to read this.

We did a bit of angling but were disappointed to find that there was a distinct lack of fish. We moved back to the gap between Great and Little Cumbrea but the results were dismal and then I noticed that the rocks on the shore were devoid of life from the high to the low water mark. On our previous visit some years earlier they had been festooned with mussels and limpets now there was not a trace of any, an ominous sign. During the week the fishing was dismal. We covered a fair amount of water and finished up in Campbeltown on the Southeast tip of the Mull of Kintyre and, having got ourselves as far as we could from Loch Goil, the weather changed, and we were advised by the trawler men to stay put until the strong Southwest winds subsided. We took their advice. They kept us updated on the radio but we were there for two days unable to leave until the third morning.

During our stay we made friends all over the place. Peter was probably the reason. We had all gone ashore and we were moored on a jetty in the harbour especially for visitors. The local kids fished from it and four of them came along three boys and little girl. Suddenly there were only the boys in sight and Peter saw from the boat that the girl was in the water and going down. He grabbed the boat hook and jumped down onto the jetty and fished her out. She was apparently alright. The boys were told to take her home and one of them was her brother. Peter told us the tale when we returned from the pub and later we were visited by the police and the family of the little girl and thanked. We never heard any more of the matter but if not for Peter, they would have been a child short.

Before we able to leave Campbeltown we checked the fuel levels and decided we had better refuel. When a boat is hired from these companies the fuel tanks are full and a fuel deposit is left which used to be £100 and is probably considerably more these days. On return the tanks are filled and the cost taken from the deposit, generally more money is required to meet the cost. However we were

short and bought fuel from a lorry that supplied the trawlers. The driver was very obliging and brought his tanker to us and handed Peter the hose, the gun was huge and the fillers on the boat small in comparison but would just fit if care was taken. The fuel came from the tanker under pressure and Peter got his carpet slippers filled up as well. I asked the driver what we owed him and he directed us to a Charringtons fuel merchants on the harbour side. I cannot remember how much fuel we had but the charge was minimal, very likely as result of Peter's life-saving prowess.
Next morning at 4am, I was awake to the radio and the voice of one of the trawler skippers telling us we could leave harbour if we liked. The weather was fine. The other three were still asleep as I started up and cast off and they did not surface until I dropped the anchor in Kilchattan Bay. We had breakfast and then decided to spend the rest of the day in the splendid new marina at Largs, where we got the boat cleaned up and we washed and showered ourselves, had a great meal and went to bed. Early the next morning we set out to return to Loch Goil. We tried to see if we could catch fish on Skelmorlie Bank but we failed again except for a small codling. We tried again at the Gantocks but got nothing we then threw in the towel and headed north to our home port. On the way we passed the Royal Navy putting to sea with one of those huge submarines; they are frightening to look at. Don caught a trout at the moorings just before we left the next morning but he had to return it as we had no freezer in the car. We also got £80 back on the fuel deposit, thank you, Campbeltown.

Responses

Bob Colquhoun._ Great recollection of my old stomping ground. With our Dad we ran sea angling trips in the Clyde for the best part of 10 years with our 56ft converted ring netter. Many stories to tell, mostly good or funny, over that time. We did this to finance having a 56ft boat as a family cruiser. Wouldn't have missed it for the world, great experiences.

David Mallett. Loch Goil and loch Long was the area that started my boating career. My enduring memory was when my wife and I trailed our small boat up there one February and took my parents so they could see where we kept disappearing to. We got snowed in for several days and even then there was only one route open. But the lasting memory was taking my late father up to Lochgoilhead so I could dig bait. Flat calm and silent and then from who knows where came the sound of a piper playing- absolutely magical.

Tall Tale 5

Boat Fishing

On occasions we had been invited to join the Divisional Boat Fishing section and had declined, but one fateful day Colin, Derek, and Pete, went along to make the numbers up. Newhaven was the venue and we made our own way there. We met at a café near the jetty and followed the other lads down to a boat that was waiting for us. We did not know any of the other lads or the skipper but that was about change rapidly.
 Rodney was the organiser. I had seen him about but had not got to know him. Another bloke named Bill who sported a scraggy beard and spoke posh introduced himself. We were led by the nose by these gents and put together our tackle. Fortunately for us the weather was supreme, warm, sunny and with no breeze; in fact perfect for boat fishing. The boat plodded on for about an hour then stopped and the anchor went down. The other five dropped their baits into the water and more or less left us four to get on with it. We were on another learning curve and several fish later, caught by the regulars, it began to dawn on us what we should be doing. At the end of the day we had a few fish in the bag mainly dogfish, there were a few spurdog and one bass but all in all, speaking for

myself, I really enjoyed the day and Bill became one of my best mates and remained so until his untimely and unexpected death in February 2001, a great shock and a sad loss.

We were now becoming an integral part of the sea fishing section at Walthamstow Nick and we entered many fishing competitions but got nowhere and in the end gave up mainly because we did not like the ethics of killing fish just to weigh them and then in the main the fish were abandoned on the beach or in a nearby dustbin. We retracted and became conservation minded only fishing for particular species and returning them as quickly as possible. This did not suit everyone in the club but we four stuck to it and eventually won them round to our way of looking at things. After all in those days the fish used to climb up your line and after having fresh fish on the table who wants frozen stuff?

The venues we fished varied and we caught fish wherever we went but as we gained more and more experience we started to spread our wings and try other methods. For instance, none of us had ever tried drift fishing with pirks so we decided to go to Folkestone and try on the Varne Bank. We had been told that the boat to get if possible was Jim Coker's or failing that his son, Mick. The call was made and we were told by Jim what we required i.e. stout rods 60lb line, feathers built on 100lb nylon and pirks weighing 2lbs. We could not take this in and to be frank took little notice of Jim's instructions and turned up on the day with 30lb line and mackerel feathers and pirks made out of ½ inch copper tube. On the jetty was another crew who had Mick booked and they had a box on wheels full of homemade and shop bought pirks plus all the other equipment required.

They saw what we had and told us not to let Jim see it. If he did the trip would be off before we started. As it turned out it should have been. We got to the Varne about 15 minutes behind Mick to see the lads on his boat pulling cod to 12lbs over the side of the boat in 5's and 6's. We tried to copy what they were doing but the gear we had brought was useless and during the first two drifts we had two small pollack. Rodney bit the bullet first and very shortly afterwards Jim's supply of pirks and feathers were quickly exhausted at a price of course. Jim was now a happy man. He had a crew of fishers who should be able to catch fish.

We later discovered that father and son were great competitors and ribbed each other mercilessly about the fishing they provided for their customers. On that occasion we were unable to satisfy Jim that we were worthy of his time and he took a lot of convincing to take us out on *Portia* again. He was a hard man and would not suffer fools lightly. However we eventually won him round and he relented but only in as much as taking us out. He still drove us hard when we were on the drift. "Hit the bottom hard lads," was his call and anyone not doing just that was barred for the next trip. The club fished with Jim and Mick for quite a few years and we had some hairy trips at times. On one occasion we were waiting on the jetty for them to turn up when two lorry drivers came along and asked if we were going out fishing.

"Yes," was the reply.

"You have to be mad to go out there, my lorry was sick on way across."

I must admit it did look a bit hairy but Jim and Mick brought the boats over to the jetty and we were invited on board. Once clear of the shelter of the harbour I knew that this was a mistake and several of us myself included started to behave like lorries; the deck was awash with tackle, bodies and vomit. It was horrendous.

Jim said, "It will be ok once we clear the land," but I noticed he was standing with his feet inside the one and only life ring on the boat. To say that I enjoyed that day would be a lie and I swore that I would never again go out when the wind was above a four and to this day I have stuck to my promise.

At about this time the crews for the Varne began to waver and we were obliged to ask outsiders in to make up the numbers. One of these was our local tackle dealer in the 'Abbey', Peter Hall. He had at that time no experience of sea angling but was a born angler and could catch fish in his bath water. He soon showed us the way home beating all of us at our own game. After a few trips from various ports and at some being given the Bum's rush, Pete stated that he was about to get a boat of his own and would require help in keeping it ship-shape and also in launching and recovering it. I was there like a shot. I had no say in the type of craft he was about to get after all it was his project but he did a lot of research and finally decided on a Pilot 590. This was a lovely boat to fish from being almost 20 feet long and 6'6" wide. It was a cathedral hull and very stable. She was powered by an Evinrude 70hp outboard and by the time we had finished she was very well equipped having a ship to shore radio, depth finder, compass and flares.

Electronic charts and GPS were a long way off in those days and Decca was a luxury only for the very few, mostly commercial boats.

Tall Tale 6

The 'Pleasures' of Night Fishing

Jim and his two brothers Andy and Richard wanted to try night fishing so Pete and I agreed to give it a go. We had intended to get offshore a bit and try for Thornbacks but as usual the best laid plans of mice and men went up the Suwannee and, as the wind grew in strength, we forced to retreat to the shelter of the river. We parked up on a bank known as Thirslet Spit, famous in its day for good fishing. Bass, smoothhound, and thornback have been caught there. However it is a different place in the dark even though street lighting can be seen on both sides of the boat. None of us were comfortable and as the night wore on heads began to drop and snoring was heard. Andy was very tired and asked if he could go into the cuddy. We made room and he disappeared. Everyone must have fallen asleep and I awoke to a loud banging. As I opened my eyes it was daylight and sun was quite high. My watch told me it was 1100. On the deck and huddled up against the cuddy door were the other three buried under waterproofs and Andy was banging on the other side of the door pleading to be let out of the cuddy.

We surfaced one by one demanding to know what was going on and why all the fuss from Drew. We let him out expecting him to dash for the side of the boat to relieve himself. This did not happen but as he came through into the fresh air he was followed by a terrible smell and hanging on the back of his salopettes were two flattened festering packets of squid. It was these that he was trying to escape from but they refused to go away even after we had rinsed the offending garment in sea water.

That was my first and last go at night fishing expeditions, some may say I don't know what I am missing but as far as I am concerned you can have my share of it.

Tall Tale 7

Another Learning Curve

Now came another learning curve in my chosen sport or pastime call it what you will, Navigation. Pete was a sailor man and had skippered a schooner owned by the Civil Service Yacht Club and had also been a keen dinghy racer before that. He knew his way around a chart and taught me all I know about getting around at sea without hitting the bottom or anything else for that matter.
During the first year of his ownership we would fish together mostly from Canvey Island where there is an easy slip at Two Trees although the creek to the open water is a bit tricky and on occasion we were obliged to wait for the tide to get home. We had no local knowledge and used the chart and sounder to determine our marks. Up to a point we did OK but only just.

It was on the return of a dismal day's fishing we met a man who opened our eyes and to whom I shall be eternally grateful. We were getting the boat back onto the trailer when he offered to assist us. Why not? The more the merrier! Then he asked if we had caught anything and if not he could tell us where to fish next time we came, "Pull into the golf range we'll have a cuppa and bring your chart."

Pete and I were a bit dubious about him but we were ready for a cuppa so we humoured him and the following 15 minutes we learned more about the Thames Estuary than we could have done in a life time. Our chart was covered in marks that had to be fished at varying times of the year with varying baits for the seasons. The fellow who was divulging this information also said that he was able to supply any bait we may require and also offered to accompany us on our fishing trips. His name was Tony Barret which he appended to our chart along with his address and phone number. He then bid us farewell stating that he was at our disposal should we ever require him.

On the drive home Pete and I discussed the proposition we had just been given, our conclusions were "He must be mad or just escaped from the happy farm." However having got home and after giving thought to what Tony had given us I saw Pete the next day and we decided that nothing ventured nothing gained was a good adage to follow. The following day I phoned Tony and we arranged to meet the following Wednesday at the slip way on Two Trees Island.

The day arrived and having arrived at Two Trees Pete and Bill and I started to get the Waltham Angler off the trailer, an easy job at high water, although Bill used to make it hard by hanging onto the transom and going all the way with the boat finishing up with a BOOTY BEFORE WE HAD EVEN STARTED. We had told Bill about Tony and he had asked if he could come along. Just as we had finished launching, Tony turned up in his battered Morris Minor van and proceeded to unload his tackle, and then three large trays each filled to the brim with in turn, ragworm, lugworm and crabs there was enough bait to supply an army of anglers. Tony's tackle looked a bit old fashioned as well. the rods appeared to be one piece boat rods with about four eyes and a tip ring, and the reels were the sorriest Abu 7000's I have ever seen painted with Blue Hammerite and loaded with what looked like 50lb mono. None of us made any remark but I am sure we were feeling a bit apprehensive about this trip and what we had let ourselves in for.

With the gear and grub loaded we set off on the most memorable day's fishing I have ever had. Pete was at the helm and Tony conned him down the Ray Gut out to Southend Pier and from there we went East and kept going, I should explain that at that time we carried only 15 gallons of fuel on the *Waltham Angler* and it used it at about 5 gallons an hour. Also we liked to keep one can in reserve for emergencies; therefore our marks were generally within an hour of the launch site. On this day all that went out of the window and Tony kept us going East, and I was getting a little concerned as the first hour came and went. However the fuel was not being used up too quickly as we were running with the tide. Even so I and two others on board were relieved when Tony told Pete to slow down and we went to the mark he had selected.

Tony explained that we would be here for about an hour and that we should use the worm bait, he did not bother to fish with us and for that hour we caught codling, whiting and dab even an odd bass. It was non-stop action.

Then he stated that it was time to move and pointed to the West but a little South of where we were. At least it was nearly the way home I thought worrying about the fuel situation. We motored for about 25 minutes and by this time we were on the second can of fuel and we were aiming at a construction standing well clear of the water. There appeared to be five or six towers joined together with catwalks. Tony explained that they were called *Shivering Sands Towers* and they were world war two defences against enemy aircraft using the Thames Estuary as a glide path to London, they had been armed with artillery and manned by soldiers and were even given the HMS title. Pete was instructed to go into the centre of the complex and then to a particular leg onto which Tony attached us with a length of rope he then let us fall off on the tide until the leg behind us was about 40 feet off the stern. The method he told us to use was as follows, The legs stand on barge like platforms that are about 10feet tall, so baited with crab and with the correct amount of weight on it is possible to trot back until the gear arrives at the base of the platform. This was where the bass liked to lie, not as I imagined down-tide of the obstruction but in front of it. We were told to wait for knocks that would be light and trembly then not to strike but to tease the bait away slowly and when all went heavy to lift into the fish, again a new learning curve and not altogether convinced we started fishing.

Tony got his rods from the cuddy and went forward onto the foredeck. He did not take any bait only a crate he had brought with him. Before he left us he requested that all bass above 20 inches be kept, the rest put back. Surely he was out of the 'Happy Farm' and by now had us convinced. Bill was the first to pull a good sized bass from the foot of the tower and as the tide continued to ebb more and more bass came to the boat and we were amazed to find that most of them were over 20 inches long. We only kept about three in ten each and returned the rest but our tally was about forty fish. Tony had caught that amount on his own and all his were in the box. He had been casting a red gill across the wreckage and retrieving it slowly along the bottom amongst the old iron and snags, hence the 50lb mono the end gear which comprised of a three way swivel, 5 feet of 50lb mono to the gill and a foot of 15lb to a four ounce lead or anything else that would permit the cast. The hook in the gill had been changed to a fine wire Aberdeen 5/0 and that was so that if it snagged it would bend out or break easier than the standard red gill hook. From there it was a case of who dares wins.

On the way home we discovered that Tony was in the process of getting his own boat and would be chartering it but he also fished commercially and as a result of this we parted company. I forgot to mention that we got back to the slipway with about a cupful of fuel left.

John Krupa

The Jumper Lure

Ed. *Keen sea-angler John from Bristol has fished many parts of the UK and has a vast experience of sea angling especially in the English Channel.*

I remember a trip over 40 years ago now. It was a trip down to Brixham and we were to get there at the crack of dawn because we were going out to fish a mid-Channel wreck on a boat called the *Paulanda* which was a converted trawler. Although very stable it was not the fastest boat on the sea.

As we arrived on the quay there were six of the regular guys and a couple of newbies, one of which was a young lad of about 14 years old. We all boarded the *Paulanda* and started the long boring trip out to the first wreck. About three and a half hours later we arrived at the wreck and the skipper set up for the first drift. By now we were all set up and ready to drop down because we knew we only had about three hours fishing before we had to leave for home.

There was an assortment of pirks, muppets and red gills heading for the sea bed but the young lad didn't seem to have any gear. The skipper appeared out of the cabin with an old looking rod and reel tackled up with a weight and a rusty hook and handed it to the lad. This was baited up with a chunk of mackerel and lowered down. After about an hour we had some fine pollack and some really big ling on the boat but apart from one pouting the young lad haven't caught anything. As the skipper went up tide for another drift the young lad was looking at one of the rigs on one of our rods intently then to my amazement he took of his coat, picked up my filleting knife and started to cut a large hole out of his red hand knitted jumper. I completely missed the next drift because I was watching what the lad was doing. He was pulling long strands of wool off and tying them to his hook and making a sort of large saltwater fly. On the next two drifts he landed a mid-double figure pollack and a ling that must of been at least 30lb.

I don't know what that lad is doing now but I bet he is successful in whatever it is.

John Taylor and others recall memories with Ivan Wellington, skipper of *Top Cat* in Weymouth

Ed. *John, from Aylesbury, has been a great supporter of the Weymouth Charter Angling scene*

I caught the tail end of the "big" man's career. These were memorable trips not only for the fishing and fun but also for being unbeatable at Pop Master.
I've heard a few tales about Ivan.
From what I can gather his contribution to charter fishing in Weymouth goes back a bit so there must be some stories/ funnies out there?
In my own experience he was better picking a good fishing mark than picking a winner in the 3.30!

Les Jones

A Lesson Learnt

Ed. *Les is the charter skipper of White Maiden based in Lymington and a man with a lifetime's connection with and experience of the sea.*

I guess we have all done this at least once but in my first couple of months I took a charter crew from Kidlington SAC to Atherfield Banks, south of IOW, and being a flat calm day with a small tide in April, I was as excited as the boys were.

Well, our vessel called *Due South* was 26' length and teamed with a 200 HP Perkins Sabre engine, would easily fly along at 17 knots. As we headed towards St. Catherine's, I spotted a sunfish. Being in a state of high excitement myself with my brain in a detached ecstasy and feeling like I was on my own again in my little Shetland, I pulled the throttle back into neutral and shouted over the roaring engine, "Look a Sunfish!"

As I said that a fella flew into the cabin smashing into my dashboard. He had a knife that luckily remained blood free. God knows how but he managed to keep hold of it safely.

At the same moment another fella hit the cabin. Gear flew everywhere!

When I said again, "Look, it's a sunfish," I realised that the deep hole I had just dug for myself was already too deep.

So I apologised and checked they were alright. None of the boys said anything and we carried on in silence. I certainly never did that again and have never forgotten it. We did have a good day afterwards and it was years before we saw another sunfish!!

The club still book with me but their last three trips have been cancelled over last three years have been on Force 8+ days.

One of them crews maybe?

Lyle Stantiford.

First Proper Rough Weather Lifeboat Shout!

Ed. *We in Weymouth are justifiably proud of Lyle's achievements. Although still a young man, Lyle has always had 'an old head on young shoulders'. Fellow classmates tell me Lyle was already 40 years old when he was just 10. Apart from being the consistently superb skipper of Supanova, Lyle spends hours in various Committee meetings and on the computer helping the local harbourside community he loves so much. His career in the Lifeboat Service sums him up as one who always puts others before himself.*

When I first joined Weymouth Lifeboat crew in May 2006 aged 18, I had been working for Chris Caines of Tiger Lily for around a year and was still working on Sundays in Andy Selby's Weymouth Angling Centre. Many visitors and anglers to Weymouth will remember Richard Garton who used to manage Weymouth Angling for Andy. Richard had been crew on the lifeboat for a number of years and was always encouraging me to try and join. It was always great to hear Rich's stories of interesting shouts he had been on, like when he was late picking me up for work on a Sunday because he had spent all night out standing by two merchant vessels in the channel that had collided! I had to try and get involved and from May 2006 I began my life boating journey.

As a very green young lad trying to forge a career at sea and training up to become a crewmember at the lifeboat station, the mass of seagoing experience I had to feed off was huge and without doubt the great individuals I have had the pleasure to learn from has put me in the position I am today.

People always ask, "Why do you give so much of your time to the lifeboat?" and yes, the obvious answer's of giving back to the fantastic local community and the feeling of helping someone in need at sea are very true and definitely big players in why I volunteer but to be honest most of all it's fun and exciting to work with a fantastic group of people that are like extended family and to put to sea in, at times, atrocious conditions with unbelievable leaders and team members in fantastic bits of kit is fun! But not always glamourous…………..

In the early days of volunteering in Weymouth every crew member starts as shore crew, then probationary crew before progressing further and, to be honest, I recall the boats putting to sea in my early days and being stood on the pontoon wishing I could be on the boat with the team beating out there in a southerly gale. Call me wrong in the head but the rougher, more challenging jobs is why every lifeboat person signs up; it's what some call "proper lifeboating!" In the days of being a shore helper when the pager used to sound, there was always a little hope that there may not be enough crew respond and I may get the chance to go on a shout.

So my first taste of "proper life-boating" came in October 2007. The pager sounded in the early hours, I forget the exact time. As normal I made my way to the lifeboat station to assist getting the boat away to sea and as I was still probationary crew I didn't expect to go on the shout. It was a pretty nasty night with showers and a strong south to south westerly wind of a good gale 8 which later turned into a steady force 9.

On arrival at the Lifeboat station I made my way down to the pontoon to assist getting Weymouth's Severn Class All Weather Lifeboat, *Ernest and Mabel* ready to go to sea. After completing my shore crew bit, I made my way into the boat house. Normally you would expect a crew room of eager volunteers ready to go but on this occasion there were five crew, myself and new shore crew Matt Green. The coxswain Andy Sargent explained that the shout was to a 24m Brixham registered beam Trawler *Emilia M Emiel* that had lost all propulsion the day before and her sister ship had her under tow in a position 6 miles south of St Albans Head. The sister ship's tow had parted and conditions were too severe on scene for her to try and establish another tow. Due to the lack of crew, myself and Matt were instructed to get some gear before receiving a thorough briefing from Andy about what we were and weren't to get involved in.

Other than us two green horns the crew were very experienced and consisted of full-time Coxswain Andy Sargent, the then full-time mechanic Hefin Roberts, the late great Deputy 2nd Coxswain Trevor Brooker, Jules Hutchings who was Weymouth lifeboat's longest standing female crew member and navigating whizz and Graham Keates who served in excess of thirty years as a Weymouth Lifeboat volunteer before retiring a few years ago. Graham was the youngest crew member on the famous Bronze Medal shout in the hurricane of 1987 that the then Weymouth Lifeboat *Tony Vandervell* launched to the catamaran *Sunbeam Chaser*.

I've got to be honest that the steam down to the Head, sat in the Dr's seat at the back of the wheelhouse was probably the most anxious I have been on a lifeboat. The further east we strayed from the lee offered up by Portland the worse conditions got and in under an hour the throttles were eased back as we approached the two vessels. As we eased back, Matt and I were instructed to rig the two search lights on the upper steering position and once complete come back down to the wheelhouse. By the time we came back down we were only a couple of hundred yards from the *Emilia M Emiel* and her sister ship.

Anyone who has had the pleasure of passing over St Albans ledge on a big ebb tide and south west wind will appreciate conditions were pretty horrendous. I could see the *Emilia* rolling from Beam to beam with her gunwales disappearing under water as she rolled heavily in the confused sea. I remember thinking, "what use am I on here?" When we re-entered the wheelhouse, Andy was speaking to Trevor about how best to go about towing the vessel. He broke conversation and said to me to, "Stick with Keatesy." I was happy with that, under the wing of the most senior crew we had; that would do me.

A few more minutes passed as Andy formulated a plan and told Matt he would be on the bridge with him to man the searchlight. Trevor made his way on deck to prep and rig the tow line. Graham was down below in the survivor's cabin so I waited in the aft end of the wheelhouse for him to come back up. At this point Andy made his way out of the wheelhouse and as he placed a boot on the steps up to the bridge he said to me, "Keep an eye on Keatesy," and my immediate reply was, "I thought it was supposed to be the other way round?"

"He needs a shit!" was the explanation.

Bamboozled by what on earth was going on, I turned to my right to be handed, by Graham, a roll of the finest quilted, (when I say 'quilted' it resembled 60 gritt sandpaper) half damp toilet roll. This was it my first real experience of "proper life-boating." In a gale of wind and I found myself clinging on in my right hand to Weymouth's most senior crewmember, a man I looked up to and admired while he offered his back end out the rails of the starboard quarter to get rid of last night's dinner and, in my left hand, the roll of loo paper that I'm sure to this day Graham regretted putting anywhere near his nether regions.

Glamorous life-boating this was most certainly not!

After this rather close encounter and relationship cementing experience between Graham and I, it was quickly on to the job in hand ensuring the crew of the *Emilia* would get to some sort of safety as soon as possible. Andy had already decided that towing the vessel was by far the safest way of saving life that night so that is what we did. Trev had the tow all rigged ready to pass while Graham was manning the line on the bollard and my job was to feed the rope off the drum that held the tow line as and when I was told to. Andy positioned the lifeboat around 20 yards from the starboard bow of the *Emilia*, slightly up wind. This was a serious piece of boat handling and seamanship to hold her there long enough not only for Trev to pass the heaving line but for the crew of the *Emilia* to secure it their end. Fortunately dealing with fishing boats does mean we don't have to give a precise brief of how we need things doing, these guys as professionals just get on with it and in good time too.

In what looked like a gentle lob from Trev, the heaving line flew through the air and straight to the hands of the awaiting crew who speedily pulled the heaving line on board which was attached to our larger tow rope which was quickly secured to the bow of the *Emilia* and the paying out process could begin from our end. This night I learned in simple terms the bigger the boat and the worse the conditions the more tow rope you let out. Easy. That night we let out all bar fifteen metres of our hundred and eighty metre tow line with a large hessian fender tied in the middle to help reduce the snatch in the rope. Once the paying out was completed Andy engaged both engines in gear, slow ahead just to take the weight and see how the boat behaved behind us and what sort of progress we could make and to where!

It quickly became apparent that pushing that weather back towards Weymouth would have been the wrong move in so many ways and add a lot more risk with the prevailing conditions so Andy made the decision to shape up for Poole. We were making a slow 2-3kts with the 150 ton plus vessel behind but things were fairly comfortable and were looking at 3-4 hrs to Poole harbour entrance punching the tide. About an hour in, a particularly large set of waves came through and I could see out of the aft window the tow line flailing around like a piece of dental floss in the breeze as the load came back on to the rope. Shortly after this there was a loud crack and a jolt in the boat as the tow line parted on the bow of the Emilia. We were quickly on deck and Andy on the bridge to manoeuvre the lifeboat while we recovered the whole tow line back on board and attempt to re-establish the tow, which we did in fairly good time.

Whilst the tow was being re-established Portland Coastguard had decided to launch our flank station Swanage and their Mersey class lifeboat. The Mersey is an older design than the Severn that we have in Weymouth and considerably smaller but still a very capable lifeboat. Swanage were quickly on scene to stand by should the need arise. Around forty five minutes in to the second tow, Bang! the same again; the tow had chafed on the bow of the Emilia and parted again. I remember thinking to myself this is not meant to be tonight! At this stage as we were well into Swanage's patch it was decided they would take over the tow and proceed with the vessel up towards Poole where they would be met by Poole's Tyne class lifeboat to assist with the tow up through Poole harbour and moor the Emilia safely on Poole quay.

At this stage we stood by while Swanage established their tow and were shortly after released by Portland Coastguard to return to station. It's always a little frustrating when you don't get to see a shout through to the end but we certainly played our part that night. It was first light before Swanage and Poole Lifeboats managed to get the Emilia alongside in Poole.

In the preceding years up to the present day I have probably been involved in more physically and mentally demanding shouts in sometimes worse conditions but this one will always stay with me and I often think back over it a have a little chuckle and enjoy telling the new crew what might happen one night when someone gets caught a little short!

FOURTH WAVE

Malcolm Nightingale

Bassing with Stuart Arnold

Ed. *Living in Poole, Malcolm knows the south coast and its skippers very well. Malcolm recalls fishing with the pioneering skipper from Brighton, Stuart Arnold, who was famous for his bassing expertise aboard his superb Lochin called Catch-Up.*

Thanks for the invite to the Sea-dog Tall Tales group. Some of the photos and tales are amazing of how the UK charter angling industry has built up to what it is today.
The skipper I admired the most and got me hooked years ago was Stuart Arnold who operated out of Brighton. I hope some people have some pictures of the Lochins he had from *Catchup* 1 through to *Catchup 3*. His book taught me a lot the art of wreck fishing.
And when bass fishing he used to make us laugh because as soon as he saw another boat heading towards him he used to spit feathers and move off before they reached his secret marks. But to this day I have still not had another double figure bass like the one I had on his boat of 16lb over 20 years ago caught on a live mackerel hooked through the nose with its tail chopped off.
One thing he taught me and I still hold to this day is that I am a firm believer of that all you skippers say: "Listen to the skipper and keep it simple".
I'm not sure if he's still alive and the last I heard was he had issues with his eyes and moved to America so not sure if that is true and hope someone can shed some light on it.
Good luck to you all and hope you all survive this pandemic so we can all go back to what we all love, fishing and laughing and making friends.

Ed. *On being asked by Seadog members if he had any update on Stuart, Malcolm replied*:

Malcolm - *I fished with Stu towards the end of his time in the UK in Eastbourne. He needed a double cataract op which I believe was largely successful.*
A top skipper who struggled to accept the massive drop off in catches on the Sussex wrecks. He was generous with his information and could still sneak out good fish but those big bass which were previously on the wrecks in numbers were long gone. His tale of a twenty pound plus bass lost at the net due to an angler not doing what he was told will live with me forever.
He did successfully relocate abroad and a friend did bump into him but I am not at liberty to divulge where. I truly hope he is still with us as I always enjoyed his company at sea.

Martin Sharp

Big Game fishing from a Tanker!

Ed. *Boatmaster Martin from Bristol has travelled the world on big ships and caught enormous critters from many of them but is just as happy small boat fishing for hounds and cod!*

I've always had a passion for fishing in anyway shape or form . I was going to do a skipper's mate's apprenticeship with Brixham and SW fisheries when I left school but unfortunately for me BP shipping contacted me and the lure of deep sea exploration won the day. Still, I had a laugh and wouldn't change it for the anything .

I caught my first ever shark from 'my' ship and by the time I secured it and ran up to the ship's bar for help and returned...just the head was left with the rest of its 200lb hammerhead body devoured by other sharks... and so I went on to catch all sorts of critters all over the world. I was even daft enough to throw a live mackerel at a marlin from a 300,000 tonne super tanker and I watched my Daiwa 600h reel empty in a few seconds.

The Mick Sands Section

Tall Tale 1

Mick's Epic Voyage; The Volunteer

Ed. Mick, known as Mikki Brikki, introduces himself below but let me add how delighted I am that he has survived and be able to contribute with this fine tale. By 'survive' I refer to the many times Mick has turned up at the boat for his day's fishing in an injured state. I don't just mean a little cut…Mick has the ability to fall off and over and under just about everything and anything on a building site. Over the years his injuries have been more than impressive…but does it stop him turning up to go to sea? No, never! So, well done Mick for surviving no matter what you manage to do to yourself and still conjure up a magical tale for us all to enjoy.

Hi Guys
I've been inspired by all the contributors on this page, and I would like to share, and hopefully entertain you with my story!

I'm Mick Sands, a bricklayer and builder by trade and have been a poor angler for many years having been introduced to angling by an old mate Chris (the bucket) Vince. We fished mainly out of Lymington with skipper Humphrey Elliot on the Compass Rose, spending as much time steaming out to sea and back again as we did fishing. Having survived fishing from Lymington, Keyhaven and around the rear end of the Isle Of Wight; we discovered a new superstar of the angling world had emerged in Weymouth. What a game changer; all trips done at a million miles an hour, with a Concorde sounding sonic boom thrown in and all accompanied by great humour.

My story returns to the summer of 1989 and one of my great clients, Chris 'Newby' Vincent. Chris' wife Maureen wanted a new car so I did a deal with Chris to take Maureen's old car (an '84 Audi 90) for my wife, Julie. Julie and I, Chris and Maureen arranged to meet up and go out for dinner. We ended up at the *Fox at Tangley* with Julie nominated the delegated driver by the rest of us before we'd even got to the bar which says a lot about Mr & Mrs CNV and myself!

I believe we had a great evening, Mr Chris 'Newby' Vince (CNV) being the generous sort and, as the evening progressed, we got onto the subject of *Eisvogel* the 1936 wooden ketch owned by Captain Vince.

Now I could go on for ever – and probably did. During our conversation Chris said the ketch was in the Azores at the Island of Faial in Horta Harbour needing a new mast and a lot of Tender Loving Care. I cannot remember much more of that night except we all had rather a lot to drink…except Julie designated driver.

About five weeks later I was at home doing some paperwork when the phone rang. Upon answering it, Maureen 'Newby' Vince said, "Hi Mick, I need your passport number to book the tickets."

I naturally asked, "What tickets?"

"You volunteered to crew, sailing *Eisvogel* back from the Azores to Blighty."

Silence followed by more silence.

I managed to stutter, "I will call you back, Maureen. There must be a mistake."

I turned dumbfounded to a smiling Julie who assured me I had promised to crew and couldn't let them down now.

I tried, "How long will I be gone?" and, "Don't you mind?"

Julie said, "No it's only about two weeks."

I was scuppered.

A short time later I found myself on an aeroplane heading for Lisbon, Portugal. When we got to passport control I discovered I could not find my passport. I searched everywhere, with no luck and no passport. The guys at Passport Control, despite much cajoling by myself and the rest of my crew mates, would not budge – no passport no entry...and the next first available flight back to Heathrow.

I had my luggage returned and was given the address of the hotel where we were due to be staying.

And now, along with 100 Rothmans cigarette, I was left behind at the airport. I sat in a stark detention room, smoking and feeling very sorry for myself when the spitting image of 'Columbo' with dark hair and a tash (just as scruffy) ambles into the room.

He said, "Your tobacco smells good."

I told him to help himself, which he did.

Referring to the cigarettes he further observed, "Good and expensive. Why are you here?"

I told him the sorry story of my lost passport.

He asked where I had flown in from, took another fag and pondered for a moment and then told me to follow him.

The Passport Control officers started shouting. Columbo shouted back and off we went up three flights of stairs and into a large office full of uniformed police. Columbo marched up to the man in charge, who looked like a splendidly uniformed general, and then there was more shouting from both sides and off we went again, this time to a telex office.

We had another smoke there and he left momentarily, soon returning with two coffees.

There were then Telexs to and from Immigration and the office I was now in before Columbo told me my passport had been found in the Duty Free area of the airport. After more exchanges, he arranged for my passport to be sent to him and all my full passport details were then sent immediately.

With my details in hand we returned to the 'General's' office who grudgingly ordered his secretary to type up an official looking document to allow me to travel, even though it was just an internal flight. I noticed that the 'General' cheered up quite a lot after a few Rothmans' cigarettes. Columbo took me through the airport and to a taxi. I assume he told the driver the name of my hotel and instructed him that there was to be no sightseeing on the way and he then bid me Adieu.

At this point I gave him every cigarette I had with many thanks. We shook hands and he ambled away.

To this day I have no idea who 'Columbo' really was but the guy certainly had power and without his help that would have been the end of this story!

Walking into the hotel bar caused a huge roar and many drinks and merriment from my fellow travellers who were astounded that I'd re-joined them.

I never did pay the cab driver ...did he charge Columbo?

And so our adventure began on Azorean Island of Faial.

Tall Tale 2

Preparing Eisvogel

   After a couple of sight-seeing days in Lisbon, a beautiful city that I cannot understand why I have never returned to, I found myself, with much trepidation, back at the airport. But this time 'Voila'… no problem. There was even a message from 'Columbo' informing me that my passport would be in Faial in three days. The man was/is a shining star!

   On the plane I had a window seat for the journey across the Atlantic to the Azores. On the four-hour flight we only flew over the sea. We flew by Faial. I was on the starboard side of the plane and looking down I could see how the runway cut into the cliffs – and how tiny it looked. The landing itself was scary although upon touchdown full reverse thrust was applied and the pilot made the landing seem like a piece of cake although I sweated buckets!

   As we descended from the plane the humidity hit hard and the air felt very tropical. I have never been to a more informal airport and we waited on the tarmac as our baggage was unloaded.

   I can still clearly remember much of the bus ride to Horta Harbour as it must be one of the most colourfully dramatic places in the world. My head was on a spring with so much to see. Every inch of the sea wall is painted with the names of every boat that was ever there and 8kms away across the sea is the massive towering land formation that is the volcanic island of Pico.

   Now I hate camping. We drove around the sea wall to the hulk that was to become my home for the next four weeks. We get out of the bus and stood looking at a wreck of a very old wooden ketch with no main mast, looking very sad and small at just 60ft long and no more than 10ft wide. Oh joy!

   There are pictures of *Eisvogel* on Google and compared to the Charter Angling boat I fished from in Weymouth, it looked an uninspiringly worrying sight. I thought FFS; time to go home!

   We arrived at the boat late afternoon on a warm day and the next two weeks of my life were spent getting her fit to sail. Everything was removed from the boat and onto the harbour wall to get dry and clean starting with our mattresses and the sleeping bags we were to use. Some hours and hard graft later we had set up our bunks so we went off to town for booze and dinner. That first night we discovered the apparently world famous 'Pete's Sports Bar' a meeting place for mariners travelling back and forth across the Atlantic. The bar had many notices on its big board and lots of the scrimshaw carvings that adorn much of the Azorean buildings. It was busy, noisy, hot and a great craic.

   It is very odd waking up for the first time in a boat; the sway and smell being alien to me. Our next few days began with unloading the boat and sorting it out and let me assure you that for such a small boat there was a lot of kit to stow. Our evenings' dinner and drinks were well earned.

   At this point, my seafaring friends, let me tell you what I discovered about *Eisvogel*.

   Built In 1935, she was a 100 square meter Windfall Ketch designed by Henry Ramussen and built by Abeking & Rasmussen, Lemwade in Germany. She was one of Goring's fleet of racing vessels built and designed for the 1936 Olympics. They became prizes of war and sailed back to the UK from Kiel in 1946 and originally named *Relthen*.

This name was replaced by *Gladeye* from the popular WW1 song *Give Her The Gladeye Now*. *Gladeye* had some racing success in the 50's and 60's including winning a 'Division Class' as a 55mtr entry in the Fastnet Race. She was bought from Inverness, Scotland, in the mid-eighties by Mr Chris 'Newbie' Vince who renamed the vessel *Eisvogel*, which is German for Kingfisher. After the Fastnet Race, *Eisvogel* was raced in The Tall Ships category in England and won a number of competitions and awards. This ketch then went on to win a Transatlantic Cup for a race between Las Palmas and Barbados. Skipper, Chris 'Newby' Vincent, was very proud to own such a prestigious craft and hired an experienced crew to sail *Eisvogel* back from Barbados to Blighty. The experienced crew lost the main mast, ran out of diesel and were in bad shape before being saved by an Azorean fishing boat, who towed them back to Horta Harbour. I understand CNV sacked the whole crew when the sad tale unfolded and he made them find their own way home! Having known him a few years by then, I believe the story to be true.

Returning to our adventure, our crew now consisted of Chris and Maureen 'Newby' Vince, myself, Robbie who was a very shy chap, but great with anything mechanical, a guy called Linton, nice guy who enjoyed a drink and had Sarson's vinegar with every meal – and I do mean *every* meal and it *had to be* Sarson's and Bobby, the youngest crew member who was a rugby player with a massive chip on his shoulder.

On our second day in Horta Harbour emptying the boat, we came across a huge holdall with diving gear, including an air tank, tubes and regulators and a couple of weight belts. This caught my interest; was it for untangling a fouled propeller and resolving other such underwater mishaps? On this occasion, with the ketch in the harbour, it was going to be used by 'someone' to clean the algae from the bottom of the boat – how hard could that be??

It was explained to me that we needed to get the air tanks filled by a specialist and to also get him to check the mouthpiece and airlines over. I was instructed to "Go find one!!" Well, I had watched plenty of WW1 films and Jacque Cousteau so I set off round the harbour with the mission in mind. Within 30 minutes I had found just the thing. After another hour the diving gear was sorted and delivered back.

A local boat builder was employed to sort out the mainmast weeks before we reached Faial. Not a clue how, but one boozy night found me, with our crew, carrying this fu**ing huge mast from the boat builder back to the harbour. Talk about being as pissed as handcarts. Insanity…but a memory I will take with me to the grave.

With just Bobby and I at the boat one afternoon a few days later, I decided to become a frogman; yes, that's how stupid I was! We dug out all the diving gear. There were no fins, so deck shoes it was. Deciding to launch in from the rubber dinghy ,Bobby helped me into all the gear. I had a tentative suck at the regulator – yep, all good. The weight belt did seem heavy and I tried complaining but Bobby directed a lot of rude comments my way ending with something like, "You're a big girl's blouse. Just jump in."

I did but hung onto the rope. Eventually with a quick prayer I let go. About two seconds and twelve feet later I am up to my knees in ooze that is the harbour bottom.

Looking up I watch a stream of air bubbles heading for the surface. The water was gin clear and looking round all I can see were great holes in the ooze, like giant eel holes. With that I grabbed the rope and hauled myself to the surface.

Bob was indignant, "You've only been down there thirty seconds!"

My reply was, "Fuck that for a game of soldiers. Your turn."

Bob helped me back into the dingy and five minutes later we are sat on the sea wall bickering. I told him I'm not doing that again! The rest of the crew returned from a shopping trip and we explained the problem. Robbie then reached into the bottom of the holdall pulling out another diving belt. Laughingly he explained that the weight belt we had used stored all of the spare weights and showed me the quick release on the weight belt. A massive lesson learnt by me!

So with a little training, I spent a few days scrubbing the bottom of the boat. It was bloody hard work but made more interesting by a shoal of very colourful fish getting a free lunch. I think it was probably later in the year than I thought, probably the end of the first week in September when we reached Faial.

After the mast was refitted, one job that scared me to death was replacing shrouds on the main mast sat in the Bosun's chair on a windy day. That's a job for a proper seafarer. Our stay on the Island was much longer than planned as one of the stipulations in order to set sail was that we had to have a six-man life raft onboard. This was ordered from England and took a while to arrive. The Harbour Master was a particular stickler for the rules, trying to get me arrested for fishing in the harbour and nearly shooting me the next time he caught me!

On the many nights when we didn't go out, Maureen would cook us dinner accompanied by beer and wine. On these balmy nights, the crew would like to sing – very loudly. I remember late one evening this Dutch guy coming out of his boat begging us to stop singing; within ten minutes, he and his wife had a glass in their hand and were singing along although his boat was gone the next day.

With much amusement to the crew, I was the boat angler. One night we were having dinner in our favourite restaurant and there was another group of Brits there. After a lot of banter between us, they revealed themselves to be journalists writing for a number of fishing magazines and were visiting Faial to go game fishing on the American boat called *Double Header* that ran fishing trips from the harbour. We had a great laugh mainly at my expense about fishing. One of the journalists was very interested that I had an uptide rod with a Daiwa Procast reel with just fifteen pound breaking strain line. After discussion with his mates they offered to take me fishing with them the next day to try and achieve a line record. Well I was very excited about this. I had to be on the boat *Double Header* at seven thirty – Alas, I woke up at 11.15 am the next day..... OOoppppss!!

It was the end of the first week when the *Gentry Eagle* motored into the harbour and moored three boats away from us. The *Gentry Eagle* had just achieved the fastest non-stop crossing of the Atlantic from the USA to GB, claiming the blue ribbon. That afternoon Robbie was tinkering with our engine and I had been set some chore when three yanks walked by from the *GE*, stopping to admire *EV*, and asking questions. Robbie came to the rescue as he knew much more than I and invited them on board for a look round which they happily accepted. Upon leaving, we were invited to the *GE*. Later we all went to look at this new superstar vessel. Robbie was in his element inspecting the engines but to me standing on the bridge was like being aboard the Starship *Enterprise*. The *GE* crew were very generous. On the flying bridge was a liferaft container that was filled with ice, beer and soft drinks. (Only the yanks!) We met on several occasions afterwards, usually in Pete's Bar, and we partied until throwing out time. Faial was a very interesting place, shopping was like going back twenty-five years; one person served, another packed and yet another wrote everything purchased in a ledger and you paid someone else. There was a volcanic eruption on Faial in the mid-fifties and I remember going to an abandoned village where the lava flow had covered over half the houses. The village was obviously at one time at the end of the island as there was a dirty great light house there. Being the hooligans we were we got into the light house and climbed to the top to take in the view which was fantastic, carving our names in the stairwell wall on the way out.

Another place I remember was a car park adjacent to an extinct volcano with a tunnel cut through the volcano wall. The crater on the other side was straight out of Jules Verne's *Lost World*. I would not have been surprised to see dinosaurs, so lush was the vegetation.

Eventually our life raft arrived. The boat was provisioned with a limited amount of fresh food as there was no fridge but plenty of tins, tea coffee and UHT milk but no booze!

Two weeks after our arrival we motored out of Horta Harbour and into The Blue.

P.S Another strange thing that happened was that about three days before we left, a sailing yacht arrived in the harbour. It was very scruffy and looked particularly unloved. It had about five crew, two being women. It wasn't long before they were on the scrounge and carrying/wheeling stuff into the town to sell and generally looking like the 'Great Unwashed'.

On our final evening sing-song at the harbour, one of the girls came and begged to be taken off the island with us. The story went they were trying to get to Denmark. Apparently the young skipper/pirate had murdered the owner to the boat and buried his body in the Caribbean!

Well who knows?? Upon leaving we searched *Eisvogel* thoroughly for stowaways.

Tall Tale 3
Sailing the Atlantic from the Azores to France

It was a Thursday afternoon when we left Horta Harbour and motored to the end of the channel between Faial and Pico, pulled up the main sail and with the engines stopped could hear and feel the lap of the Atlantic against the hull; turning North-East we started for home.

That same afternoon we were each given a harness with a rope attached and told that these were for 'Rough Weather'. We had to clip onto a galvanised steel cable that ran around the perimeter of the boat – a safety lifeline!

The 'Watch Schedule' was worked out between us five blokes; we each had a three hour watch, with 12hrs off, around the clock with the skipper going first. The watch began at 3pm so First Watch was 3pm to 6pm, second 6pm to 9pm, third at 9pm to midnight and so on. Being the 'newbie', I was given the third watch. This meant keeping a good look out and an eye on the compass. As it got later, the crew would stay in the day cabin and it was down to the watch to look after the rest of the crew! Skipper Chris stayed with me till the end of my first watch, which was very comforting.

I can remember our first meal at sea; steak, potatoes and green beans, we ate on deck as the light was fading and Pico was sinking below the horizon; this was the last land we saw for some days.

Being built for racing, the *Eisvogel* is a very sleek 3ft from the water line, perhaps a little more; with the steering wheel set in a cockpit behind the mizzen mast. Your feet are about water level when sat in the cockpit; the cockpit being approximately 6ft wide and 12ft long with some wooden seating.

My first night sleeping on the moving boat was somewhat different. We were not going that fast as we were heading into an easterly breeze, about eight knots, with the propeller in neutral. As we glided through the sea the prop made a continuous ticking sound which was very therapeutic!

On the boat was a sea toilet and Mrs Skipper ensured that it was kept spotless. Woe betide the crew who failed in the vital task of maintaining its sparling appearance. After witnessing Robbie get a tongue lashing from Mrs Skipper, no-one made the same mistake. Ablutions were carried out on deck with salt water and saltwater shampoo and soap. I have to say that after a couple of days of feeling a bit all over salty, I got used to it. We (the crew) took it in turns to make breakfast, lunch and do the washing up. Mrs Skipper, Maureen, cooked dinner with the crew, in turn, washing up and keeping the cabin ship-shape.

The first morning was the start of a beautiful day. After breakfast I sat on deck sunning myself.

I watched the skipper entering the cabin and returning with a black sack, tied at the top with a bit of weight in it. Our skipper shouted at me to stay where I was but to watch carefully and with that tossed the sack, representing me on this occasion, into the briny at the same time shouting, "Man Overboard!"

The crew sprang into action, one person keeping a constant eye on the bag; the rest of the crew were bringing the boat around, resetting sails and chasing down the black sack, which under constant surveillance from the watcher shouting directions (and me as well as I didn't want to drown). Within fifteen minutes the bag was back on board and we were on our way again! Another valuable lesson learnt.

The journey settled into a routine but we were making slow progress as we beat against a easterly breeze. We played a lot of card games and I did a lot of reading. Bob loved his music and ,after he did a late watch, he would leave his Walkman and some tapes. I listened to Dire Straits' *Brothers In Arms*, Simply Red's *Picture Book* and my particular favourite was George Michael's *Faith*. It took away the monotony. Oh, little did I know!

On the fourth day out, I was on the 6pm to 9pm watch, which was on quite a calm night with the usual easterly breeze. I was watching a ship about four miles away on our starboard side and I told the skipper who went below to contact the said ship. He returned asking me to remain on watch until 21.30pm. No worries, skipper came back checking to see if all was OK. By then, it was getting very misty and the lights of the ship had disappeared. Returning to me again at 21.45pm and after a bit of a chat he took over the watch. A bit strange I thought as it wasn't his turn to be on watch but being the newbie I never thought any more about it. I went below, had a coffee and turned in.

I was very rudely shaken awake at about 3.30am by Bobby. The first impression on waking was the noise of the prop, which was a very fast whizzing sound. Bobby shouted at me to get my floatation suit and harness on. I bought the floatation suit especially for the trip and had it all on and up to the cockpit in swift order. What greeted me was a maelstrom of wind and sea spray. The skipper, still on watch, was calm but <u>Really</u> firm; telling Bobby and I to clip on the lifelines, get on deck and reef in the mainsail. Bloody difficult was an understatement as the boat was being tossed about all over the place with waves breaking over the boat. Being a lot younger and both of us as strong as bullocks, we got the mainsail down and reefed to the boon. My memories are of it being dark, noisy and wet. The skipper praised our efforts when we returned to the cockpit and then got us to drop and set the mizzen sail; so he had a way of steering and controlling the boat.

I felt great relief as the skipper gained some control of the boat. When I went to my bunk, we were heading North east at three knots. After getting the sails in, I slunk down next to the skipper. We were heading south with the knot meter now off the scale as it only went up to 12.5 knots!!

Bobby, as with the other three crew members, went down with mal-de-mere. I stayed with Chris marvelling at how he handled the boat in such appalling weather and handing him fags.

It got light around five am; the dawn bringing a clear, sunny but windy day with a very rough sea. The waves were enormous, way beyond what I could have imagined. We slowly climbed up each wave to quickly slide down the other side into the trough, surrounded by a wall of water.

This continued for another few hours and began to slowly abate, the wind easing and the waves becoming like an exciting day in a race. The squall eventually passed us by, or us away from it. The gas stoves were on gimbles so I was able to make Chris and I coffee.

We had survived a squall thrown out into the Atlantic from Hurricane Hugo. Chris had contacted the ship I had sighted, which turned out to be an Indian freighter. They had told him to expect some bad weather, which was why he had taken the extra watch. The freighter stood by all night, disappearing about seven am. By mid-day, other than massive rollers, one by one the crew appeared and by 2.30pm the sails were reset and we were heading towards home again; albeit now a lot further south than we intended. From then on, for the next four days, we saw not a thing; no planes, no ships not even a seagull. We were miles away from land with miles of water below us. At this point, Dear Reader, I realised just how big the sea is and we were considerably less than a flea on an elephant's rump.

At around Day Eight, the skipper made the decision to head for France, as we had already been at sea for a long time.

We were having dinner in the cabin that night. Robbie was on watch. The other five of us were sat round the table all eating. It was very quiet when we heard footsteps walking on the deck above us.

Bobby shouted to Robbie, "What are you doing?"

"Steering the boat, you buffoon," came the reply.

More footsteps heard and the hair on the nape of my neck rose up.

Maureen piped up with, "It must be Hans – or a ghost."

"Oh yes," the crew responded as we'd heard the sounds before.

Well, I never saw Hans but I did hear footsteps again that night. I know I know, but I know what I heard.

We made it into the Bay of Biscay and the weather was kind to us. I had a few fishing lures with me and thought I would throw out a line and try trolling. Much to the merriment of my crew mates, I caught a large tin of Portuguese sardines! Yes, very amusing ha ha...although when I landed a couple of strings of mackerel the next day, they laughed no more and we ate fresh fish for dinner. So, on a Sunday afternoon, after eleven days at sea, we motored into Camaret-sur-Mer Harbour on the furthest west point of France and north of the Bay of Biscay. We were berthed on a floating pontoon and after tidying and covering the sails, we all raced to the showers. What a treat to have hot fresh water. Once changed, we set off to the town for dinner. There was a fair on the harbour side and it was very busy. We ended up in a very nice hotel restaurant where good food and wine was consumed in great quantities. Much to the angst of the Management, loud singing started at which point we were bribed to leave with a box of booze. We had been in the restaurant for a long time so walking into the fresh air, I for the first time and only time, found myself legless – and once down I found it impossible to get up. I was helped to a harbour bench and much, much later, I made it back to my bunk. We spent the next day, Monday, getting over hangovers and cleaning the boat.

On Tuesday we all piled into a mini-bus and drove up to St. Marlow; catching the ferry back to Portsmouth and back to normality.

P.S. Revenge is a dish best served cold..........

My business did very well when I returned thanks to the wisdom of CNV.

At the time I banked with Lloyds and my bank manager was a great bloke who looked out for me but his Second-in-Charge was vertically challenged and suffered with short-man syndrome as well as being a first class twit. You know when things are going well when the Bank starts to invite you to civilised Soirees and one was at a nice hotel that Julie, my better half, wanted to attend.

The manager could not make it, so it fell to the Twit to take over. At one point in the evening, he condescendingly engaged me in conversation which was all about him! He told me that he and his friend owned a small yacht and that he loved sailing, going on to tell me how they had sailed to The Isle Of Wight to have lunch and were planning to sail to the Channel Islands in the summer. He dreamed about Blue Water (deep water) sailing. He then told me how he would love to visit this famous bar in the Azores.

At this I pounced. "Do you mean Pete's Sports bar overlooking Horta Harbour?" I asked innocently.

"Oh yes that's it; how have you heard about it?"

"Because- thinking you smug, little rat as I looked at him- I have been drinking and socialising in there before sailing home across the Atlantic. As his jaw hit the floor, I walked away, saying to my wife, "Time to go ….."

Dear Editor, *just a few postscripts. I didn't put in much detail about how much work there is involved in sailing with the number of ropes, winches and other running gear along with handling two masts and two mischievous booms with the constant trimming require when actually sailing.*

You, Dear Editor, will know how damp a wooden boat can get especially after being moored in warm climes. After the great squall, we had a drop of water in through the deck and as we sailed further North East and it got cooler, sleeping bags needed airing every day. Expansion and contraction, I suppose. The last two nights before France, I found myself sleeping in my flotation suit as it was dryer and warmer. Camaret is just south of Brest, on the north-west corner of France.

One other memory comes to mind. When on watch we would sit with our backs to the cockpit with our feet on the helm. We were in the Bay of Biscay and I was on the 6am to 9am watch. It was a very calm morning and I was admiring the sunrise when I heard a splash on my port side. We were slightly heeled over that way and I saw a pod of dolphins frolicking alongside the boat – man they were so close. I swear they were looking straight at me as they came alongside – it was indeed a magical experience! Mick Sands

Nick Crouch

Toed Off

Ed. More recently Nick fishes with Ryan Casey and Lyle Stantiford, Weymouth charter skippers of Meercat *and* Supanova *respectively and is an angler of lengthy experience recounting here a grim experience from 1988.*

Whilst steaming in after a day's charter in 1988, I was asked if we could stop and get a few fresh mackerel for the party to take home. Drifting past Sun Corner at the Needles, a steady flow of mackerel was coming aboard plus a few pollock. Having decided they had enough, we called it a day and were just about to head back to Keyhaven when two canoeists caught my attention. They were waving their paddles frantically at us.

I headed towards them to see what was up and was informed by one of them that they had seen a human leg floating close to the caves near Tennyson's Down. I asked if perhaps it was a dead seal or part of one but no this had a walking boot on it, I was assured. I wouldn't risk getting in too close so I gave one of the canoeists a landing net and off he duly set. He returned 15 mins later with the net and catch draped across the canoe's bow. He was retching, the poor chap.

The guy passed me the net handle and I started to lift the net and contents aboard but the stench was too much. I lashed the landing net to the gunwale and kept the leg in the water.

I contacted Solent Coastguard and explained the situation and they informed me they were sending *Freshwater One*, which was a medium sized RIB, out to assist.

I established radio contact with *Freshwater One* and within a short time they were with us. They tied up alongside and two of the crew jumped aboard with a black body bag and placed it on the deck. Although this was all very interesting for the anglers, I just wanted the leg gone. A mate had found a body in Southampton water whilst clamming and there were sorts of rumours that he would be responsible for burial costs etc if it was not identified.

Bulls**t or not, I didn't need that.

There seemed to be an issue with the body bag zip. It was corroded and the zip was stuck closed. The lifeboat guy was giving it some encouragement verbally. I said I had some WD40 and a pair of pliers and fetched them from the wheelhouse. This did the trick and the zip tab sheared clean off!

I said I had a roll of bin liners on-board and would they help? The body bag was rolled up and fired back into the RIB.

A bin liner was made ready and I lifted the net and leg clear of the water and swung it aboard. The stench was horrific. I was retching; so were the lifeboat crew as were the anglers... although they were still catching a few mackerel off the stern. I had to catch hold of the bottom of the landing net in order to flip the leg out and into the bin liner; never have I wanted a ring at the bottom of a landing net more.

We managed to get the leg in the liner first go and everyone was quite relieved. It was kinda out of sight so out of mind...that was until the Lifeboat crew man lifted it and started to swing it over the gunwale. The bag ripped and the leg hit the deck and slid off down towards the stern and the anglers had kindly washed the deck down on the way in and this aided the leg on its tour of my boat. To this day I can still see the Hi Tec walking boot on the foot.

We double bagged the liners and eventually got it off my boat to my relief. I thanked the lifeboat crew; they thanked me and off we set for home.

Over the next few days a torso and bizarrely two more legs were found in the area.

Back then our area (Needles) was home to many great characters and friends such as Ray Pitt, Ron Bundy, Ron Cowling, Roger Bayzand, Chris and Arthur Savage, my Father Bob, Robby Russel, Wilf Maybe and many more.

At 22 years old, I was a young charter skipper and naively told my friend, Ron Bundy, all about my day. The next day while we were at anchor south of the Needles. The fishing had gone quiet over slack water. The skippers were chatting about this and my father was in a conversation with Ron Bundy. These two were well known for having hilarious conversations over the radio and usually fitting each other up. The conversation centred around Ron Bundy trying to buy rag worms off my father as he'd heard his son had caught a nice sole off *Tennysons Down* yesterday. My father had ever so slightly over valued these ragworms but pointed out that the sole his son had caught was so immense that he had to get the lifeboat out to assist in landing it.

Ron agreed and admitted he'd heard that his Nipper had gone aground at the sand bar on the way in due to extra weight of this fish and had to be 'Toed' off.

Great characters...miss them both.

Chris Ponsford. *Quite a story, Nick Crouch. Was there any back story to the body parts and bodies, murders, gangland killings?*

Nick Crouch. *Hi Chris, I believe it was someone walking who fell off the cliffs. The spare leg, however, is still a mystery to me.*

Chris Ponsford. *But at least it's not sinister. But still a horrible experience for you.*

Nigel McLoughlin

Inkgate and the Things it Taught Me

Ed. *Nigel, from Reading, is a well-known angler, supporting many charter boats along the south coast of England. He often appears on Facebook sharing fine catches and an infectious good humour.*

A big 'THANK YOU' to those who have set this page up (referring to the Sea-dog Tall Tales Facebook page). The posts on here have been a tonic to the rest of us in these troubled times.
I'd like to add my "tuppence worth" in the hope that it may amuse a few of you. I guess I should call this *'Inkgate and the things it taught me'*.

For a number of years I'd book three days of tope fishing with Spike Spears, who operated *Bessie Vee* out of Langstone. The trips were for a group of five or six of us who wanted to catch the May-time run of these wonderful sporting mini sharks.
On day two of our trip in 2004 we were anchored on the *'Utopia'* grounds to the South East of the Nab Tower. The fishing was rather quiet, so we were contemplating a move to a Smoothound mark for a while before coming back to the same mark to catch it at a more productive state-of-tide.
We were on the 'ten more minutes 'til we move' warning when one of the guys, Andrew, said he'd got a weird bite and had started to wind something in. The usual remarks about plastic bags and rocks started to come out but a minute or so later Andrew exclaimed, "Sh*t! It's a nice cuttlefish!"
We needed some bait for a bream fishing session the following morning and this would do the job nicely. Spike was not in the best position to grab the net so he shouted for me to do the job. I grabbed the landing net and went to the stern, telling one of the other lads to get a bucket of water, then scooped up the cuttlefish. I lifted it over the gunnel and dropped it into the bucket.
Afterwards I stood there looking admiringly at the cuttlefish - a decent sized one of at least 2 kilos. I was leaning on the landing net handle feeling pleased with myself, naively believing that I'd avoided a case of *'Inkgate'*.
How wrong I was ...the events that followed took only seconds but seemed to unfold before my eyes in slow motion. The cuttlefish inflated itself to roughly the size of a FIFA regulation football with a loud sucking noise then belted its ink load out against the side of the bucket with considerable force. The side of the bucket acted as a baffle which resulted in an ink explosion. This went up the side of the fish box and over the deck, but mostly up my left leg, even managing to find its way up the inside of my shorts ...... and coming close to giving the compilers of the Oxford Dictionary an additional meaning for the word *'Blackball'*.
There followed a short, silent pause before it dawned on us what had happened ... then we all burst out laughing - but not just a bit of chuckle, or short belly laugh - this was the real 'piss-your-pants/can't-stand-up/need-oxygen' variety'!
Gasping for breath, I sank to my knees and used the side of the engine box to stop myself from falling any further, oblivious to the fact that I was spreading ink around the deck but unable to do anything about it anyway. Out of the corner of my eye I could see Spike doubled over, using one of the grab handles outside the wheelhouse door to support

himself. The rest of the lads had either knelt down on the deck like I had or were clinging to the gunnel rail for support, tears of laughter streaming down their faces - all thoughts of fishing forgotten for the time being - and pretty much impossible in the circumstances.

After four or five minutes of this, most of us managed to gain a little self-control. I pulled myself up using the end of the fish box and stood there with my left leg looking like I'd knelt in a mechanic's oil drain pan.

Spike said, "Shall I turn the deck wash on then, Nigel?"

"Yes please, Spike."

As he was about to step back into the wheelhouse, he turned to looked at me. We had a moment's eye contact ... big mistake ... it set the laughter off again - all of us laughing uncontrollably but this time mostly at each other's futile attempts to gain at least a little self-control .... priceless moments on a priceless day.

I learned two lessons that day - one practical, the other moral.

The practical lesson was: "Don't bring the cuttlefish into the boat until it's dumped its ink load (- *you messy bastard*)!"

And the moral one? It's a cliche - but it's true: Laughter really IS infectious ... and it's just the sort of 'Infection' we need at the moment given the current state of the World.

The Paul Maris Section

Ed. Paul Maris. *Whoever has met Paul from Takeley in Essex will surely have vivid and unforgettable memories of him. He is a true 'Essex Lad' and 'full of it'. His saving grace is his delightful and ever patient wife, Jackie, who is one of the three women I have personally nominated for the coveted 'Bravest Wife Award'. Paul has fished everywhere and with everyone and has enjoyed remarkable angling success at all levels of sport fishing from congering to International Bill-Fish Fishing. Not bad for a self-made lad who made his fortune from over-priced Garden Sheds.*

Tall Tale 1

Beware the Drop Off

Hi one an all. Those on here that know me will say I have been around for a long time maybe too long. I started back in The Sixties. In that amount of time you have so many memories and stories to tell. Back then the fishing for cod off the Essex coast was excellent. This was fishing reasonably shallow water, long before up-tiding, just lobbing our baits out off the stern of the boat. The one thing I remember about the winter fishing back then was how bloody cold it was. Our winters seemed so much colder back then and what didn't help was the clothing we had then compared to now is so different. Plus the tackle we used then was archaic to what is available now.

The tale I must tell you about was in the early seventies. I fished a lot with a guy called Michael Clark (Nobby) who was a water bailiff for the National Trust. We both ran Shetland Suntrips mainly out of West Mersey and towed them to other parts of the Essex coast. Nobby contacted me and said he had been talking to a guy called Bill Roberts who had a tackle shop In Leigh-On-Sea. It was suggested Bill would supply the bait and his local knowledge and we would supply the boat or boats. Nobby and I was aware of the cod fishing in the Thames and Southend in the winter but he introduced us to bass fishing especially at the *Red Sand Towers*. These were observation towers in World War Two that were also used by the pirate station *Radio City*. There was lots of rusting superstructure that was a haven for bass. Bill was the first guy I met that specialised in light line angling, casting small lures and jellies while we fished on the bottom with rag worm. Our catches of bass were back then exceptional, no monsters but nice fish up to about six pounds. Nobby and I often went out on our own when Bill couldn't make it from Two Tree Island and gradually learnt the area of where to fish.

Now we come to the story. One day Bill asked if he could bring his bait digger along to fish with us, no problem as four could fish comfortably on our boats. So along came a young lad called John Rawle. He was quite a nice lad back then and soon fitted in. On this day in question I can't remember how the fishing went but we were on Nobby's boat so he was at the helm. Now the one thing you needed to know when you came into Two Tree Island is there are a few sand bars you have to watch for. These were ok at high water but you ran the risk otherwise. Yes, you have guessed it. He decided to cut the corner and ran aground. He raised the outboard and John and Bill got out and started to push the boat. It started well their trousers rolled up and the water was knee high but they weren't ready for the 'drop off'.

Warning shouts came from the stern but they were too late as already there were two guys with water up to their necks coughing and spluttering out a few choice swear words. We managed to drag them in but the tears were running down our faces.

Happy days!!!

Tall Tale 2

Cod Galore

What instigated this piece is the story by Scott Belbin and the tales about his dad and how he started going from a pleasure angler to a charter skipper. Well I was a part of how it all started which was a long time ago.

The fishing back in the late 60's, 70's and 80's off the Essex coast was amazing compared to how it is now. Well, there is no comparison really. To give you an idea, we had a run of catches topping 200 cod a day with fish well in the mid 20lb bracket. I remember going out with an angling party on a number of occasions and seeing them getting smashed up, spools shattering and rods broken when they were not prepared and came under-gunned.

I feel extremely fortunate to have fished in those amazing days. Can I see it coming back? Sadly, the answer to that is no. Fishing back then there were no quotas and there was an abundance of fish all around our coast. The wrecks were full of quality fish. You see old photos of decks awash with fish.

Stewart had three sons Scott, Lee and Dale. Cheeky little buggers and they still are! They all like their fishing,

I hope I am proved wrong but I think the future of our seas and sea angling looks bleak; what with pollution and over fishing.

Going back to the old days, I remember a trip I had with Stewart and Mick Toomer out of West Mersey. We decided to anchor an offshore wreck at anchor to see if we could catch some conger. Now this might be a surprise to a lot of you but we didn't catch conger but did enjoy a nice catch of cod and some double-figured ling. Ling off the Essex coast was a bit of a surprise. It was on one of these trips with Mick Toomer when I said to him I fancied a wrecking trip off the south coast and who would he recommend.

He said his first choice would be Weymouth on a boat called *Offshore Rebel*.

Now that's another story methinks.

Tall Tale 3

"Maris, you're dead!"

Following on from my previous log on Mick Toomer's recommendation, I contacted Paul Whittall and booked a trip aboard *Offshore Rebel*. I can't remember how many of us went down to Weymouth on our first trip but one trip lead to another and it soon became apparent the diversity and quality of the fishing was second to none. We were fishing methods us Essex boys had never done before. It soon became apparent that if you went down there on a general trip you needed to take a variety of baits and gear depending on the states of the tides.

What I loved when inshore fishing was the Shambles Bank and the mussel beds. We couldn't believe the size of the plaice there was back in the eighties and so on. Then, when the tide picked up, you went for the turbot and brill. Then of course there was the Kidney bank with its huge blonde and undulate rays plus there was always a chance of a turbot or brill. But then there was the wrecking whether it was on the drift or at anchor. Paul also mentioned his trips to Alderney so we had to give them a go, stopping on the odd wreck on the way out and back. What a lovely place to visit and fish and the restaurants where pretty good too.

It was coming back from one of these trips that Paul said about the three day conger trip that had just started up. They had just fished their first comp and it was a great success so they hoped to do it on a regular annual basis. So we booked our places on the next one. I was a member of our local Takeley Sea Anglers Club. We had been telling some of its members of the great trips we were having in Weymouth and the Club was keen to give it a try. Well it was a great success. The amount of new club records we achieved and PB's was outstanding especially the conger.

Now that was a big wake up call for a lot of the members. The photo shows a couple of paper cuttings, one of our club trip and another of a successful Weymouth Conger Comp on *Offshore Rebel*. A couple of funny things I must mention on this particular day. We were gilling with live sand eels for pollack and cod and we were having a reasonable day and were on our way to another wreck when we saw *Tiger Lily* fishing on it. Paul called up Chris Caines and asked how he was doing to which he said he had had a few cod off it but nothing big. Paul said we would have couple of drifts and leave him to it.

My gear was an upside rod reel loaded with 15lb mono a 10ft trace with a 4/0 hook. We started the drift and at a given moment Paul said we were showing the wreck. Within seconds my gear locked up solid, sod it I've hooked the wreck but then it started to move. This was a bloody monster. Paul said to just try to hold on until we cleared the wreck. All I could think was I am never going to land this thing. Well, Lady Luck was on our side and slowly but surely I managed to gain line on it. I think we were about just over a mile from the wreck when it surfaced. It was the biggest cod I have ever caught. As we went back to the wreck and past *Tiger Lily*, I hung the cod up and shouted we had caught the big one so we were moving on. You should have heard the language. I often reminded Chris of that cod. I don't think he ever forgave me. Ha ha. It weighed 32lbs.

Those of you that know me know I like a bit of a laugh and a good windup. This particular trip was our club's two day weekend away at Weymouth. This time we had 18 members that wanted to go, so I contacted Paul and asked if he could find another boat for us. He came back and said he had got *Top Cat* skippered by Ivan Wellington. We had a draw for the two boats I had drawn the *Rebel* for the Saturday and *Top Cat* on the Sunday. My old sparring partner Dave Hawkeswood was on *Top Cat* on the Saturday. I had a quiet word with Ivan and said was he up for a laugh, which he was so the plan was set.

Now picture the scene... the crew was making their way on the boats when Dave, with all his tackle, just cocked his leg over the gunnel when this giant of a man came out of the wheelhouse, grabbed him by the scruff of the neck and said, "I've heard you wanted to be f****d by a black man!"

All I heard were screams of, "Maris, you're dead!!!"

Those of you that fished with Mr Whittall will know it was like going back to school. You knew if you made a mistake you would get a bollocking.

They were great days Paul that I shall never forget.

It was a blast mate.

Tall Tale 4

Televised Conger Comp

There was a documentary on the many activities taking place in the English Channel both work and leisure related. It was decided to cover the Weymouth three day Conger Festival filming the first and last day on *Offshore Rebel* with Adrian Brown's *Al's Spirit* on the middle day.

Now included in the film crew were two gorgeous young ladies. That was a bit worrying that they were going to be exposed in a confined area to a group of randy fishermen.

However the day arrived for them to be on our boat and what a day it was. We had never seen the outer harbour alive with mackerel. The whole fleet of boats filled their boxes before we had passed the end of the end of the pier. The weather was fantastic. On the way out the girls were in the wheelhouse interviewing the skipper but before we started the competition it was suggested that the girls interviewed me. They miked me up and there I was trying to have a sensible conversation in front of the camera with the rest of the guys behind the camera giving me a lot of rude signs, like give it some of that !! and a lot ruder. Well, the fishing was great we had a lot of eels and I was lucky to get a sixty pounder which won the day. But the bit I must mention is I spoke to one of the girls at the weigh in and asked her what she thought of the skipper?

She said she had never met anyone quite like him before. Ha ha ha !!!

Ed. *We were fortunate to win on both days that the TV crew ladies joined us...and to win overall. Usually the fish disappear when a camera crew are on-board!*

John Rawle. *The truth probably was, Paul, the girls came in the wheelhouse and asked you who that short assed little pervert was that they had just been talking to. And for Maris to win you must be a super skipper.*

Ed: John, you promised me you wouldn't reveal the contents of the wheelhouse recording!!!

Paul Maris: *If you dish it out you have to be prepared to take it. It is nice to have a bit of banter with all the crap that is going on in the world.*

Tall Tale 5

First Involvement with Game Fishing

It was back in 2001 that Dave Hawkeswood and I got involved with big game fishing in a serious way. It kicked off when we saw on Sky Sports about Xmas time 'Marlin fishing in Mauritius' featuring the *Marlin World Cup*. This had a number of sponsors, mainly Air Mauritius, Sky Sports and World Matchplay which was run by Barry Hearn who always brought a celebrity out to fish.

Keith Arthur was there as well being part of *Tight Lines*. I got on well with Keith. He was a down to earth guy and full of info that he was willing to share. It was while I was having a beer and a chat with Keith that he asked me if I ever had fished for tarpon to which I replied I hadn't. He told me of his exploits in the Florida Keys, mainly Key West, and said I had to give it a go.

A few weeks later I was fishing out of West Mersey with my old mate Stewart Belbin who runs a charter boat. I told him about the tarpon fishing and with both of us knowing John Rawle, who had set up a charter fishing operation in Florida, Stewart said he would give him a call. Well three of us booked John for the next spring. He told us not to worry about bringing any gear, just to get our arses down there on the given date.

First and foremost what a place the Keys are to visit and fish. Well the Sat Nav got us to John's easily. Carole and John showed us around the place and we met the other people that were staying for the week. If I remember correctly we had five sessions on the tarpon and two on the shark. There were mainly two boats doing the night sessions on the tarpon, John and a guy called Geoff and occasionally another guy called Kip.

I believe I did six trips out there, some with Stewart and fellow Takely SAC member, Whiskers and some with my friend, Sid. The one thing that that stood out that I admired was John's knowledge of the area and the set up. He had bait suppliers and also there was a fish market where he got the fish carcasses for the shark fishing. The fishing was world class. All I can say is those of you that haven't got tarpon on your bucket list, do as it they are something else; you have got to experience it. As for the shark fishing, it's amazing. It's so visual as you are only fishing shallow water. One tip on the tarpon fishing is if you can, do it at night when there is not so much activity on the water.

Now for the story, Geoff had an aversion to anything black. He wouldn't have an outboard if it was black. If you wanted to wind him up, just mention Barack Obama and he would go into one. The one thing he liked was sweets, especially wine gums. I got a large box before we flew out there and opened it and took all the black ones out...and ate them...sealed the box and the next time I was out with Geoff, gave him the box. He didn't open it until he got home. Next time I saw him he said there were no black ones in the box, so I told him I ate them cos he didn't like anything black. Well, that didn't go down too well.

One of our trips I was out there with Stewart and my wife Jackie. The week we had booked the weather was crap, wet and windy and the fishing was hard work. However, this was when we had the ash cloud from Iceland. It soon became apparent that our flights were cancelled and we were unable to get home. Luckily for us the people that were due out the following week couldn't get out so we stayed another week. The second week was unbelievable, the weather was beautiful and the fishing was the best we ever had. One tarpon session, Stewart and I had ten fish that probably averaged 150 lbs and when you consider that most fights took 30 minutes, it was non-stop action!
What an Experience!

Paul Muffett

Bananas

Ed. *Paul from London is another great supporter of the south-coast Angling Charter Boats and very much a member of the sea angling fraternity with many friends in common incljding the late and very much missed Chris Caines.*

Another story about bananas following on from the marvellous tale related by Tom Bettle.

This relates to the late great Chris Caines aboard *Tiger Lily* from Weymouth.

I had chartered the boat along with seven friends for four days' summer fishing around the grounds, banks and marks off Weymouth.
On the second day of our trip, Chris was sitting in the wheelhouse along with my regular angling partner, Malcolm Quick having a jovial chat, when he produced one of the so called *yellow devil fruit* and ate it for his lunch.
Later in the day, again whilst chatting with Malcolm, Chris produced and ate another. Now Malcolm is not one to miss a trick so when Chris ate another couple of bananas the following day, Malc starting to sing, "I'm the King of the Swingers" from the Jungle Book movie.
This went on for a little while until Chris realised what Malc was doing and howls of raucous laughter was heard from the cabin.
That evening, in the pub, a plan was hatched to wind up our poor unsuspecting skipper the following day.
A bunch of bananas was purchased from a local store and smuggled aboard in readiness for our plan to be put into action.
As Chris readied the boat for the first drift of the day, each angler was given a banana which was duly hooked onto our lines and lowered into the water. After a few moments fishing this drift, I called out that I had a fish on. Chris very swiftly exited the wheelhouse to be met with sight of eight anglers all swinging in the most marvellous specimen sized *yellow devil fish* you can imagine.
I cannot possibly repeat the words uttered by Chris but those of us that had the pleasure of knowing and fishing with him can imagine what was said. Imagine the great man as he stood at the wheelhouse door with that famous expression of his that said it all.

Ian Bagley. *Ha ha ha ha ha. Great story and Chris was an absolute top guy and even when he said to me there is no point going wrecking today as the May water was so bad, I said, "Sod the fishing and let's go anyway."*
It was not all about catching fish some days to me and my group. It was the company that we all keep that matters most…. especially now as time goes fast and nothing lasts forever.

Rich Rickman: *I'm with you in the bananas bad Ju Ju belief. Whilst fishing the Lymington Cod Open with George Phillips ,who arrived late, we steamed out to the Shingles. After three hours fishing we had caught nothing. George opened his lunchbox and, yep, a banana ffs.*

I threw it overboard and 'boom' a 21lb cod was on immediately and he won the competition.

Paul Thompson

An Original Tall Tale

Ed. *Known as Geordie, Paul is retired from the Army, Artillery Regiment. As such he has spent a lifetime yelling commands over the noise of hefty bombardments. This has made Paul extremely loud. When he is on a charter boat, Skippers dread him coming in the wheelhouse for what will be a deafening chat. Paul has organised charter trips including the Channel Islands and has been a loyal supporter of charter boat fishing for many years.*

I remember the time my mate Jed Bottomely and I were fishing the Dragon's Teeth at Abbotsbury and he turned to me and said, "The last time I fished here I had a 10lb cod."

I said, "That was a good one, mate," and I began telling him of the time I fished out of Weymouth back in the early seventies.

I can't remember the name of the skipper but he was getting on a bit. Anyway we were drifting off Portland bill and all of a sudden I had a tight line.

"Here we go," I thought but on reeling in to my astonishment I had hooked the lamp from an old Spanish Gallon. Even more to my astonishment the lamp was still alight.

At this point Jed said, "I don't believe it was still alight after all these years."

I said, "OK, mate. Knock 5lb off the cod and I'll blow out the candle."

Just a light bit of fun in these sad times. Stay safe everyone and we will have tight lines again.

Tall Tale 2

Frying with Washing-up liquid.

As the weather has taken a change for the worse it has reminded me of the time myself and two friends were fishing the SAMF Masters on Chesil Beach Dorset.

It was one of those weekends when the weather was that bad that you really don't want to be near the South coast. Anyway, Jimmy King, David Gavin and myself booked into our Caravan at West bay to fish the SAMF masters. We had done our shopping at ASDA in Weymouth and had plenty of provisions to last us three days. As we had to book in for the match that evening, we decided to eat out in Weymouth and have a few beers before having an early night to be at our best for Match One on West Bexington the following day.

I had volunteered to be duty cook for the weekend so next morning after a hearty breakfast of bacon sarnies we set off to the first match venue. Now as I have already stated the weather was horrible and after about three hours of trying to hold bottom the match was abandoned which was a bit like the first day in the SAMF Masters in Wales but that's another story. Anyway, on returning to our caravan in West Bay feeling very wet, cold and bedraggled, we sorted our tackle ready for what was promised for the next day to be a much better day, weather-wise, for Match Two.

I said, "OK, I will start the dinner while you two have a shower."

Jimmy, being Jimmy, retorted with, "I'll shower first," so Paddy sat having a cup of tea while I got busy with the frying pan.

"OK," I thought, "Cheese burgers sounds good." So in goes some oil and four burgers and all of a sudden the oil has gone. "Funny," I thought adding more oil.

Yet again the oil disappeared. At this point I looked at the bottle of oil. Now why anyone would want to make washing up liquid the same colour as cooking oil and put it in the same kind of bottle is beyond me.

At this point as Paddy and I were in hysterics with laughter.

Jimmy exited the shower looked at me and said, "What have you done?"

Why do people always think I have done something wrong?

After explaining to Jimmy the mix up with the washing up liquid and the oil I said not to worry as we have loads of burgers. After ejecting the spoilt burgers into the bin and cleaning out the frying pan, I said to Jimmy, "So where did you put the oil?"

"In the top cupboard," he said, so I took down the oil and as I went to pour some into the frying pan I said, "Hang on this is still sealed."

Jimmy and Paddy both said together, "It will be you just been cooking with washing up liquid."

I said, "Yes I know, but I also cooked the bacon for the Sarnies we had for breakfast this morning".

We did laugh! Well, me and Paddy did. Stay safe everyone!

Paul Whittall on Chris Tett, skipper of Weymouth based *Peace and Plenty*.

Ed. *I know I said I would not write anything...but I have to include this story as this could have all ended extremely badly had it not been for the prompt action and outstanding seamanship of Chris Tett, skipper of the* Peace and Plenty.

The most amazing, courageous and unselfish display of boatmanship I witnessed was by Chris Tett when we were both in Alderney Harbour in a stiff north-easterly. We had just moored up when a mass panic on the Alderney Harbourside broke out. The Dockies had let the wrong ropes go on the Island supply ship (I think it was Burhou). The stern was swinging away from the wall very quickly and pivoting on the bow lines. It was swinging in a huge arc that would have seen the stern crash onto the rocks at the end of the 'Ferry' pontoon. Chris let go his moorings quickly and told me he was going to position *Peace and Plenty* right at the stern of the ship on the leeside and use his boat like a tug to try and push the ship against the wind and back to the wall. Chris had fitted out my boat and I had a prominent bow roller. He told me to stand clear as I would rip my foredeck off if I tried to help. I watched him push that ship inch by inch back to the harbour wall. It was an unforgettable lesson in assessing a very dangerous situation and risking his boat to save it. And he had time to tell me to stay clear because of the damage I would do to mine.

Amazing courage and skill.

The Phil Reed Section

Whales and Tigers

Ed. *Phil is one of those fortunate anglers to have fished with the amazing Frothy de Silva out of Madeira as well as other exotic locations plus supporting many 'home grown' skippers*

This is a tale from a land, far far away and quite a while ago...
Me and a couple of mates headed out on a winter's day off south-east Queensland, Australia, to try and catch some reef fish known as Pearl Perch, the closest thing to a cold water fish there and probably one of the best eating.
We were heading out to a reef with a soft 1.5 metre swell running and out of the corner of my eye I clocked what I thought was a capsized boat so we changed our course and headed towards it.
The closer we got the worse the smell got and we realised that it was actually a dead humpback whale that looked just like the hull of a capsized boat.
Once we were close to the whale we realised that there were sharks feeding on the whale. We counted for tiger sharks and they were all between 12 to 15 feet in length. We all came close to a change of underwear when one broke away from feeding on the whale and swam under the boat but I did have a camera in my hand and got a shot of the fish as it appeared from under the boat. Its head looked like a diving board and only added to our nervousness. It was an eerie feeling to see fish of that size slowing munching on a whale.
We left the sharks to their feed and headed off to try and catch ours but later heard on the radio that a local charter boat visited the whale and that there was a great white that had joined the feeding frenzy and that the shark gave him a visit and nudged his outboard a couple of times.
I never went swimming in the sea out there!

Tall Tale 2
A Thresher in the boat

Seeing pictures of Dale Edmund's thresher sharks that he seems to catch regularly reminded me of a very hot summer's day in June 1981.
Me and my two mates all booked up a day out with Dave Adams on *Torbay Belle* out of Langstone. We had all caught a few fish before so thought we were well prepared for the day. Unfortunately none of us were prepared for the force of the initial run from a smooth-hound. I think we all hooked up at once and no sooner had we hooked up our lines snapped because our drags were all too tight on our Penn Seaboys or Delmars. Moments later another old bloke, well he was at least 25, boated a smooth-hound and we quizzed him about his enviable catch and he helpfully told us about setting drag and the best bait being crab.
Full of disappointment but determination to 'up our game', we sorted out our terminal tackle and went crab collecting in Pompey Harbour. We collected a bucket full of crabs including some edible crabs that were probably five inches lengthways across the back. We

booked up with John Baker on either *Joy* or *Bessie Vee* and headed out on sun drenched August day in mill pond conditions. The journey to Selsey seemed to take forever. It probably did at 8 knots!

Once we were there we watched a few good smooth-hounds get caught and in my excitement and a bit of envy, I tried to put on one of the edible crabs and had to ask John for a pair of pliers to pull the hook through the shell. He laughed and gave me that 'are you sure?' look. I'm not sure if it was the size and type of crab or the black plastic coated multi-strand wire that I had for a trace.

I hooked up on the crab much to my surprise and his 10 minutes later of a panicked tussle an 18lb smooth-hound landed on the deck out of his net. I was elated and he was pleasantly surprised. My moment of glory was stolen though by the news on the radio that a large thresher shark had jumped into another charter boat and broke one bloke's leg and another's arm. A large debate was entered into on the boat by all the customers and the skipper and it was decided that it was *BS Banter* on the radio that often seem to be the case in that neck of the woods.

My Dad picked me and my mates up from Eastney and had the radio on. The news came on with a report that a large thresher shark had actually jumped into a charter boat and that two men were taken to hospital with broken bones and that the shark had been killed as it was too lively and heavy to get out of the book and was taken to a local fishmonger. An article followed and it was apparently quite a regular occurrence for a thresher to mistake the dark hull of a boat for a bait school on a flat calm day and to jump on to the boat thinking that it was stunning all the unsuspecting bait fish.

This however wasn't the only questionable tall fishy tale in this story.

A couple of years later I was collecting peeler crabs to go bass fishing off the beach and was letting all the large hardbacks run off. I was told in no uncertain terms by an older bloke who I think was a police officer called Colin, nicknamed *Colin the Copper* anyway, that I should keep the biggest crabs possible as John Baker had told him that a young kid had been on his boat and caught a good hound on the biggest crab he had ever seen used. He looked put-out when I told that I wasn't fishing for hounds but for bass and he looked completely scandalised when he thought I was lying about it being me that had caught the hound on the crab.

Tight lines to one and all and hope this adds a little humour to your isolation.

Tall Tale 3

Alderney; Old and New

Having lived overseas for a little over a decade and returning to the UK, I had heard from a few people that the multi-day charters to Alderney were not what they were with regard to the catches; well, is anything ever?

I had a great time in the years that I had visited there fishing with David 'Spike' Spears on the *Bessie Vee* and *Sundance 2* with Lymington based, Roger Bayzand.

After I left to go overseas my dad and his mates carried on the annual pilgrimage with Spike and I recently found a photo of my dad with an 18lb turbot that Spike insisted on netting even though he was in the latter stages of his battle with his illness. The photo brought many memories of the fun times we had fishing and the entertaining nights in the *Harbour Lights,* that fine establishment not far from Braye Harbour.

One particular memory of a week in Alderney was when the fishing was particularly lean on a trip with Roger Bayzand, I think there was a case of lock jaw for the local population of turbot, bass and brill that week. In an attempt to avoid the despondency, one of our crew, who shall remain nameless, decided to put the contents of a bottle of Jack Daniels into a half full bottle of coke. He seemed to hold it together until the end of the day when he made a minor slip.

The minor slip involved his brand new gold Penn lever drag reel. As we all set up for a flatfish drift everyone had their rod and reel in their left hand and weight in their right....when, with an obvious momentary lapse of sanity he threw his rod and reel in and held onto the weight at the start of the drift. The reel was correctly in free spool so the brand new gold reel headed towards the sea-bed of the Alderney South Banks.

There wasn't a straight face on the boat or a dry eye other than the owner of the brand new gold reel who couldn't remember how well he tied the mono backing to the spool.

Fortunately for him the knot was a good 'un and after hand lining 200m of mono and 300m of braid he retrieved it but I think if he hadn't we would have all chipped in to buy him a new one for the entertainment value during one of Alderney's slow fishing periods! We did finally find some fish on one Roger's 'last resort, never fail' drifts and the reaction and elation of some people who caught quality fish was nearly as funny as the gold reel show!

I have returned with thanks to Alistair Munn for arranging and Jamie Pullin (Offshore Rebel) for putting us on as many flatfish in the last couple of years as we used to get when it was fishing well over a decade ago. I can't comment on the bass fishing as there's been a ban on.

Although it's not the same it is just as good for the fishing, watching the WAFI's getting stuck on rocks and the craic off the boat in some old haunts and new venues.

FIFTH TIDE

Raymond Crowe

Wait for the Fat Lady to Sing!

Ed. *Raymond, from High Wycombe, recounts a story from ten years ago from the same Weymouth boat he still charters now. The loyalty many anglers show to their skippers is humbling indeed. Without the support of anglers like Raymond, the charter boat industry would struggle.*

I'm really enjoying all these great stories and glad to be part of this group.

As a keen lifelong angler one thing I have learned: "It's never over till it's over." A very good example of this was a Turbot Day in April from Weymouth. I think it was around 10 or 11 years ago and the Boat was *Fish-On* skippered by the inimitable Josh Simmonds.

There were reports of good sized turbot on the grapevine so we were all very keen! I fished with a regular crew and we always had a fiver in the pot for best fish of the day. Collecting that money from your mates was always a great feeling! We stuck at it on the Shambles Bank &and finally Brian Roberts landed A 19 pounder. He was beyond happy and started to tell us all "cough up ya fiver" and how he would get the first round in with his winnings. However, the day was not over and although a fish that big would take some beating the next drift through up a 21 pounder for Rick Loranis!

Poor Brian's 15 minutes of fame was over! Lesson learnt. Always "wait for the fat lady to sing!"

Ric Pitkethly

'Our' Sea Monster.

Ed. *Ric, originally from Brighton and now living in Poole, Dorset, has many years of experience on the sea in many vessels and is a great supporter of the Dorset Charter Angling fleet.*

The following story happened to me over 30 years ago and was submitted to a *Sealife* competition some 20 years ago:

It was August 1987 as we eased out of Brighton Marina heading for Cowes I.O.W. I was at the helm of my 36 foot twin screw trawler yacht *Saracen*. Our party consisted of my young son Scott and friend and manager of my Brighton Health Club, Laurie. We had intended to set off the previous evening but the wind was blowing 5 or 6 so we took early to our beds. In the early hours of the following morning the wind was rapidly dropping and we looked set for a pleasant trip.

We were heading down to Cowes to see a friend of Laurie's competing in the I.O.W. power boat event. In the dark the shore lights twinkled reassuringly. As the light of day flooded in we entered the Solent cruising at around 8 knots. We crossed the Solent and entered Cowes Harbour. We found a berth close to the town centre and made fast for the night.

Laurie's wife Jean had to work that day, Saturday, so she was joining us in the evening coming down in a small fast boat owned by our mutual friend, Reg who owned the local vacuum cleaner centre. The hours ticked by and Reg and Jean were very late. We tried to raise them on the radio time and time again, but to no avail.

I had a small fault on one of the ship's heads. During this period of waiting, Laurie took it to pieces and totally rebuilt it. He said he was not too concerned about his wife's lateness but he just had to keep his mind focused. I had my doubts. Reg and Jean duly turned up during the evening having had to make a late start There were no mobile phones in those days so communications were far less likely.

Reg moored his boat next to ours. Having spent a pleasant evening together it was early to bed due to an early morning start. After a peaceful night and an early breakfast we slipped back out into the Solent to gain a good spot to watch the powerboat racing. When racing had come to an end and we had enjoyed a good lunch onboard, Reg headed back to Brighton Marina and we crossed the water with the intention to berth overnight in the comfort of Langstone Harbour Marina.

Disaster! Somebody had removed a Channel navigation stake. We found out later that another boat had hit it and destroyed it a few days before and I inadvertently cut a corner in the channel duly running aground on a falling tide. Oh dear we were soon high and dry even after efforts from the chaps from the marina in a brave attempt to tow us into deeper water with the aid of a RIB. We thought we may have need needed "propping up" as I felt, due to the shape of our hull, we may topple sideways. However we took the ground quite successfully but it did mean a night spent on the mud rather than in the comfort of the marina.

In the morning we were due to sail back to Brighton but a strong wind had come up overnight putting pay to that. So we entered the local marina ,moored up and made arrangements to leave her there for the week and the four of us caught the train back to Brighton and a week's work.

The following Saturday night Jean drove Laurie, Reg and myself back down to Langstone by car returning to Brighton on her own. We made an early start Sunday morning, settled our bill and proceeded though the strange lifting lock gate that was peculiar to that marina and this time taking more care in the channel but to be fair there was a lot more water so one did not need to be quite so accurate. Leaving Haying Island to our port side and turning east back into the Solent we started our journey back to Brighton.

Somewhere off Littlehampton we decided to stop for breakfast. We just let the boat drift and after a hearty fry up and coffee the three of us were just sitting on the upper deck taking in the magnificent views. The morning was hot, the sea was that oily- calm which you rarely experience when one of us noticed that about 100 or so yards away something was floating. With the sun behind it we could not make out what it was, but there was a fairly large dark shape out there.

The discussion started, "Was it a dead body?"

Did we really want to go over and find out? No, it's an inflated black plastic sack.

There was only one way to find out.

"We had better go over and have a look then."

I started up the engines and we slowly motored over in that direction. As we got closer we were all dismayed to see it had disappeared. Had we all imagined it. I took the boat to the spot we thought we had last seen the object and I cut the engines and let the boat drift. We looked all around searching the sea…..Nothing.

Then All of a sudden, not more than two or three yards from the boat's side, surfaced a huge head with a large orange spot on the top. This head was quickly followed by an equally huge body. A creature such as that none of us had ever seen before. It was close to six feet long and four foot or more across its four huge paddles. It had a series of strange ridges down its back. We did not have a clue what it was.

There had been a number of T.V. programmes over twenty years ago about this creature. It was just 'Our Monster.' We stayed with him or her for an hour or so. We lost track of time. We were amazed! The creature would go under the surface from time to time only to surface again shortly after but still next to the boat all the time; *it* and the boat just drifting along together on the tide. There were some boats fishing about half a mile away and we were concerned we would drift in that direction.

We were becoming very protective and we did not want anyone else to see 'our monster' in case they harmed it! Time passed and we had to get back to Brighton so we said our goodbyes, still not knowing what this creature was.

The next day now back in Brighton, I started my quest to find a name for our creature. I first rang our local Natural History Museum. There were no Sealife Centres around then. The curator could not solve the mystery from my explanation; his only suggestion being a Green Turtle. I knew at least that was not what we had seen.

Out of the blue that afternoon I received a call from a chap at the London Natural History Museum, the local curator having given him my number. He told me what we had seen was a Great Leather Back Turtle. The gentleman was very interested and interesting. He told me many facts about the Leather Back and the great age which it could attain, where it came from and other fascinating facts. He also told me of the sightings of the turtle over the years in the U.K. waters. Not many had been recorded at that time although the first went back a couple of hundred years or so.

Today there are apparently far more sightings. I wonder if this is due to the advent of far more T.V. programmes and the emergence of Sea Life Centres educating the public to a higher degree. People are now far more aware of these creatures. Or could it be down to Global Warming?

The gentleman from the N.H.M. then went on to say did I notice anything unusual in the water on the day.

I replied: "Yes! There were _loads of Jellyfish _- Huge dustbin lid jobs more and larger then I had ever seen before".

"THATS IT!" he exclaimed. That's why your turtle was there and he went on to tell me that this was their main food source and how they would follow their prey for thousands of miles in this case right up the Gulf Stream. I learnt a lot that day about the Great Leather Back Turtle. The local newspaper, The Evening Argus, did a piece on our adventure that week and a couple of weeks later I saw a report in the same paper that a Leather Back Turtle had been washed up dead somewhere on the South West coast. I telephoned the paper to see if I could find out any more information, but I was unsuccessful.

I hoped that was not 'Our' turtle. I would like to think he is still roaming the oceans gorging him or herself on giant jellyfish to this day.

Richard Hinton

Fishing with Geordie

Ed. *Well Done, Richard. This is a great retelling of fishing with Geordie, the pioneer of long distance wrecking and inspiration for many of us that tried to follow in his footsteps.*

Although our wreck fishing out of Gosport with the HMS Dolphin Sea Angling Club was improving we were struggling to find the wrecks using the old Decca chains. We wanted to learn more and catch more and expand our knowledge and experiences.

We were drawn to an advert from a Geordie Dickson out of Plymouth who stated – 'if you pay peanuts you get monkey' (Ed. *I remember that Ad*!!) along with many other sales pitches about the promise of big catches. We thought that now as we were experienced wreck anglers we should give it a go and we booked a trip! I can't remember the exact date but it was all arranged to meet up on a Friday evening, probably way back in 1981/2, with the trip booked for the Saturday, leaving the Barbican in Plymouth at 7.00am.

So we all met in the pub in Gosport for a few drinks. Once time was called we set off to Plymouth! Arriving about 4 am at the Barbican Sea Angling Centre all excited at our new venture. Geordie turned up with Dale Entwistle as crew early, so we set off 6.30 ish.

We asked where we were going and was told to look at a chart with prices on it . It was showing that the further we went out from Plymouth the dearer the trip.

Well we were up for it; "Top of the Shop for us, please."

"Fine," said Geordie. "You'd better hold on as we would be going at some speed!"

"Yer, right," we thought. "We're hardened anglers. We'll be fine!"

With that as we left Plymouth sound Geordie opened up *Artilleryman 2*. Well we didn't have to be told again to hang on as we were all over the place. After about an hour, we asked Geordie if there was any tea? The reply came back, "This is a Fishing Vessel... NOT a F***in'...... Cafe!!"

Well that put us in our place! We were a new group of anglers to him, and we were a bit rowdy so thought we'd better shut up. However, one of our group Ray was well known to have a bit of a temper with a reputation to back it up and was now spitting feathers! Oh dear, you can imagine the mood out the back of the boat was now somewhat fraught.

Anyway with some guidance from Dale about the preferred rigs to use, we were shown the 'Killer rigs' using a pirk on the bottom and three red gills or delta eels above. We were only used to a boom with a single red gill or a perk on its own. But we listened and learned, taking advice from the experienced expert. We had plenty of gear so embarked on making up Killer Rigs to pass the time.

All set up, we waited to arrive on the wreck in expectation. Eventually we arrived at the first wreck and all six of us dropped together with the killer gear! Bang! All six of us hit the big time with two, three or four fish each at once! Ray hit the Big Time with a full house! Didn't his mood suddenly change! Geordie was miraculously now his best mate; the best thing since sliced bread! Ha Ha. We did take the piss big time out of Ray for that and still do after all these years.

Bloody hell what a day! Cod, pollock, ling, and the odd coal fish and all mostly double figured fish as well. This was the most knackering day's fishing any of us had had. It was absolutely fantastic.

We arrived back at Plymouth Barbican Sea Angling Centre about 6 - 6.30pm with a boat full of large fish where we were boarded by Mike Millman who was a reporter for either Sea fishing or Sea Angler magazine at the time. He wanted to take pictures of us holding up the bigger fish.

We were well impressed and whilst thanking Geordie and Dale for a great trip, we booked our next trips before we left the boat. All are original thoughts were so wrong about Geordie. All his efforts were just to catch fish and he wasn't interested in spoiling the anglers. You just had to prove that you were up to it and respectful then he would mellow a bit after you'd proved yourself.

Anyway after a few beers in the Sea Angling centre we set off back to Gosport! Whoever was still awake drove. Christ knows how we made it home we were so tired but we had a great time! Thanks to Geordie who after many years of fishing charters became a great friend.

Robert McQuillan

Stay in the Boat!

Ed. *Robert, from Portsmouth, 'remembers' this particular incident...but was it Lymington or Weymouth; a dogfish or a huss??*

I clearly remember fishing out of Lymington on a charter boat *Albatross* skippered by Pete Treadgold. We anchored up just south east of the Needles Lighthouse.
  My mate Mike was sat on the rear transom with his back to the sea when he had a bite. He struck the rod and toppled backwards into the sea but managed to throw his rod back into the boat. He surfaced and was recovered. His first words were whether the fish was still on the line. He wound it in and it was a small lesser spotted dogfish. This brought back good memories!

  Roger Bayzand.   *I remember hearing that, a very lucky guy!*

  Mike Northcott.   *Now from the horse's mouth. Bob, you are misremembering. It was out of Weymouth and the fish was a bull huss of about 4lbs. Luckily, it was in mid-August so no harm done! I have a pic somewhere. I will dig it out.*

The Roger Bayzand Section.

Ed. Roger Bayzand is one of those rare people who is extraordinarily talented at everything he does. I remember reading a number of times from different anglers that Roger was generally regarded as the Best Skipper in the UK by those who knew him. His pioneering angling adventures, for bass in particular, were regularly featured in Sea Angler. His journalism was superb and his photography was really on another level..bordering on Art. His enthusiasm and energy were amazing...I never understood how, after we'd both had a hard day around Alderney, he would leap off his boat and run up the quay to take my lines and moor me up. Now retired in Australia, his amazing paintings have built up a considerable following of mainly adoring female fans. He is indeed a very special and talented man.

Before becoming a charter skipper, Roger led an exciting life aboard various yachts as crew. He has that magical ability to describe scenes and lands in a mesmeric way that leaves the reader wanting more. I REALLY hope Roger writes his own book as he has such a fascinating story to tell and he does it with colourful memories written with such wonderfully evocative detail. Roger has kindly submitted a number of his stories here....so...sit back and enjoy the Roger Bayzand section!

Early Days of Seafaring before the Chartering started.

To Sea at Last!

The breaking of my apprenticeship was I am sure a disappointment to my parents but it had been my choice to start it, so I guess I had a right to end it. They were concerned about what I was going to do and Dad arranged an interview with Fox and Sons real estate agents. They took me on and I stuck at it for a while. It really was not my cup of tea so when Eddie an old skipper friend of mine said, "Come and join my crew on a yacht I am skippering in the Mediterranean," I was off like a shot!

The sale of my Mini paid for a flight on a Vickers Viscount to Malta then a taxi down to The Britannia Bar in Gzira to catch up with Eddie. The only trouble was no one knew where he was and had not seen him for months. After a couple of days I gave up searching and walked the dockside asking each boat if they needed crew.

I got offered a job on the first day aboard a beautiful 72-foot Fred Shephard designed yawl built in 1914 called Thanet, my time at the marine engineering college was a bonus point for the skipper as he could sail but did not know much about engines. In a few days we were getting ready for our first charter, the crew consisted of the Dutch skipper, his young Maltese wife who would be the cook, some old black bearded rogue from the Caribbean as mate and me.

Our charterers turned out to be a honeymoon couple. He was some sort of minor British aristocrat, grossly obese and a completely pompous oaf and she was a fragile looking English rose.

Off we set with our interesting blend of characters and it was a pretty uneventful motor sail in calm conditions to our first stop, the tiny Italian island of Linosa.

Our arrival caused quite a stir and people started to come down to the shoreline to see our yacht and soon a couple of men came rowing out to greet us. It turned out that one was the Mayor of the island and it seemed we were the first yacht they had seen for a long time.

The pompous oaf demanded to be taken to a restaurant as our dear cook's Maltese version of garlic chicken had not gone down well with him. It turned out that there was no such thing as a restaurant on the island but the Mayor very kindly invited us to dine with him. So at sunset we piled in our tender and went ashore. It seemed like most of island had turned out to see us and we were led up the sand street to the Mayor's small stone house.

It was fairly dark inside only with small unglazed window openings, we sat around a bare wooden table and I guess the mayor's wife brought out the first course, a boiled egg. His Lordship's face was a treat to see, I don't think he had ever had an experience like that before but I was thinking how generous it was for these strangers to share their food with us.

Our next stop was Lampedusa, the largest island in the group which had a restaurant, so our charters were able to dine ashore. The crew got invited to a meal aboard a local fishing boat and as our skipper knew the boat owner so we were treated to a feast. First a huge platter of pasta was passed around as we sat on the aft deck, I was starving and went for a second helping only to realise that this was just the first course and to be followed by an equally large tin bath filled with freshly cooked langoustine, all this was washed down with copious amounts of rough red wine. Another evening to remember!

Then on to Sousse Tunisia; quite an eye opener to walk around the souk for a young lad form the Isle of Wight. After a couple of days visiting the sights His Lordship announced that he had to get back to Malta immediately as one of his horses was running in the Derby. It was blowing pretty well and the skipper was not at all keen to leave but the ultimatum was thrown down. "Either get me back to Malta in time for my flight or forego your charter fee!"

So off we went with a gale of warm wind blowing off the desert behind us. That night as I was on the helm and we surfed down the following sea someone put on Ravel's *Bolero*. What a stirring piece of music that seemed to suit the exhilarating moonlit atmosphere.

The occasional wave would break on the counter and slosh up the deck. Our charterers were in the aft cabin and I had warned them to keep the skylight closed but they rather typically ignored me so I must admit having a little chuckle to myself when an errant wave slid on board and dumped itself through the skylight and onto their bed. The resulting squawks were music to my ears.

We made it back to Malta in time and he reluctantly paid for their trip.

Tall Tale 2

Getting Started as a Charter Skipper.
A New Boat and a New Life.

Getting started as a charter skipper is never easy. My very old commercial boat would not be good enough to carry passengers, so it was time to take the plunge. I gave up my job running the ferry and angling charters for Sean Crane at Hurst Castle Ferries and decided to buy a new boat heralding exciting times!

After looking around at what was on the local market, I eventually found a 28-foot Berry boat called *Sundance* for sale in Poole. She was fitted out in 1976 and had been very lightly used. The only drawback was a very old Ford 4D engine but the owner offered to throw in a "reconditioned" spare, so we shook hands and a deal was done.

Ron Berry was a very well-known Dorset boat builder who had built a large number of fishing boats and most harbours along the south coast had a few, especially Poole and Weymouth. Mine was Iroko planked on good sized sawn oak frames with lighter steamed frames in-between. She was just what I needed with plenty of deck space to fit 12 anglers and it did not take me long to get going. I have to thank Mark Bingham, who was working at a New Milton tackle shop, for organizing many bookings that really helped keep us afloat in those early days.

I also have to express a deep debt of gratitude to Trevor Housby, an angling writer who got me some very valuable publicity in the local and national angling press. Trevor and I became really good friends and we often used to fish together. I remember the idea was to find a pub that did a really good lunch then seek the nearest trout fishery.

With a busy summer angling season and a winter of oyster fishing topped up with angling trips at the weekend, we kept our heads above water.

The thing I loved most about skippering a boat is that you are your own boss and every day is a fresh adventure. I took any opportunity to explore new grounds, ranging far and wide off the southwest coast of the Isle of Wight even as far as St Catherine's Deeps, a notorious spot for very strong tidal currents and overfalls and quite a trek in my chugger that could make 6 ¾ knots flat out.

Each day brought a different batch of customers many of which have become lifelong friends and are still connected today via Facebook. A lot of the groups would book one trip a month throughout the year and gradually my diary became full. It was so good to have the security of these regular bookings.

New angling techniques were being discovered; one prime example was uptide casting which had been perfected by skipper and author, John Rawle. A group of us went for a trip with John out of Bradwell, Essex just to learn his method. This revolutionised fishing on shallow banks like the Shingles and Freshwater Reef.

Technology was changing rapidly too and I grabbed every opportunity to add or upgrade equipment as things were developed.

At first most boats were just equipped with a compass and a VHF radio. Next came an echo sounder and these progressed from a flashing light on a dial to indicate the depth to a paper chart that recorded depth which led on to a colour display unit. The ability to see the recorded depth gave an indication of the type of seabed and what's more, see fish 'echoes'.

The next revolution was the Decca system. Until it became generally available we were using landmarks or radar ranges to find our fishing marks. Decca had been developed as a navigation system during WW2 and consisted of an on-board receiver that picked up radio signals from 3 land-based stations. The triangulation of these signals gave a read out that corresponded to a position that could be found with charts that had the curved Decca overlay. The problem was that you had to rent the receivers from Decca at a cost of £1,500 a year which around 1980 was too expensive for me to consider.

Eventually a Danish company started to produce a "pirate" receiver that they would sell for about what a year's rental would be. There were threats from Decca that they would shut the system down but in the end the UK government took it over as the Navy had a need for it. This opened the gates for other manufactures to join in and eventually reasonably priced sets were available to anyone. Accurate (20 – 50 metres on a good day) navigation enabled us to start to discover shipwrecks and the fish that congregate around them which is the start of another yarn.

Tall Tale 3

We need a Bigger Boat

The advent of accurate electronic navigation opened up a whole new world to us. We knew the potential of wreck fishing in our area as Anton Proctor had already fished some of them with his boat *Avon Valley*.

A small group of local skippers decided to make the 40 mile trip from our home ports to see for ourselves. It turned into a marathon journey, six hours steaming out to the wreck, four hours fishing and another six hours home. The results were good but it was obvious that most passengers would not be happy traveling for 12 hours to get four hours fishing. It was exhausting for the skipper too, as the day starts well before the clients arrive and ends well after they have left. It really was time to get a bigger and faster boat.

I suppose I had always been looking and assessing the different options to suit my needs and within my budget. The Mitchell 31 was a bit too small, the Lochin 33 was not quite right and too expensive, the Offshore 105 was a cheaper option but I did not like the ride. Eventually another boat came on the market, the Starfish 10.

I had a good look at the lines and the semi-displacement hull looked like it had really good sea going potential. The fiberglass construction was very strong as the simulate clinker hull had great longitudinal stiffness whilst the numerous internal frames gave it immense strength. If anything it was overbuilt which was a comment made by the DOT Loadline surveyor; not a bad thing when the sea is rough, although the extra weight meant a sacrifice in speed.

The yard was very amenable to providing a bare hull with a wheelhouse of my choice attached, so we placed an order and waited for the truck to arrive some months later.

I was lucky to find space in Aquaboats building shed to do the fit out and we were joined by Sean Cranes Aquastar hull for *Wild Rose*. Even Ray Pitt was working in the shed for a while doing their electrical wiring. It was like a meeting of old friends and I happily recall a series of birthdays that winter where buns at tea break were the order of the day.

The first time I climbed up the ladder and looked into the cavernous void of the bare hull I wondered if we had bitten off more than we could chew. Heather and I fitted deck beams, built the deck, installed the rudder, prop-shaft and engine, fitted out the wheelhouse including the windows; in fact everything. We worked late into the evenings during that freezing winter but completed it in time and on budget. It was only the fibre-glassing of the deck that we got help with and of course "Stainless Steve" did all the glistening rails and fittings. Finally in March of 1988 she was pulled out of the shed and we had a wing ding launching party .

Sundance 2 turned out to be all we hoped for; it cut our journey times in half and opened up a whole world of possibilities.

We fished further from Lymington and some wrecks were now closer to France than England, so we did a few overnight stops in Cherbourg.

Boats from Weymouth were doing the same thing in the Channel Islands, mainly Alderney, whilst the vessels from Devon such as Geordie Dickson and Ted Cooke favoured Guernsey.

It was an article written by Trevor Housby that alerted me to the inshore fishing around Alderney and when I asked him about it he said get in touch with Roddy Hays he will help you out. Roddy did exactly that and on our first trip to the Island came with us on the boat and showed us how to catch bait and where to fish. What a kind and generous man. This was the start of yet another long term friendship.

Alderney became a regular haunt and we soon established the *Harbour Lights* as our base for the anglers to stay. It had everything they needed with accommodation, really good food and a well-stocked bar. Howie and Rowie Gaydon, who ran the family business, were great hosts and really made the Island experience for my customers.

I stayed on the boat, converting the wheelhouse seating to a bed each night. Waking up at dawn in a calm anchorage was lovely. I could potter around on my own and get on with the constant maintenance jobs that go with running a boat.

I made friends with Paul Whittall, a skipper from Weymouth, who was a regular visitor and between us we started to explore the banks between Alderney, Sark and Guernsey . Having someone to share information with gave us the opportunity to be in two places at once. The very strong tidal currents have a huge influence of where the fish are and when they are feeding, so gradually we started to build up a picture of where to be and when.

These currents were strong enough to produce standing waves as they ran through channels or over banks, definitely not the place to be in bad weather.

The Alderney trips ran from three to seven days and I found that the bigger (spring) tides definitely fished the best. This left the smaller tides to work out of Lymington on a daily basis.

In amongst all this fishing I was taking out parties of divers, mainly to dive the hundreds of shipwrecks that litter the English Channel, many from the two world wars but a lot that had floundered in the 1800's and before.

Dave Wendes had started me on my wreck hunting quest many years ago when he gave me a sheaf of Hydrographic Office printouts listing wreck locations. In exchange for all this information, I offered to take him and his pals out for a dive when I found something. Many of the positions were inaccurate or just plain misleading and although a few were easy to find most took a fair bit of hunting. It was tantalizing stuff watching a sounder screen for any signs of debris that could indicate that the wreck was nearby, then a surge of exhilaration when it was spotted.

To mark the spot we dropped a 70 lb weight attached to a rope which tethered a string of floats on the surface, the divers could then follow the line to the wreck below.

They aimed to dive over the turn of the tide when the current stopped for a short while, so we would be watching the buoys to judge when the time was right, then they would enter the water in pairs.

The next bit was an anxious time for me. They were totally beyond my help so it was a relief to count the inflated markers that showed they were near the surface. Many of the dives they undertook were at a depth that needed decompression, so they would hang at the required depth until they were OK to surface. I always had the kettle boiling ready for their return as even in the middle of summer the sea temperature only gets to 16 C.

Dave and his crew started discovering that many of the names that the Admiralty had given to these ships was wrong, by finding nameplates, crockery with crests and even ships bells with a name they were able give the them their true identify .

Dave Wendes has now published two excellent books about his extensive research called *South Coast Shipwrecks*. They contain the accurate position combined with the history and photos of many of these wrecks. (Email wightspirit@btinternet.com if you are interested).

Two of these were clipper ships bound for Australia with cargo manifests that read like the contents of a hardware store like Bunnings. Sheets of glass, corrugated iron, oil lamps, rolls of lead, tiles and even a traction engine. At one time I had a stoneware flagon destined for Sydney Brewery that had been recovered from the depths.

For many years things went really well, my bookings were full from year to year and I was also busy writing for the angling press and making videos and TV program, more of which another day.

Tall Tale 4
Pirates of the Caribbean

Roddy Hays of Alderney invited Shimano's John Loftus, Chris Cole, wife Heather and myself to come and visit him in Anguilla. I admit when Roddy had first talked about moving there I had no idea where Anguilla was and he had to show me on a chart. It was a speck of an island just north of Saint Martin, east of the British Virgin Islands and forms the NE corner of the Caribbean Islands.

In early 1999, we flew into Sint Maarten on the Dutch side of the Island and got a taxi to the French side where the name changes to Saint Martin. The taxi driver said, "I can't take you all the way; the French have blockaded the border as they are having a strike".

Evidently as Saint Martin is a Department of France, the government was trying to introduce the sales tax that applies all over Europe. When the taxi dropped us off we walked up the road towards the ferry port. In the distance there were pops and bangs going off, which we thought were fireworks. Then a car came racing down the road towards us and the driver leaned out of the window and shouted, "Go back! The riot police are shooting up there!" We set off at a trot, toting our baggage to the nearest hotel on the Dutch side. In true French fashion by the next morning everything was over and we were able to get our ferry to Anguilla.

Roddy had set up a fishing operation there and had a couple of boats moored in Road Bay. Before we arrived the area had been battered by a monster hurricane. Roddy, Susan and a very young Izzy had been hunkered down in their shuttered house whilst the fabric of the community was torn apart. They said that it was a very frightening experience and that the constant noise from the wind was one of the worst things. By the time we arrived in the New Year, things were starting to get back in shape although there were signs of damage everywhere.

We had a wonderful time on Anguilla. The weather was warm, the sea was clear and we explored the beaches and settlements. We had a few days fishing with Roddy on his new Glacier Bay 22 foot catamaran. She was a wonderful little boat that performed like something much larger, particularly into a head sea. Roddy told us that they were going to leave the island as they could not face another hurricane season with a young child.

On the way back to England, Chris and I talked over our trip and how we had enjoyed fishing on the small boat and decided to see if Roddy would sell it to us. When I mentioned this to John he said, " Well, count me in." And so it happened we became owners of a boat in the Caribbean.

We thought we would try and charter it to cover our expenses and with the help of Roddy's friend Max got a little business going which initially was quite successful. Unfortunately more hurricanes hit and we nearly lost the boat when the lagoon at Sandy Ground broke through the beach. I remember seeing a photo on the internet of *Gecko* poised very close to a river of water just waiting to suck it out to sea. These disasters really hit the tourist industry that these islands rely on so we stopped chartering and decided just to use the boat for ourselves.

Heather and I had a holiday on Tobago and I went fishing with a very well know Captain, Frothy De Silva. Frothy invited me to come back and spend some time crewing on the boats with him over the next winter. I joined up with another English skipper, Dicky, to run Frothy's boat whilst he went to fish the Spice Island tournament in Grenada. Dicky and I had a great time. The fishing was brilliant with loads of dorado and wahoo around the bamboo *fads* (fish attracting devices) that Frothy had put out. On Frothy's return, he regaled us with tales of Grenada which started me thinking. The southern Caribbean from Grenada south was considered to be out of the hurricane zone, the fishing was great and it was much cheaper than the northern Caribbean. Maybe we could move the boat there.

So it came to pass Chris and I sadly said goodbye to all our friends on Anguilla, including Maxo, Hezron, Francois and family, then set off on the 400 mile run south. As Chris says, that was a true adventure.

Our first stop was St Kitts for fuel. We really should have filled up and left but trying to the right thing I went to the customs to clear us in and out of the country.

Here I came across a jobs worth of the first degree. The customs officer took my paper work, chucked it on his desk and covered it with a sheaf of other papers. I stood there for an hour biting my tongue whilst he ignored my presence before finally picked them up stamped his stamp and sent me off to Immigration who with a smile dealt with me in minutes. Off we went past Montserrat, half of which had been wiped out by a volcano, and on to Guadeloupe. It was just on dusk as we neared the entrance to the marina at Riviere Sens that we spotted a marlin tailing nearby but had no time for that as we needed to get through the clearance formalities before we could go ashore as we had no accommodation on what was basically an open boat.

In the morning we refuelled and got a real shock when we went to pay. Petrol here was the same price as mainland France and much more than the other islands. Our next stop was due to be Martinique but as it was French with the same prices we decided to push on to St Lucia.

The trade winds in this part of the Caribbean blow from the north-east and can be brisk, often 25 knots in winter and even more between the islands. As we rounded the southern end of Martinique we ran into a fairly good sea. We were racing the clock to get to St Lucia before immigration closed so we could get ashore so we pushed little *Gecko* pretty hard, leaping over the waves with spray flying everywhere. Chris and I were just wearing shorts and as we pulled into the harbour we looked at each other and laughed. We were both caked white with salt. There was no time to waste so I just pulled on a T shirt and raced up to get us cleared in. I remember a particularly nice shower when we got to the hotel.

Our next night was at Bequia, which proved to be a gem of a spot and as, we were nearing the end of the journey, we treated ourselves to a couple of days there.

We found accommodation at the Auberge des Grenadines that had a really nice restaurant. We went out early the next morning and caught some black fin tuna which we offered to our host, as these were beautiful fresh fish. She cooked us a lobster omelette for breakfast and that evening we dined on tuna tartar and seared tuna steaks. The Grenadines are real jewels in the Caribbean and a beautiful cruising ground. After a couple of days poking around we headed off to Grenada.

Finding a place to leave the boat was not easy. We knew we could get into Trinidad and have it put ashore in a boatyard whilst we were not there but many places have time restrictions. So when we cleared into Grenada and the lady said, "How long do you want to stay?" and I replied ,"I am not sure."

Her friendly reply of, " Stay as long as you like." I knew then that we had found a new home.

The boat is still there and Chris is still using it when he can. Grenada turned out to be a very friendly island and a great place to stay. If you ever go there I highly recommend the Aquarium for a long Sunday lunch, sit by the beach, enjoy the band and eat some fantastic food perhaps with a beverage of choice.

Where are the Pirates you ask? Well when we were in St Vincent they were filming *Pirates of the Caribbean* and asked if we would be interested in running the crew to the set in the next bay.

Tall Tale 5

Crewing on the Lymington Lifeboat

The Royal National Lifeboat Institution has been saving lives at sea around the coast of the British Isles and Ireland since 1824, it is a charity funded by donations not government money.

I was honoured to be asked if I would like to join the volunteer Lymington Lifeboat crew by the then Senior Helmsman Chris Carrington.

In those days things were considerably different to the way they are today. Then all crew training was done on the boat by going through drills at sea with the senior crew, we would get regular visits from the Inspector who would ensure that the crew were up to scratch.

We often exercised with other lifeboats mostly Yarmouth and the rescue helicopter, which initially was a Navy unit but then was changed to the Coastguard and provided by Bristow Helicopters. After the really good relationship with the Navy I was a bit apprehensive if the privatized service would be as good. I need not have worried most of the crew were ex RN or RAF search and rescue personnel and they were as good as ever with better kit. The photos are of Coastguard helicopter India Juliet a Sea King from Lea on Solent and one of me on board having been winched up from our Lifeboat

When our launching authorities got a call from the Coastguard requesting the assistance of Lymington Lifeboat they would fire off two maroons to summons the crew. Maroons are similar to a parachute flare to look at but instead of projecting a flare they send up an explosive device that goes off with a huge bang, loud enough for the whole town to hear.

The crew would drop what they were doing and rush to the boat house, the first helmsman and two crew to get there took the shout unless it was really extreme weather when the crew might be selected. Whilst they got their wet weather gear, boots, helmet and lifejacket on the rest prepared the boat and pushed it on its carriage to the top of the slipway ready to launch. There the crew clambered aboard and took up their positions as the boat was sent down the slip gathering momentum until it hit the water. Once it floated off the bed of the trailer the engines were fired up and we sped off down the river towards the casualty. In my early days the outboards were 55 hp Evenrudes and even though they were well maintained they were sometimes difficult to start. Often one would go and the other remain dead, we discovered that we could partially drag start it by putting it in gear, which helped the starter spin it over.

Whilst this was going on one of the crew would be on the radio to the Coastguard to get the details of where we were going and what the problem was.

A lot of the calls were fairly routine especially in the busy yachting season, boats aground or broken down. In my view not really Lifeboat jobs but we turned out any way, the rational was that it would be better to help them sooner rather than have them in real trouble later.

It was the calls that came at 3am in the middle of winter when it was blowing a gale and pouring with rain that the adrenalin really started pumping. One such night we pulled a very frightened French couple off their yacht that was stuck on a lee shore with waves breaking over it.

I can remember walking them up to the boathouse after we got ashore, cold shocked and shaking the woman asked " How much do we owe you?" When I said "Nothing, it's all free." She looked amazed and started crying. Evidently they had been in trouble earlier in the night when they were off the Needles and had called the coastguard but turned down the offer of the Lifeboat because they had very little money. Thank goodness they were tears of gratitude.

One of the first shouts I crewed on was to a yacht spotted by the Needles lighthouse keepers that was floundering in the surf on the SW Shingles. It was blowing a full gale from the south west; Yarmouth Lifeboat were tasked with searching the Needles channel and we were sent to the shallow water to the north of the Shingles bank. We rounded Hurst Castle in the usual confused chop but it was not until we got into Christchurch Bay that we felt the full weight of the seas that were rolling and breaking across the bank. One of these cresting breakers reared up in front of us and as we went up the face it started to break, the boat was stood up on end and I though "This is it we are going over backwards." Miraculously we fell sideways and surfed back the way we came. Sadly, it turned out the yacht was completely destroyed and there were no survivors even though we spent all the daylight hours left searching.

There were the occasional humorous ones. I was the helmsman on a shout to a boat behaving strangely off Keyhaven river. The Isle of Wight ferry has spotted it stationary with sails flapping.

As we neared the yacht we could see someone on the helm but it was not moving and obviously aground. We pulled alongside and asked if he was alright.

"Yus I'm fine jus heading for Keyhaven," in a very slurred voice. The old boy and his mate were completely plastered and unaware they were going nowhere.

I missed the best one when the Lifeboat was called to a boat seen drifting in Alum Bay, with no sign of anyone on board. When our crew pulled alongside a very startled and undressed couple appeared.

Over the years kit was changed and one of the real improvements was a dry suit, now we could stay warm and dry even if we had to enter the water. The boats grew in size and weight and now require a tractor to launch instead of 4 people pushing. Training is very organized and they even have a college at Poole headquarters.

In the 15 years I served on the Lymington Lifeboat we had a very close crew who worked so well together and like so many services that put their necks on the line they liked to blow of steam with a good party.

I ended my time with them as Senior Helmsman as my busy work life had got in the way of being as active a participant as I felt I should be so it was with a real tinge sadness that I handed over the reins.

Tall Tale 6
We need a Tackle Company..... and an even Bigger Boat!

It was the advent of a new type of fishing line that got us started in the fishing tackle business. Gel spun polyethylene or super braid as we came to know it had two remarkable properties, firstly was its very low stretch and secondly it was very thin for its breaking strain; both being qualities that anglers looked for. The major drawback was that it was very expensive.

I could see the advantages that it would give my customers so we went looking for a wholesale supplier that we could buy from in bulk. In our search we found that one of the few manufactures of this material was based in Holland and was willing to supply us directly if we could place a big enough order. They would also make it to our specification and our colour. The line is braided from very thin filaments and it's that slow process that makes it expensive. We went for the maximum tucks per centimetre, which pushed up the price but gave us a premium product.

The number of spools we had to order would take me years to shift if I just sold them on my boat so Heather and I decided to take the plunge and start selling by mail order, however starting a business with just one product was not going to work.

For some time anglers visiting the USA had been bringing back soft plastic lures designed mainly for freshwater bass fishing, they found them to work extremely well in the sea particularly for pollack and cod. Another search found Action Plastics in the US and we placed an order for many boxes of lures. These needed hooks and it was through a British agent we were able to get a supply of high quality Japanese hooks. Thus *Bayzand Sportfishing* LLP was born.

We launched with a special offer that was included in the packaging of a cod fishing video produced by *Sea Angler Magazine* and John Wilson, that featured some of our tackle being used on board *Sundance*. The result gave us a kick start as many people who purchased the video took up the offer, in fact people were still sending in the order forms many years later, perhaps after they picked up the film from a second hand shop!

Our good relationship with *Sea Angler* paid off and we were able to get a prime spot for our adverts, always vertical on the right hand page and generally next to a relevant article.

Heather used her considerable computer expertise to build a website which was way before social media was a major selling tool. She would post news from the boat on it every couple of days and in its heyday was getting 10,000 hits a day.

We kept expanding our stock lines always looking for new innovations and manufacturing some items such as plastic booms and traces at home. Whilst visiting a tackle trade show in London, I found a small booth with a Chinese firm offering a line in moulded soft plastic lures. I asked them if they would manufacture lures to our specification to which came the reply, "You will have to pay for the moulds."

"How much is that?" I asked.

He came back with, "150 U.S dollars."

How I kept the grin off my face, I don't know. I had costed a 6-impression injection mould in the UK and was told £20,000. We took a punt and placed an order half expecting to be a fiasco but it turned out to be completely the opposite. We dealt through the Hong Kong office who were really efficient emailing photos of our designs and Fedexing samples overnight for us to test. Heather designed the packaging and when the truck arrived with boxes and boxes of lures we were amazed that everything was as we requested and first class quality.

The business took off and Heather gave up working at the chandlery to run it full time. She made a point of getting any orders in the post the same day. She received many compliments from customers for the speed of service, with some ordering one day and getting it the next.

On the boating front, since being on Roddy's catamaran in Anguilla, I had started to look at cats available in the UK that would make a good charter vessel. Cheetah, in the Isle of Wight, made a cat influenced by the Australian Shark Cat, I had a ride on Geoff Blake's Cheetah Cat one day off Ventnor. The word must have spread as soon after I had a call from John Kennett, a potter from Yarmouth, who said, "If you are interested in a cat you should go and see what South Boats are building me."

So off to South Boats on the Isle of Wight I trotted. They were just building the hull plug for this new breed of catamaran which looked really good. It was designed by TT boats at Bembridge, the same firm that produced the lines for the Nelson, a famous semi displacement powerboat favoured by pilot authorities around the world for its sea keeping abilities.

I said let me know when John's boat is in the water and I will come and have a look. It proved to be a great sea trial, loads of deck room and hulls that were easily driven, thus needing relatively low horsepower. So a discussion was had and an order placed. My deal was that I would buy the hull and wheelhouse and employ the yard to help me with the fit out. One strange but nice connection was that their yard was part of the old Groves and Gutteridge shipyard where my Father worked as a naval architect during the war. The building shed was the old Lifeboat shed.

When my the hull was finally out of the mould, I did a daily commute from Lymington to East Cowes first using *Sundance 2* then by ferry and a car I kept in Yarmouth. The first things we installed were the deck beams, so very different to the solid hardwood beams in *Sundance 2*. These were glass fibre moulded around square section PVC downpipe and very lightweight and stiff. They were attached to the hull with a two part adhesive used in the aircraft industry. Even though tests in the yard showed the glass-fibre would fail before the glue joint we still tabbed them in with some glass. The fit out proceeded well and my main man was Ian Dobson who skippered his own boat out of Bembridge. In March 2000 we launched and I can remember pinching myself as I sped down the Solent on my way home, I just could not believe we owned such a beautiful vessel.

In truth we did not own all of it as Barclays Bank had a major share in it at that time. Heather has always been great at handling the books. Soon after we launched *Sundance 2* in 1988, interest rates shot up to 18%. We had a boat loan and a house mortgage but we managed to make the increased payments and when the rates came down she kept on paying the same amount, thus being able to settle them early.

The new boat was a dream, tons more room and a few knots more speed without an increase in fuel. I had figured that 15 knots cruise would be enough considering the average sea state in the English Channel so had fitted her with a pair of 212 hp Sabre Perkins diesels. They turned out to be more than sufficient and our cruise was more like 16 to 17 knots.

So the years went by, backwards and forwards on the 70-mile run to Alderney or the 80 plus mile round trips to mid-Channel from Lymington. Life consisted of many long days and even on days off I had plenty of maintenance jobs to do.

Heather said to me one day, "You are looking grey and I don't mean just your hair. I think it's time to stop."

She was right, I was feeling exhausted and although I still loved the life it was wearing me out. Both my parents had gone and we really did not have anything to hold us in the UK any more so we decide to retire somewhere warmer.

The question was... Where should we go?

Tall Tale 7

Moving to Australia.

"You bought a boat before a house!" These are words that I have heard a few times since we moved to Australia. I just put my hand up and plead guilty but it was Phil Reed's fault!

When I was still in England and getting close to moving I had been in contact with Phil, an old customer and good friend who was living in Brisbane. I had told him that I had been looking at boats in OZ and was thinking of a Steber Craft monohull with a diesel inboard. He suggested having a look at a Blackwatch 28 and there are were couple listed on *Boat Sales*.

So soon after arriving in Sydney I went to look at one of these at Pittwater just north of Sydney. It was blowing fairly hard so a good time to take a sea trial. The broker took me out in a tender to the mooring and we hopped aboard. Even though she was a few years old it looked very new, the 500 hours on the engine told a story having done only 100 hours a year. Evidently she had been owned by a wealthy family who owned a waterside house in Sydney harbour. They only used her for harbour cruises hence the large cockpit table and seating. She was a proper little pocket game boat equipped with outriggers, rod holders and a live bait tank.

We fired up the 230 hp Yanmar which drove a straight shaft and prop. This was another of my requirements. Many of these vessels are fitted with outdrive legs which are a pain in the proverbial. As soon as it was warmed up, I pushed the throttle forward and she popped up on the plane cutting through the chop with ease.

That was enough for me to have her hauled out for a bottom inspection. As I tapped and prodded my way round underneath, the boat the broker gave me a quizzical look and said "Are you a surveyor?" I grinned as I had spent plenty of days watching Dad do surveys and after building and running a number of vessels, I knew my way around. She was in really good condition so a deal was done and I got the broker to arrange transport to the Sunshine Coast in Queensland.

Blu Reela turned out to be just what I needed. The express layout gave me instant access to the deck so that I could fish and moor on my own if needed and she was also very economical to run.

I joined the Sunshine Coast Game Fishing Club and made some good friends who were very helpful, particularly Rob Smith known by everyone as Smithy. Rob runs a charter boat out of Mooloolaba and is the fountain of knowledge for what is happening on the coast; in fact he really has his finger on the pulse of fishing all over Australia. He really helped me get up to speed with local tactics and marks. No matter what you have done and where you have fished, you can't beat local knowledge.

Although black and blue marlin are the main quarry in the Club, I really enjoyed light tackle snapper fishing using soft plastics on the relatively shallow inshore reefs. Quite often I would head out at 4pm with a friend or two and sometimes on my own. Snapper come on the feed as it nears sunset and by 7pm I would be heading home, perhaps with a fish for dinner.

When it came time to move to Perth I had to make the very reluctant decision to sell *Blu Reela*, something that I regret to this day.

Soon after moving to the west coast I got a call from Russ Housby to ask if I would like to help him deliver a boat.

I have known Russ since he was a small boy; his father Trevor and I were good friends as I have written about before. Russ and I had fished together many times and he had crewed for me for a short while before getting his Skipper's Ticket and heading off to join the game fishing boats in Madeira.

Russ is one of those meticulous guys that are fastidious about doing things in the best possible way. Watching him tie intricate trout flies as a lad was amazing. His dedication to detail led him to become a very sought after crewman that has taken him all around the world including Madeira, Ghana, BomBom Island and Australia. Russ had been living and working in Vanuatu for some years and was asked to deliver and skipper a 40 foot Blackwatch from the Gold Coast in Queensland over the 1200 plus miles to Vanuatu.

I jumped at the chance and joined Russ at boat broker *Game and Leisure Boats* dock, at Runaway Bay Marina. There was a fair bit of running around to do before we set sail and the brokerage were really helpful, even lending us their Ute to do numerous shopping runs. Eventually we were joined by Steve Tedesco, filled up the tanks and deck bladders and set off for the four day run to New Caledonia. Everything went to plan. We transferred the fuel from the deck to the main tanks with no problem and stood our watches as we chugged along at 8 knots.

That was until 2am on the third night. I was just taking over the helm from Russ and was probably a bit dozy having just turned out of my bunk. I got a bottle of water from the cooler and was heading for the helm seat as the boat lurched and I took a swan dive off the flying bridge down the ladder to the deck 8 feet below, bouncing off the fridge on my way which helped slow my fall. I landed flat on my back on the deck and soon had two worried looking faces saying, "Don't move, where does it hurt." Amazingly all my limbs worked and apart from some nicely bruised ribs I was OK. I was dismissed back to my bunk to recover and still feel guilty that Russ had to stand a double watch and then some!

By the time we pulled into the little marina at Koumac on the northern end of New Caledonia, I was up and about. The weather took a turn for the worse and we were stuck there for 10 days. Whilst we were waiting we did a crew change. Steve left and we were joined by Troy Neel, a well-known baseball player from the USA who now lives in Vanuatu. We really made the best of our time in Koumac enjoying some good French food and catching every jack in the marina, even helping out locals with engine problems.

Finally we got the weather window we needed for the run to Vanuatu and headed up the coast to some very remote reefs way off the beaten track. I don't think these places see many boats because as we put out a couple of lures a heap of dogtooth tuna piled on them immediately. We got one to the boat but the next hook-up was eaten by sharks, which were now homing in. Even though this horseshoe shaped reef looked like an ideal spot to spend a few days we had to get on our way as the weather was turning again.

A slow overnight cruise brought us to another reef that was just showing as a line of breakers, the sort of thing that boats hit when the weather is calm. At first light we put out the lures and immediately caught some yellow fin tuna. As the light improved we could see the reef properly and moved the boat into shallower water. There we caught some bait and started fishing for dogtooth tuna or doggies as they are known, just a tad feistier than the Needles doggies! They are experts at getting away and will take you straight through the coral bommies given half a chance. Troy was in his element fighting these dogtooth tuna, being a well-built sportsman. I was more than happy to catch the 5lb to 10 lb mackerel for bait. All too soon we were on our way to Vanuatu and pulled into Port Villa late on the second night. What an adventure!

Russ now owns the boat which is called *Nambas* after one of the local tribes. He runs very popular live aboard trips through the chain of islands. I can't wait to get back to Vanuatu. The people are really friendly, the fishing is great and you can buy real French food!

Ed. *Roger's adventures are far from over. I did recently ask him when he was going to write his book. He told me' "When I get old"!!!!*

SIXTH WAVE

The Scott Belbin Section

My Story: Watery Reflections

Tall Tale 1.

Ed. Scott is the young skipper/owner at Essex Sea Angling. Inspired by the Seadogs Tall Tales, Scott has worked hard here to tell the fascinating story of his upbringing amongst the fishing folk of his childhood and then stage by stage, boat by boat through his journey to becoming a where is is today as a full time charter skipper. This is all set in the Mersea/Blackwater Estuary/River Crouch area and is a tale full of fascinating detail and supportive family and friends. It's a great read. I hope Scott will be another skipper to write his own book one day when the time is right for him.

I was lucky and fully appreciate I had a privileged upbringing which enabled me to become a skipper. When I say privileged, I didn't come from money (although that would have helped), but from an early age I was taken fishing by my Dad. He was a charter skipper long before I was born and so I was brought up on my dad's charter boats. Really to tell you my story I feel I should first tell you a bit about Dad's story.

Dad, Stuart Belbin, grew up in Upminster. Where my Grandad was a keen angler he took my dad and his two brothers angling from a young age. This would have mostly been fresh water fishing near to his home. My Nan and Grandad acquired a beach hut in West Mersea when he was very young. With a front row beach hut it was only a matter of time before they invested in a small rowing boat to fish from. As the years went on the rowing boats progressed into larger dinghies such as their Shetland Suntrip.

With the Shetland being fast he could now fish further out and tow it to other places if he wanted. While he had this Shetland, named *Miss Grace* after my nan, he got his first licence (of sorts) in 1973. This meant he was able to take small parties, up to four people, out for the day with him. During ownership of *Miss Grace* he made some good friends who were also running Shetland's at the time such as Paul Maris, Richard Parkinson and Nobby Clarke. Both Paul and Richard later became some of my many godparents. Eventually dad and grandad traded in their Shetland for their first inboard boat. *The Miss Grace II,* their second vessel, was a 26ft clinker boat with an aft wheelhouse.

At some point in the mid to late 70's the *Miss Grace II* was chopped in for the Crusader which was Dad's first boat on his own. She was another clinker boat, this time a 36ft Naval Pinnace which he had the wheelhouse arrangement changed on to make more suitable for angling. One of the local boat yards has a hull the same as the Crusader called the Norden which they use as a harbour launch. Dad was taking regular parties by now as well as working other jobs too. By the early 80's Nan and Grandad had sold their house in Upminster and moved to Mersea. Dad was still living with them at this point. The Crusader wasn't a big boat for the length although she was 'of her time'.

With his boat now fairly well booked, he invested in something with a bit more room for angling parties. This came in the form of the *Researcher*. This boat was another clinker vessel. Although this one was 32ft she offered a nice clear deck with plenty of room. The Researcher was still moored in Mersea until a few years ago and I always thought she had nice lines. He kept the Researcher until the mid-80's.

Angling had seen a few changes during those 10 years or so with people like John Rawle and Bob Cox bringing boat casting to us and putting Bradwell, opposite Mersea, firmly on the angling map. The Blackwater and surrounding area had some fantastic sport to offer at this time. The Bradwell boats made headlines with some of the fantastic catches of bass they had seen offshore with thornback rays in the spring and autumn, hounds and tope in the summer and some big stingrays to name a few. In the winter they could offer the cod fishing from the Blackwater right off to the Barrows. As ever, the Blackwater Estuary was a great asset and meant they could fish in all but the worst conditions. The boats from Mersea had access to the same rich waters with all of the benefits and had a healthy number of charter boats too.

Dad was quite well booked and established by now. The boat was pretty good in its day and the lads caught fish. By this time he also had a licence to sell fish on the boat too. This was quite common among charter boats back then. When he wasn't booked, he would often work with his friend Derek Mole sometime using gill nets but often using longlines. They would take turns with whose boat they would use and hand hauled the lines. As they progressed, they invested in baiting machines and line haulers. These lines were baited with squid and in fact it was the high-quality Falkland's squid they used, which found its way onto their charter boats. The squid soon proved to catch many different species and is now a must have bait on most charter boats.

By now Dad had several regular parties, some of whom he had known for years. Paul Maris was one such angler; I know it's generous to refer to him as an angler. Dad and Paul had been friends back when they both had Shetland Suntrips and used to trail them around. Paul now fished on Dad's charter boat regularly as well as many other parts of the country. The story goes that they were doing a 24hr trip offshore, cruising at 8knts as this was the best way to make the most of an offshore trip. They fished The Knock at first which is around 30 miles out. With the weather very fine and some keen, experienced anglers on board Dad suggested they try punching a further 10 miles out to the next bank, the 'Galloper'. It was now somewhere around 1984/85 and at 40 miles out this area was near enough untouched. With most boats having limited navigational equipment, limited sea keeping and limited speed they didn't head this far out. Plus, there was normally no need to. On this first trip they anchored on the bank itself and on a calm summer's day they had numerous decent cod along with an unexpected variety of fish. On that first trip off there, without trying, they had over 15 different species of fish.

This first trip set the wheels in motion for Dad to move up a gear and invest in a faster, more modern boat and he had always wanted an Aquastar. After they were first made back in the 70's, both Aquastar and Lochin were the boats to have. Looking back today, most well-known skippers had one of these boats at some point back then. To get one of these he would be stretching himself financially and had to offer a share to one of his good mates; Steve Bateman, also to later become one of my many god parents. After searching around he found what he was looking for in the shape of the *Deva*. She was a twin engine Aquastar 32, one of two built for Trinity House - the other being the *Tamesis* which ran from Plymouth for many years. They had been made to go alongside navigation buoys so in turn were very heavily built and a high spec. These boats had a short career with Trinity House and by the time dad bought the *Deva* she was under private ownership in Scarborough. She cruised at a much faster 12knt rather than 8knts and this speed would make these offshore trips more sensible. By now he had made a couple more runs off to the bank and was keen to try some of the surrounding wrecks. This he did, and it was a resounding success. Over the next few years he gained a lot of publicity for big catches of cod, ling and pollock around the Galloper and beyond. He was particularly thankful to keen anglers such as Paul Maris and Dave (Whiskers) Pucil for putting the time and effort in with him on these exploratory trips.

It was around this time that mum and dad were blessed with me. The *Deva* features in some of my earlier memories. Some are of being aboard, stood on deck as a toddler unable to see over the gunwales. Others are of bright sunny afternoons walking along Coast Road with Mum to meet Dad as he came ashore. Dad would be followed by dozens of noisy gulls as the lads would often still be gutting cod after a 3-4hr steam home! Dad had some cracking hits of fish on the wrecks.

He may be ageing somewhat now but it's fair to say Dad was my undeniably hero as a child. As well as bringing home some huge catches of fish and running what to my mind was the best charter boat in the port. When he wasn't on the boat, he would be coxswain on the lifeboat, a race marshal on the British rally cross and working other jobs when he wasn't at sea. Back at home he had my two brothers and I to keep him and Mum busy. I don't know how they had the time!

By 1992 with interest rates stupidly high, a young family at home and after a succession of bad weather it looked like the *Deva* would have to go. Dad says he had enough of paying the bank managers wages and needed more financial stability. The *Deva* went to Ireland where she has stayed to this day. She now has a single Caterpillar engine in her.

There was a short break after he sold the *Deva* before a friend of his, Don Taylor who used to fish with him, asked if he would run a boat for him. A couple of other people had offered before to, no avail, but this time he came through. This time he would be running another Aquastar, this time a later 33ft model purpose made with a slightly shorter wheelhouse for angling. The wrecking continued, as did the inshore boat casting trips. At this point I was a few years older and I have slightly more memories of the *Silver Lady*. I can remember a bit of fishing and being a bit older and taller I could just about see over the gunwales now. I vividly remember being on board when Dad would run trips to the *Ross Revenge* aka *Radio Caroline*. It's funny, as the *Ross* has now returned to the Blackwater and Dad is once again running trips to her. When I went back, I could even remember much of the layout. Running the *Silver Lady* worked fairly nicely for both Dad and Don. Unfortunately, once again finances put a stop to the fishing as the stock markets crashed and once again financial stability was needed. The *Silver Lady* was sold and went to Belgium, Dad and Don delivered her in some awful weather which only helped to further Dads trust in these boats for their sea keeping abilities.

Watery Reflections: How I got into Chartering
Tall Tale 2

As you will remember from part one the *Silver Lady* had been sold and we pick up the story from there.

Dad was once again without a boat and now working on a building site where he had been gradually working his way up from a site labourer in-between running trips on the boat. Over the next couple of years he was boatless. This meant more time was spent by all of us coarse fishing. On the odd occasion we were able to get out fishing with Derek Mole aboard his fishing boat and once Dave Weaving kindly took me out on the *Jenna D* for the Golden Cod competition. Just a few short years later Dad found himself once again in the position to buy a boat. I must admit to me at the time it seemed like this was many years but looking back it was only 2-3years.

Mum and Dad were now divorced and Mum was living near Manningtree. As Dad would drive us between Manningtree and Mersea we would cross a bridge over the Colne at the Hythe on Colchester. As we went over this bridge each time we used to look across at an 8 meter starfish which sat unused and on the mud for most of the tide. We often used to comment on her being a nice little boat and how she didn't seem to get any use. Dad put a note on her asking if the owner wished to sell her. A short while later the owner got in touch and it wasn't long before he had a boat again. This time dad had no intention of chartering. He had the boat full with just him, grandad and us three boys on board. The Starfish was named *Bluebell* and this was not going to stay! Us 3 boys were very much co-owners of this boat, that is in every way besides running costs, maintenance or anything that couldn't be deemed 'fun'. We all sat around and very likely after much bickering chose the name *Razorbill*. The *Razorbill* went through many changes under our ownership.

She wasn't fast but it didn't matter too much as we used her as a private vessel for several years. We made many great memories with family and friends aboard her and she served us well. The speed was improved with a couple of engine changes and eventually she was making 25 knots flat out, cruising at 16-18 knots and inevitably became licenced for charter fishing.

By now us boys had grown up and started getting our own boats. I had spent many days and hours on this boat with my Grandad Stan, or *Flash* as I often affectionately called him when I found out his nickname in the war. I had also taken some of my friends and my Dad's friends fishing while he was at work and I was on school holidays. By the time I was 17, I was told I had a wealth of experience for my age and many hours under my belt so at 17 I got my Offshore Yacht Masters Certification just as dad got the boat licenced for charters. I will tell you more about me later but for now I will bring you up to date with Dad's story. When I would let him get a look in, Dad was working his way back into chartering. Shortly after the *Razorbill* was licenced, he and I bought another boat together and licenced her too. This was the first *Galloper*. By now he was working towards chartering again.

At a different time of life and with a bit more security it was a realistic option where he could semi-retire and work the boat just a few days a week without having to worry. The Starfish was a great little boat, she did very well for 26ft but they are wet and it was tight even with 6 anglers on board. The best way to make it work would be to get a bigger boat again. Around this time one of Dad's friends told him about their boss who had taken an Aquastar in part exchange for his boat and wanted to sell it if Dad was interested. We went to view her and with a 300hp Ford she went well. She had just undergone a major refit and Dad was able to buy her at half the price of the re-fit! Both the *Razorbill* and the *Galloper* were sold shortly after. Dad re-named this Aquastar, formerly *Celtic Dolphin*, the *Razorbill II* and I bought my own Aquastar shortly after and stuck with the name *Galloper*. The *Razorbill II* had been fitted out more as a gentleman's cruiser. She had an extended wheelhouse up to the engine hatch, a bow thruster and even derricks on the stern to pull a small dingy up on. Dad didn't have make too many changes to her for licencing though.

He ran this one for a few years before another Aquastar came up for sale in Yarmouth. Once again, we had looked down on this boat on her berth in Yarmouth a couple of times. She was originally *Private Venture* and then *Southern Star* which were both well-known boats in the Solent. She had a rough time at Yarmouth. As a mark of this, when he bought her she had stainless steel griddles bolted over all of the windows! Dad was able to buy this at a reasonable price. This boat was a better boat for chartering. She has higher decks so no engine box in the way, seating at the stern, a shorter wheelhouse and more deck room as well as being built like the proverbial brick toilet. He still has this boat today and it has served him well. It's nice to fish off and built heavy enough to lay alongside the ship *Ross Revenge*. Dad is 67 now, that's 47 years chartering, give or take the odd break, and so he is certainly one of the longest serving licenced skippers in the area and maybe the country! Not too bad for a lad from a council house in Upminster. Longevity doesn't mean he is the best in the world, maybe just the maddest.

Watery Reflections
Tall Tale 3

To tell you my story from the start we will have to back track a bit on Dad's story and join him with the *Deva*. As I mentioned before I have several fond memories aboard this boat. As I grow older they become a little more hazy but those of seeing her steam back along the beach surrounded by gulls will stay with me forever. Times may have changed a bit but even now when you see a boat being followed by flocks of gulls you naturally assume they have had a bountiful day. I am grateful, not only to my Dad for providing the spectacle but also to my Mum for letting me witness it. As far as I can remember I always wanted to go fishing. I don't mean as a living but just fishing, anywhere. I have and would again, particularly right now, fish any available bit of water. I have fished in bits of water you could almost step across. I've spent hours catching sticklebacks and flounders from dykes and minnows from flooded streams, give me a bit of water and I want to try and catch a fish from it. I was no different as a child and no doubt gave Mum and Dad grief for it. I can remember pestering to go wrecking with Dad when I was clearly too young. I was allowed on the boat and allowed to fish as I got big enough to actually handle a rod. I'm sure I ruined several anglers' plans of a child-free days charter boat fishing. I can remember fishing more on the *Silver Lady*, by this time I was just about big enough to handle a rod and even peek over the gunwale. Eventually I was allowed on a trip offshore. I can't remember if it was wrecking, or even what we caught. I do remember it was flat calm and when we got a long way out Dad stopped the boat to show me how clear it was and that we could just about see the bottom. This must have captured my imagination for me to remember it so vividly. It was probably the first time I had seen such clear water as everything close inshore in the Thames estuary is normally clouded with silt. Another trip I can remember is an evening/night trip I went on. I won the whip on the boat for the biggest fish but refused to accept it as I was convinced it was a fix! Obviously now I know it was very likely my natural angling talent shining through!

Looking back, we really were lucky not only to have a father and grandfather who not only enjoyed angling but were happy to share it with us. I could recall endless stories of our fishing trips both fresh water and sea fishing. It's a wonder Dad has a single hair left on his head after loading the car up with enough tackle for me, my two brothers and very often my Grandad as well as his own! One occasion I am very often reminded of was from when I was quite young. We were fresh water fishing and using maggots for bait. It was a chilly winter's day and I had a Parker coat on. I don't remember what we were fishing for but we were getting through bait quite quickly. Dad asked if I needed any more bait as it had been a while since I changed it. I said, "No, it's alright I've got some in my pocket thanks". This clever use of initiative wasn't met with the praise I had expected as I remember when we got home Mum wasn't too keen to hear I had a pocketful of maggots either.

I don't really remember when the *Silver Lady* went really. As I mentioned in an earlier instalment, we had a couple of trips out on Derek Mole's commercial boat the *Talon*, although a much later version than the one pictured the other day. We had one trip in the Blackwater Estuary with good numbers of codling and one trip further out as far as I remember catching the odd roker or cod. Dave Weaving also took me on the *Jenna D* which at that time was a Bullet 38. This was for a local charity competition called the Golden Cod and I don't remember what I caught. I was with Dad's friend, Adrian, known as Uncle Adrian - everybody is an uncle this or auntie that when you're young. I remember Uncle Adrian had a sea scorpion of some sort which he took back in a bucket for the weigh in.

In these years between boats we did lots of fresh water fishing. Dad was in a small syndicate that fished a couple of farmers' reservoirs. They were stuffed with carp, roach and rudd along with the odd pike. We were truly spoiled fishing here as they would still produce at any time of year provided they weren't iced over. The water was about 30ft deep in the middle so the temperature was fairly stable in the winter and come the summer they were drained to just three feet or so deep. I have seen carp literally climbing up the banks after ground bait we had spilled at our feet, they were that ravenous and densely stocked. We pestered Dad into a trip here night fishing and he eventually gave in. I was a little older so I was allowed to fish all night but my two younger brothers had to pack their rods away and sleep. The next morning came and 50 odd carp later I was knackered. Apparently when we got back to Dad's and I climbed into bed I pronounced that 'I never want to go fishing again' and promptly slept for the next day and a bit.

In Part 2 of my story, I mentioned how we came to view and then buy the Starfish 8 we re-named the *Razorbill I*. It was barely more than two years between the *Silver Lady* going to Belgium and the purchase of *Razorbill* but that time seemed like an age to my younger self. It was only when we started looking through pictures and dates that I realised it was only two years. Very shortly after this my brothers and I were to purchase our first boat. I had dreams of getting my own boat for a while before hand but finances were a little tight as I was still at primary school!

By now Mum had moved to Lawford, just outside Manningtree. Her house was a short walk from the top of the tidal Stour across a road, through a folly and over the sea wall. I had ideas of getting a little boat and mooring it there so I could head off wrecking. We dreamed of lots of little boats, various things with inboards or no inherent buoyancy but at the right price. As it happened Dad heard that one of the local lads was selling his Orkney Longliner *Boy Lew* which he had used for gillnetting and we could buy it without an engine for £550. Between the three of us we scrapped our savings, emptied our piggy banks, sold a kidney or two and bought her. Without an engine we were going nowhere though. This is where our lovely Nan and Grandad helped us out and offered to get one. For our combined birthday, Christmas, tooth fairy and whatever money, they bought an old two stroke Evinrude 7 hp from one of my many godparents, Richard Parkinson. The shaft was a bit too short and it made a right racket as we steamed around but it got us along for a couple of years.

We looked into mooring the *Boy Lew* at Manningtree but she would have been afloat for just a short amount of each tide and to be honest Mersea offered better fishing. I was 11 when we bought her and the oldest out of the three of us and when I look at 11year olds now I find it frightening to be honest. We learnt quickly and managed not to kill ourselves or each other. There was always somebody around keeping an eye on us. The Orkney turned out to be our biggest asset to be honest. In all of the time we owned her, I never felt unsafe and I can't think of a better 16ft boat. Now between the *Razorbill* and the *Boy Lew* we would enjoy make happy family memories.

Watery Reflections
Tall Tale 4

This was a time of many changes in my life. Mum had moved to Lawford and we would be between there and Mersea. This opened up new fishing opportunities over the coming years. I finished primary school at Mistley and then went to Manningtree High School. I had a new baby sister called Millie so there was another person to drag around while fishing at every available opportunity. Luckily mum was good at finding a nice bit of beach or some kind of water to keep us occupied so everybody was happy. Mum has always been keen to broaden my interests to stuff other than fishing. That said when push came to shove, she just wanted to see us happy. There have been many times when she has saved the day, like the time she removed her shoe buckles to use as fishing weights. Or the time we were on a strict non-fishing holiday in Tenerife and she ended up asking hotel staff for champagne corks to act as makeshift floats for us. We certainly kept Mum and Dad busy between the four of us. They near enough let us go where we wanted between Mersea and Manningtree. I'm sure each of them appreciated a rest when we were gone for a few days though. We had some great fun exploring Manningtree and the surrounding areas but the freedom of the boats took us to Mersea as much as we could.

Over the years the *Razorbill* got faster which allowed us to venture further and eventually we got back off to those wrecks where Dad had made his name. Sadly times had changed somewhat by now though. Those uncharted wrecks were now firmly on everybody's charts. GPS was now commonplace rather than luxury and far more reliable. Boats had become faster too and it seemed that every man and his dog could now access this special place. One of the first times we headed off, the first wreck we arrived at had a 20ft rib anchored on it and several people diving it. We were well over 40 miles from home! The boat we were on was too small for a journey like that really let alone an open rib!

The nail in the coffin for Dad was when we arrived at one of the furthest wrecks he used to fish only to find this too was plastered in nets. It's a big wreck and he was able to anchor it to try and make the most of the last of the tide. While we were anchored a Belgian charter boat appeared from over the horizon. They had been fishing somewhere back towards the English side out of sight and made a bee line for us. They drifted the same wreck as us and came past very close. It was flat calm; he had his engine running and there was very little tide left so he was perfectly in control. Sharing a wreck isn't something we are used to around here and Dad certainly wasn't as he had rarely seen any other boats out here at all when he first ventured off. As it happens, although we were miffed, we exchanged little more than a polite smile towards the 10 or so anglers on his boat. I do remember it was an old Offshore and we were surprised how the decks were awash on such a calm day.

The skipper started pointing and waving his arms out towards the North East. We didn't understand him and he didn't speak English. He only had one or two drifts but kept gesturing in the same direction towards what we could now see was a boat bearing down on us. Whatever the skipper on the 105 was saying it seemed he didn't like the looks of the boat heading our way and he wasn't hanging around any longer as he headed off pretty sharpish.

The other boat grew ever closer and as it did the sheer size of the thing came apparent. Before we knew it, Dad had to start the engine and run the boat ahead to avoid being struck by the oncoming vessel. Dad came back on deck offer his appreciation to the other skipper for his boat handling. The other boat was a massive commercial boat around 80ft long towering above us. The skipper leaned out of his window and said, "I hope your anchors are not in my net." We hauled our anchor and watched him pull his set nets in. The boat was vast with decks 10-12ft out of the water so they had to use a grapnel to get hold of the marker buoys. She had a shelter over the working deck and we watched them haul countless cod and the occasional ling aboard. As soon as they had the gear aboard another load was shot from a pound in the stern. This one day put a stop to any dreams I had of witnessing catches like Dad had seen years before. The wreck netting boat with all of its size and catching power, clearly undeterred by weather due to its size, would be the demise of this fishing. We heard several years later this boat had in effect put itself out of business in the end. I will add that I don't see those wrecks netted much anymore although there isn't much for them to catch nowadays.

The Starfish 8m we were using at the time was a bit small to head right offshore and very often better fishing is to be found inshore off the Essex coast anyway. The shallow banks and estuaries provide a breeding ground and nursery area for many species. Often fish are feeding on the shore crabs and shrimps which live very close inshore. This means that much of our time is spent less than 10 miles out in the winter and less than 20 miles out in the summer. Winter fishing would be for codling, whiting and the odd thorn-back ray. Summer fishing would be bass, smoothhounds and maybe a tope if we could go off far enough. Bass could be hit or miss as they had a lot of pressure on them at the time but we did have some very good trips on them. In the early summer when the shore crabs start to moult, they are very vulnerable to predation. This moult normally signalled the first push of smooth hounds in numbers. These fish are great fun to catch and we often target them in just a few feet of water. The Starfish is a semi-displacement hull which roughly means although it could go faster than a trawler, it could handle weather better than a speed boat and was easy to manoeuvre. This made it an ideal boat for me to graduate from the Orkney with. We still had the Orkney and used her for all sorts from playing around with nets and eel fykes to hand picking oysters and angling for bass or cod.

As well as my brothers and I using the Orkney we were often joined by our Grandad. I was lucky as not only was he my Grandad but he was my mate and angling buddy too. If my brothers weren't up for fishing with me then Grandad would often come along for the day. We didn't go far at first. Often, we fished the creeks around the moorings which can be full of small bass at times in the summer. one such time we were fishing and he inevitably needed a pee. It's not easy going over the side of a small boat, particularly when your over 80 years of age and not so steady on your feet. It was common for him to use the bailer for this which was an old bottle with the bottom cut off to scoop water out of the boat. I passed him the bailer and carried on fishing only to hear cursing and swearing coming from his end of the boat. When I asked what was wrong it turned out he hadn't realised the bottom was cut off of the bottle so had removed the top and proceeded to make a mess over the deck! I couldn't help him for laughing.

The small boat was becoming too awkward for Grandad to get in and out of and I was ambitious to venture further afield. It wasn't long before Dad let us head out on our own while he was at work. I was 14 years old when I took Grandad out for my first trip 'on my own' as such. We used to fish in the estuary at first and were happy just being out there. Grandad loved to eat fish, he would eat any fish we put in front of him. He even ate a mullet we gave him once and enjoyed it! On our first trips I often used to cook up something we had caught like whiting or dab, even mackerel in the summer.

Over the next couple of years I was lucky enough that I got allowed to venture further on my own. Often with Grandad but also with some of Dad's mates who became my mates. Carl Sealey and Steve Bateman would often join me and I learned a lot from them while also clocking up my hours at the helm and gaining boating experience. While looking through pictures the other day I found a couple from a trip in early summer. I would have been 16 or 17 and we were starting to look at getting the boat licenced for charters. On this day it was myself, youngest brother and Grandad on the boat. We had a great day there were plenty of thorn-back rays, some nice hounds with the biggest hound over 17lbs and a good few bass with Grandad taking the biggest at just under 10lbs. Trips like this filled me with enthusiasm and confidence as I took my Yacht Masters Offshore ticket over the coming year.

Back then in the early to mid-2000's the numbers of thorn-back rays were at a real low point. In the spring when they first arrived, we would often travel over 20 miles out to try and catch them. We often didn't stand much chance closer to home as the fish had to run the gauntlet of bottom trawls or a barrage of set nets or drift gear. Happily, shortly after I gained my tickets and the *Razorbill* was licenced there was a commercial ban bought in locally on thornback rays. The effects of this for us were positive and immediate. As the next spring arrived, we were seeing numbers of thorn-backs in and around the Blackwater Estuary that I couldn't remember seeing before. To put it into context I fished the estuary most of my life and didn't catch my first thorn-back from within the estuary until I was 18. Since this ban was bought in along with the restrictions over the following years, we have now come to expect them to be here and all year around. At the same time the numbers of cod were good too which made winter bookings plentiful. The fish were there in pretty good numbers which improved for several years along with a general increase in their size.

Aside from fishing I had left school and started as an apprentice carpenter. Dad was still working as a site manager and helped to line me up with an apprenticeship with the firm he worked for. I was a busy boy for a while, did 1-2 days a week at college, 3-4 days a week on site, weekends on the boat, volunteered as a Coastguard Rescue Officer and somehow found the time to get my driving licence and Yacht Masters ticket in the evenings.

On an 8m boat with a party of 6-8 anglers, there's no room nor a real need for a crew so by this time Dad and I were taking it in turns to run the *Razorbill*. If I wasn't taking a trip, I would be on the Orkney messing about with nets or angling. It was at aged 18 that Stacey and I first started courting. I say courting but really, she talked her way onto an evening fishing on the Orkney with me. She had grown up netting on her Dad's small boats so who can blame her for being blown away by any attractive hunk with a boat and natural ability to find fish. That's how I remember it anyway. Over the next year or so Stacey joined me on my Orkney or when I was running the *Razorbill*. It turned out her upbringing made her a good angler and she would often outfish the lads onboard. I hadn't been seeing Stacey very long when my Grandad passed away. Unfortunately they only met a couple of times. Grandad was fortunate enough to keep enough of his faculties that he could still come fishing until a matter of weeks before he died. I had lost one of my fishing buddies but in Stacey I had gained a new one.

After the *Razorbill* had been licenced, for a couple of years we were quite busy and I was on about getting my own boat. I was 19 and approaching the end of my carpentry apprenticeship so expecting to be earning more on site. Dad was also hoping for a career change as he now had his sights set on retiring from site into semi-retirement on the boat. We ended up getting another boat between us. This kept Dad happy as he knew he would still be roped into maintenance so at least this way he was earning out of it. It also meant Stacey and I could still save for a house so he wouldn't be lumbered with me living at home for too much longer.

Watery Reflections
Tall Tale 5

We looked around for a while and ended up getting a Brinkliner 28. There are a few around and they are a variation on the Starfish hull, just stretched 2ft more. We brought her back, made some alterations and named her *Galloper*. The choice of name should seem obvious now as this is the name of the offshore bank around which Dad had made his name years before and the place that still captures my imagination today. The Brinkliner has higher decks and more room than the Starfish although she was a little lacking in shelter as well as speed though. Fortunately, we had her at a time when fishing was very good inshore. In the winter we averaged around 100 cod a trip and come the spring we could catch plenty of roker within 10-15 miles from home. I still wanted to head offshore though. The wrecks may have seen better days but there were still other fish to be caught. In the winter we had some cracking fishing for cod on the offshore banks. Most boats didn't head off here as there were plenty inshore, but the stamp of fish was far better offshore.

The boat was not really fast enough but the fishing was good and having a slow boat made me appreciate it more as I got faster boats later on. One of the most memorable days that winter, and of my career as a skipper so far, was on a glassy calm sunny day just before Christmas. We headed off 30 odd miles with just three on board. Myself, Uncle Paul (Maris) and Tom who was one of my work mates at the time. We left early and caught the tide out. Even with the tide that boat would only make 9 knots or so at best. Best part of four hours later we arrived at our chosen mark. We fished two rods each and had 40 odd cod. All but one were double figured and the biggest fell to Tom at just over 18lbs. This had been Tom's first time sea fishing and Paul told him not to bother again as he wouldn't see a better days' up-tide fishing for cod.

A few months later we were to head back offshore to try and catch the tail end of the cod as they left us for the summer. We had a few more people on board this time and our sights were lower as there were now very few codling inshore. Again, time off here was limited by the boat's speed, or lack of, so we anchored our first mark. Stacey was into a decent fish shortly after we stopped. It put a good scrap up before surfacing. It turned out to be a spur-dog and a good one at that. It pulled the scales around to 21.3lbs and is still the biggest I've had on the boat. It was the first one I had seen alive and as we hadn't expected it, we didn't have any suitable end tackle to deal with their sharp teeth. We were bitten of by several more throughout the day but had 14 to the boat and a dozen cod mixed in with whiting, pouting and rays. These trips were good considering we could only fish for 4-5 hours due to steaming time.

For some years now we had been trying to catch plaice off of Essex. Dad had caught a few accidently while wreck fishing but we wanted to target them. The previous year Stacey and I had succeeded when we headed off on our own one day. Now I had my own boat I was keen to prove it wasn't just a fluke and try to catch some more. A long time ago plaice were caught inshore and they still are in nets, even now, but we were having to head 40 miles out in order to find them. That summer we put a few trips in with some good anglers on board including Mick Toomer and Uncle Paul Maris and Uncle Steve. We had a few plaice for our efforts although most were small. True to form, Stacey had the biggest at 3lb something. Once again our time fishing was limited by the boat's speed.

After trips like these it's understandable that I was keen to get back offshore and had a serious case of 'dieselitis' which I haven't quite recovered from yet. The Brinkliner was a nice little boat and boats are always a compromise but this wasn't the right compromise. Needless to say, I made plans to get a different boat. Dad really wasn't keen on this idea after the time and money we had invested in this one. He may also have worried it would mean I couldn't afford to move out for a while longer but he needn't have worried as Stacey would make sure that wasn't the case.

Watery Reflections
Tall Tale 6

By now Dad had been offered the orange Aquastar and offered me the Starfish to buy. It was tempting as she was fast and with a good, nearly new, engine in her. However, we didn't buy her. I don't like buying from family and friends if I can help it, she was sold and the Brinkliner put up for sale. Stacey and I looked around for a long time for the second version of the Galloper, we put a wanted add out for an Aquastar, Lochin or Bullet and had replies from several people. We had a couple of Bullet 38's offered to us in Scotland and went to view one. That is another tale in itself! A while later we were offered an Aquastar in Rhyl North Wales. She was an old boat and needed work but the engine was fairly new and clean with low hours. She was also cheap enough that we could afford to buy her and still have a deposit for a house. With nothing better offered to us within our budget we went ahead and bought her. We spent a few months working on her when we moved the wheelhouse door over, put new windows in and generally bought her up to scratch. We did lots more work to her over the course of the next 5 years that we owned her including updating electrics, a new spray cover, having the hull spray painted and the engine reconditioned to name a few things.

The Aquastar served us well over those years. She had her ups and downs, but she offered space and sea keeping speed that the Brinkliner couldn't. The cod fishing was good over the next few winters and this made life easier. The roker were not only getting more plentiful but closer to home too. They also became a year-round standby for us. The hound fishing was good but tope proved to be a problem. The numbers were ok for the first year or two but then the numbers declined dramatically. Although this was a pain, we could change our offshore trips to target bass from June/July time into the autumn and had great success with them. The Aquastar may have been faster than the Brinkliner but with an average cruising speed around 12-14knts it meant over 2.5hrs to reach the banks we normally fished for the bass. I was pushing to get offshore bookings in throughout the winter too. The weather restricted what we could do a lot more at this time of year but we had some cracking days on the cod at this time. We took a run off there for an article in Boat Fishing Monthly with just a few of us aboard. Once again, I was joined by Uncle Paul (Maris) as well as Dave and Jim who would be doing the article. Myself and Paul cleared up that day with a dozen doubles between us many around 15/16lbs.

Speed isn't everything by all means and I will happily plod around at 12 knots if I'm not going far and it means I will arrive at a good time of tide. However, this isn't always the case and one year in particular we often had to steam some 15-20 miles along the shore to reach the best fishing inshore. This would be a particular problem when pushing the tide and speed could be down below 10knts so best part of 2hrs steaming on an inshore trip. When all of the boats are slow this isn't an issue but when everybody else steams past several knots faster, then for the good of the business I felt the need for speed.

While we had the Aqaustar we had a lot of other things going on ashore too. Shortly after the boat was launched Stacey and I got engaged. Stacey had also been offered a job operating a launch service that the local yacht club have. This would mean she would be working in Mersea and on the water so she took it. Over the course of the next year we would get married and buy our first house too. Moving into the house and our wedding coincided perfectly. The only thing that spoiled it for us was the loss of my dear old Nan just a few months before. I would have loved her to have been there but we did get married in Scotland and I wore a kilt as was her wish as she was originally from Cambuslang. Shortly after our marriage, Stacey suffered some health problems and her work signed her off until it was sorted. When she was signed back to work, they promptly sacked her and she was devastated.

Stacey found other work and I carried on running the boat and doing the carpentry in the week but Stacey had enjoyed her dream job for just a few short months before it was taken away from her. Stacey is a determined young lady and wasn't going to give up that easily. We looked around for a while and eventually purchased a Matlow 21 which we stripped out and re-configured as an open launch. I won't go into all of the details but over the course of the last 8/9 years the boat has had several re-fits and engines and is better now than ever. Stacey built her business up over several years and was able to rely on the income of the boat alone. Now certified and nationally recognised for 'Learning Outside the Classroom' and with several published books along with the other schemes, my wife can come up with the *Lady Grace*, named after my Nan, has evolved to offer boat trips and much more.

Watery Reflections
Tall Tale 7

The Aquastar had seen us through our wedding, purchase of our first house and setting up Stacey's business. However, with much of the rest of the fleet being faster and the popularity of our offshore trips for cod and bass, we wanted something faster and more modern. After owning her for 5 years and making many improvements, she was sold quite easily. She went to Hartlepool and I gather the new owner, Trevor Newton, is offering charter trips aboard her this year. Trevor very kindly gave us a few weeks' grace to find a new boat. There was nothing that tickled our fancy being advertised so we put a 'Boat Wanted, Ad up. There were several replies and one offered us an Evolution 33. I liked the Evolution boats and being 33ft this would fit on my mooring too.

Thanks to Trevor's generosity we were able to tie in the lorry taking the Aquastar going to Hartlepool and straight to Weymouth to pick up the Evolution. I was without a boat for no more than 24hrs! We had the Evo up and running in time for my next trip. There were a few changes I wanted to make in the wheelhouse layout, and have since. Our first trip was offshore and we even found some spurdogs. The Evo made life easier. We could cruise at 16-18 knots and she provided a drier ride and she had flush decks so she was deceptively roomy. She came into her own on the offshore trips where many of the lads prefer a smaller group onboard. We had great success on the offshore bass trips despite having to work around a windfarm that was under construction. This windfarm also seemed to play its part in the demise of the tope fishing too. When I got offshore in the winter we still had some nice cod and the spur-dogs as we got into the spring.

I was now offering most of my offshore trips to target bass from the end of June onwards as the tope were very sporadic. This was all well and good until there were strict bag limits put on bass. The initial bag limit of three fish per angler was not an issue as only once or twice in my whole career had I seen a party keep more than three per angler. If anything, it stopped those that were being greedy. When they reduced it to one per angler and then a ban on anglers keeping them at all it meant the end to the majority of my offshore bass trips for a while.

The inshore fishing is our bread and butter here and the Blackwater Estuary comes into its own throughout the winter. We can often be catching while other ports are forced to cancel. The Estuary itself provides great fishing and shelter from most wind directions. We don't always have to stay in the Estuary either as there are many sand banks as well as the coastline of Jaywick, Clacton or beyond also offering us sheltered fishing too. One thing we haven't been able to offer the last few years has been cod fishing. The last year with any numbers was around 2015 into 2016. I sincerely hope they return as I personally enjoy catching them. There are many theories surrounding their disappearance but I won't go into detail. All I hang on to at the moment was, they were here not so long ago. After all, in the spring of 2015 some boats had over 80 in a day in the Estuary! Happily the thorn-back rays have filled a gap for the time being. We now expect them in varying numbers throughout the year. When they move inshore in numbers in the spring we can have some impressive numbers and the best I have seen is over 120 between six anglers!

It's fair to say the Evolution's speed has helped with our hound fishing too at times. We often have to steam 20 odd miles around sand banks to reach some of our smooth-hound marks. There is usually a certain time of tide to be there and we are guaranteed to push the tide for half of the journey. We have seen some great fishing for hounds aboard her and the time saved steaming made evening trips realistic too.

The tope fishing has come back slightly over the past couple of years and our hardcore anglers have still put in the effort and got some good results. The same is true of the bass. I don't think I did any offshore bass trips when they were banned from anglers keeping them back in 2018. Even with a one fish bag limit, bookings were hard to fill but we are slowly getting given a bit more of an allowance and this year the bag limit is two per angler and the season is longer.

Watery Reflections
Tall Tale 8

I have wanted a catamaran since I was at school. They were just becoming really popular as I was starting to run the *Razorbill*. We used to call into Gemini Workboats every now and then and dream about what we might buy if we won the lottery. Every now and then they might bring a Gemini around to Mersea for see trials and we would marvel at their size. As I said at the very start of 'How I got into Chartering' which has now turning into 'Watery Reflections', I don't come from a moneyed background so much as I would have loved to buy a big catamaran as my first boat, I simply couldn't afford it. Luckily, I have been able to work my way up over the years with lots of support from family, friends and a loyal customer base many of whom are now friends more than customers.

I reached the point a few years ago where I could now afford to stretch myself and buy a catamaran. When considering investing such a huge amount of money into a business, Stacey and I had many things to consider. Firstly, I had to be able to work it from Mersea. This may seem odd to those that haven't been here but our boats are moored within the creeks that surround West Mersea. These are tidal and can be both narrow and shallow at low tide. Put a few moorings and some boats swinging around and suddenly a boat can become awkward to work. A catamaran also requires a wider, deeper channel than a traditional 'v' hull which naturally has its deepest part in the middle of the creek. Some catamarans are wider than others so would a narrower design suit Mersea better? This was soon put to rest as one of the commercial fishermen moored next to me invested in a Sutton catamaran which was as wide as any boat I might buy and he worked it from Mersea with no problems.

My mooring was another point of consideration. I have purposely stuck to 10m/33ft boats so I don't lose my mooring which is about the best one I could hope for. The budget would restrict what we may buy as with anything, although most 10m catamarans are of a similar price. Then there is fuel economy to consider as this plays a big part in most charter boat purchases. Make the wrong choice and I could easily use twice as much fuel each year! Although I may have always had an eye on what I may buy and various running costs it still took us a couple of years pricing boats and comparing fuel consumption which is often hard to get reliable figures on. We had decided that a Blyth catamaran would best suit our needs and we knew several people who had already run successful businesses around here with Blyth's, so that helped. The only problem was with the cod vanishing and restrictions on landing bass it didn't seem worth the extra investment on a new boat. I didn't want a second hand boat as we could potentially buy somebody else's problems especially with a second hand vessel would include its two old engines and that could be two lots of grief!

As it happens a second hand Blyth came up for sale that already had two new engines in just a year before hand. In addition to this, she had new hydraulics, wheelhouse and windows. So we had a good start. We viewed her and she needed a lot of work doing but it seemed like the best compromise in uncertain times. Over the coming weeks we bought her and even sailed her back from Weymouth to Mersea. Some journey of over 200 nautical miles, in January! Fortunately for us the weather played ball and despite a dusting of snow over the chalky cliffs of Kent, it was a pleasant journey back. This was the longest journey I had ever had on a Blyth by some margin. The only other time I had been on one was for a quick ride in the River when John Rawle first had the *Daphne Carole*. I was pleased with how she performed but a little daunted by the work ahead.

We then spent over nine months stripping the boat back to little more than an empty shell and re-building her how we wanted. It is a time I would rather forget which included many late nights and early mornings and vast amounts of fibreglass dust in between working two jobs. I had lots of help from too many people to mention for which I am grateful. Our Blyth was re-launched in time for the beginning of November last year. She has performed very well through all of the awful weather of an Essex winter and is every bit the boat I have worked towards over all of these years. We may not be allowed out to play at the moment but when we are we have many exciting adventures planned aboard her.

As I write we still have the Evolution for sale. She was made well in the first place and I have made a few changes to make her even better. Her straight forward set up and manoeuvrability made her a pleasure to use over the last 6-7years. I will be sad to see her go but I'm sure she will go on to serve somebody else just as well.

As for me, I am still as keen as ever to go fishing. This lockdown is the longest period I can remember when I haven't held a rod. Let's hope we can get fishing soon, even if we can't run charters it would be nice to get out. Over the last couple of weeks my ramblings have skimmed the top of how I ended up chartering. They have covered a bit of my Dad's life and a bit of the first 32 years of mine. Hopefully there will be plenty more ramblings in another 32 years.

SEVENTH WAVE

Simon Dando

The Shooting Party

Ed. *Simon comes from Somerset as has been bringing groups of excellent chaps to Weymouth and other south coast ports for years. He has even been generous enough to step in as crewman for me when I needed two onboard. A fine angler himself, Simon has that great sense of fun and love of cider that makes Somersetians the smashing chaps they are!!*

Several years ago the shooting season had come to an end and a group of us were gathered in the local pub. One thing led to another and the conversation turned to fishing. After several pints of Somerset's finest it was decided a fishing trip would have to take place.

We were fortunate in as much as one member of our group not only knew of a good boat but was also well versed in the procedure of booking said boat. With the financial details taken care of, it was now a case of waiting and hoping the weather would be in our favour.
The evening prior to our departure the skipper contacted our chap telling him the weather would be good and we would leave the harbour at 7.30. Our chap then explained that he too had been keeping an eye on the weather via the internet. This piece of information seemed to have a profound effect on the skipper who then burst into a tirade of expletives and other unmentionable language and that everyone with a computer was a Meteorologist and that it did his head in.

6.30 am arrived and we were all stood on Weymouth Quay looking down at a huge blue and white catamaran charter boat.

Although we were a full hour early, our chap told us the skipper would be impressed by our punctuality and it would show him how committed we were to the task at hand. Just as we put the last of our gear aboard the boat a slim gentleman clutching two carrier bags came walking along the pontoon and just as he got to the boat he stopped looked up to the heavens and then down at his feet all the while shaking his head before springing aboard with a loud, "Morning, gentlemen."

Cups of tea in hand and moorings cast off we were on our way under the Town Bridge and then on the starboard side down to the mouth of the harbour All that stood between us and our quarry was twenty nautical miles and twenty to thirty fathoms of water.

It was during this part of the journey it happened. Two of our group were chatting about a previous hunting expedition and mentioned the "R" word! Yes, the"R" word and the skipper had heard it.

A total silence fell over the wheel house, extremely tall tales of extremely large fish ceased mid-sentence. The skipper knew only too well the gravity of the situation and began to chant some kind of ancient incantation in a garbled West Country accent I'd never heard before.

It must have worked though because we had a great trip and a good time was had by all!

The Stephan Baker Section

Tall Tale 1

Fishing recollections on-board the famous Mistress

Ed. Stephan, despite his best efforts not to be, is actually a pretty good angler. Renowned for his towering intellect, he definitely falls into that category of 'Madman or Genius?' Having spent a good deal of time with him, I know which way my opinion would sway! His Dear Wife is the second of the three incredibly patient women I have nominated for the Bravest Women of the Year Award.

After a few years of working 12 to 16 hour days, setting up a landscaping business, I realised I was on course to become a well off dead person. I decided I'd get back to my roots before it was too late and enjoy my passions of nature watching and fishing.
This revelation occurred in the early 1990s. At that time, as now, I was fortunate to meet some brilliant skippers. I fished mainly from Exmouth with Colin Dukes on Smuggler 3. It was with Colin that I managed, on one trip, to land my heaviest trio of pollack of 20lb, 19lb and 18lbs respectively. I also fished out of Plymouth in the days when there was easy parking and before the Sutton Harbour Corp. ruined the place. I had the good fortune to fish with Graham Hanniford and Bill Warner aboard Graham's famous boat, *Mistress*. I caught many large pollack, ling, conger and some fantastic coal fish. It was Graham who made me realise the importance of a well-adjusted drag when fighting a big fish.
On one trip Bill Warner's boat, *Mistress,* broke down 32 miles out from Plymouth. That was a very long day.

Austen Roger writes: *Please tell us more!! The early 90s were the best years and Plymouth was the mecca for charter boat fishing when specimen sized fish were common. Had some cracking days fishing back then; days you could only dream of now. Great memories indeed.*

Stephan Baker added...*regarding Lymington based Roger Bayzand...Firstly, Roger, I must say one of my regrets is not having fished with you. You were yet another legendary skipper.*
Graham's Hanniford's boat was an Offshore 105 named Tiburon. It slammed a bit but got the job done. He then went on to buy a monster of a boat, Size Matters. When I write part 2 later, I will also mention some of the brilliant crew members who were trusted to captain the boats. Alan Bennet comes to mind .

Glenn Hook I had many a good trip with Bill Warner. He was king at anchoring a boat. Amazing! He was indeed a great skipper that I had the pleasure of fishing with. The first trip with him ,we introduced him to wire line fishing. He wanted to ban us using it swearing we would lose our fingers. He took some convincing that we knew what we were doing and used it all the time to fish strong tides. I remember the first bites coming and he couldn't believe how positive it was. He was telling us to wind down and strike into fish that were just nuisance pout. Then, when the congers and ling came out, he was amazed at how hard they hit the rods but we could get them away from the wrecks quickly with no stretch in the line like nylon. After a couple of trips on the Mistress we came down to find Bill had bought wire line for at anchor fishing. He was converted along with us until braid hit the market and that changed everything. We certainly had some eventful trips out with Bill.

Colin Bryant I fished with Graham for many years and caught some and lost a few big ones as well along the way. Met some great characters and had such a laugh and great crack. I will never forget those days. Also fished with other skippers on the day and had good times with namely Alan Bennett and Shaun Brett. Love to hear some more of this.

Tall Tale 2

Stand-in Crews

Whilst thinking of great skippers and their boats, it occurred to me that the stand-in crews should be given a mention. Al Bennett comes to mind. He was stand in skipper for the Ginger Monster, Graham Hanniford. We both agreed that it would be very unwise to upset Graham. He was an ex-Cornish rugby player. Alan was also a very tough man who also would take no crap from anyone either.

It was on one wreck trip that Al's strength saved the day. It was early March when the water temperature could not have been more than 7C. T*iburon* was dead in the water, due to the prop being fouled by some heavy duty rope. Al proceeded to strip to his pants, secure a rope around his waist and fortunately the boat, grab a blade and jump into the freezing mid-Channel water. Maybe ten minutes later the prop was freed, and we were able to get fishing. The new flag the *Tiburon* was flying that day was not the Cornish flag but Mr Bennett's jeans!! Much respect to you, Sir.

Plymouth had some great characters and skippers back in the day. Dave Brett, *Scorpion's* skipper, was a lovely man. It was his son, Sean Brett, that Graham trusted his new, Canadian built boat *Size Matters* to. I used to get up at three in the morning and drive to Banjo Breakwater to board the boat. At this time the Sutton Harbour Company had made parking difficult so there was no more *Capt'n Jasper's Breakfasts* for me.

Sean was always able to put us on the fish so the four hundred mile round trip was worth it. I had many great times in Plymouth as my sister-in-law lives there and we had great parties. I remember one such occasion after a successful trip resulting in a bathful of pollack ling and cod.

By 1am, I was barely able to stand up. Oh happy days!

I'm running out of drinking time now, so other skippers...Colin Dukes, Jim O'Donnel and Hayling Island's Colin Johnson tomorrow.

Austen Roger. Don't forget Paul Descombe from the Electric Blue *and Dale Entwhistle from* The Mistress. *Both were fantastic crew and great characters.*

Stephan Baker. Nearly forgot Dale. He was a big character, great fisherman, story teller and too good at the pool table. He always beat me.

Tall Tale 3

Final thoughts on my Plymouth Trips.

I used to fish the yearly British Conger Club Competitions. One year the competition was over-subscribed so other boats were enlisted. I ended up being drawn to fish from a boat named *Westward*. This boat was more usually fishing for whelks. The gunnels were very low and the super structure high. There had been a big storm in the Western Approaches so the boats were limited to fish within a 20 mile radius of Plymouth. The swell that day was enormous.

As mentioned the *Westward* was top heavy and rolled and rolled. The deck was soon awash and tackle boxes etc were all over the place with inches of water covering it. With the boat loaded with anglers, it sat low in the sea. The swell was rolling in and the gunnels were no more than a few inches above the sea. Thank goodness the Skipper decided to come inside the breakwater where things were a bit safer. I managed to catch one strap conger and my biggest catch of the day, the Trans-Atlantic cable. The cable put up a good fight before finally breaking me off.!

An honourable mention should go to Jim O'Donmell who skippered the *Tiburon* when Graham changed boats. I again caught some nice fish when fishing with him.

I was impressed by another Plymouth boat, the *Electric Blue*. She was, I think skippered by Tony Allen or Paul Drescombe. *Electric Blue* was a very fast boat, probably the fastest boat around. It was this speed that was nearly its undoing. It was making its way back to Plymouth at twenty knots plus when all of a sudden it came to a rapid halt. The crew etc were thrown all over the place. Both props had caught a length of leaded rope!! This had caused the *Blue* to come to an immediate stop. Both props and shafts were caught and the bottom of the boat damaged. Fortunately the boat didn't sink!

Steve Black

The Sexiest Boat in Weymouth

Ed. *Steve was a young man that the Weymouth Skippers 'took to their hearts', especially Pat Carlin who saved Steve, a non-car driver, countless hours of travelling on Public Transport to reach the outpost called Weymouth. Steve used to stay overnight on Pat's boat and came to look upon him his 'adopted Uncle'.*

I'm not a skipper............... just your average fishing nut.

My angling passion arose from being posted with the Forces to such exotic destinations as Singapore and Hollywood (Okay, it was Holywood, Co. Down), four years in Dortmund and two in the amazing city of Berlin. Obviously I didn't get my Scottish accent from any of these postings.

My earliest recollections of sea fishing are those from Holywood - situated a stone's throw from Belfast Lough and I remember watching huge shoals of mullet - that I found impossible to catch - using a pair of binos from the bedroom window. I also remember seeing a flamingo. I think it must have escaped from the nearby Belfast Zoo.

There was an access road to Kinnegar pier that stretched out into the Lough and gave instant deep water fishing for those of us willing to run the gauntlet of the authorities.

Entry to this road was made by climbing round the 'green gate' that was almost always locked. The sewage boat used to dock on the concrete pier at the end of the road and this in return is what attracted those elusive mullet . This was 1983 and the IRA were still very much active and I recall a nail bomb detonating outside a pub called The Deep in Holywood town centre.

My first ever charter trip saw me travelling as a complete but keen as mustard novice to Carnlough with members of the military band and spending the majority of the trips either asleep or wishing I wasn't feeling so green.

I'll never forget the skipper shooting a net at the end of the trip if we hadn't been that successful and me selling fresh plaice, pollack and coalfish to my neighbours to recoup some of the small outlay I paid for these trips which was a fiver if I remember rightly. That was it. Fishing was for me and provided, in a way, an escape that most people can't comprehend. Hitchhiking, sleeping in public toilets, being hunted by the police as a missing person, suffering a gambling addiction and most recently serious depression and anxiety have all been relieved to some extent by my love of fishing.

Two years of coarse fishing on the mighty Havel Lake in Berlin saw the family move to UKLF at Wilton and where I spent my adult life in and around Salisbury. Having never taken my driving test saw me in the early nineties relying on public transport to get me from Salisbury to Weymouth which was an absolute arse of a journey by either bus or several trains.

Shortly after I'd left my basic training at Princess Marina College, I was to fish on a boat from Langstone Harbour and had checked the train timetables for my plan of attack...or lack of it. Anyway, I arrived at Portsmouth Harbour sometime in the early hours of Saturday evening and took a local bus to Langstone. At the end of the road opposite the mooring was a large toilet block and this was to be my sanctuary for the night until the boat left at 8am Sunday morning.

Fruit machines were to play a huge part of my early 20's and would leave me skint pretty much most weekends. Most of my fishing kit had been donated from more Senior anglers or picked up on the cheap and my pride and joy was a gleaming Mitchell 624 reel and a 20lb Daiwa Cruiser Deluxe MkII rod with top and butt rollers.

Four South Coast skippers were going have to endure me for the foreseeable future . One of them doing more for me on a personal level and forever being my adopted Uncle.. although I'd hate to think how many times he shook his head or muttered under his breath...

> He also owned, in my view, the sexiest boat in Weymouth ...all 38' of it!

Steve Harder

Bonwey and the famous Shambles turbot

Ed. Steve Harder from Southampton gives a wonderful description of catching his first ever...and still best ever..turbot from Ken Leicester's Bon Wey. *There was something about the big, beamy boat that made it drift perfectly for flatfish. Ken was usually top boat on the Shambles Bank by a long way over the rest of us. Steve captures the achievement of the catch superbly.*

Being primarily a shore angler myself, I haven't really boat fished a great deal, although I do enjoy the odd trip afloat now and then. My first trip out of Weymouth was aboard Ken Leicester's Bonwey targeting the plaice on the Shambles Bank. On one of those trips, 9th April 2001 to be precise, we'd been drifting all day and I'd caught a few plaice to around 3lb 8oz (which at that time was my P.B) when Ken said he'd do a couple of drifts down the eastern end of the bank to see if we could find an early Turbot.

I'd anticipated this possibility, so had brought along a pack of Ammo mackerel fillets just in case. The first drift, I put on half a mackerel fillet on a 3/0 hook (the biggest I had on me) and lowered it over the side, hoping a tasty turbot would sniff it out. Everyone else on the boat carried on fishing for plaice with big ragworm and squid strip baits and a succession of better sized plaice came aboard in the 4lb to 5lb 8oz range along with a couple of 4lb to 6lb Turbot!

When we motored back uptide to start the final drift of the day, I was torn between putting the plaice rig back on or continuing with the turbot rig. As I'd never caught a turbot from a boat before, I thought that dragging a fish bait along would give me a better chance of picking one out, so down went another mackerel fillet. I sat biteless as I watched several more good plaice and even a couple more small turbot come to the net to the plaice baits and I was beginning to think I'd made the wrong choice as Ken shouted out we'd be giving it another 10 minutes before heading in.

I thought about reeling in and putting down a plaice rig instead but again decided against it. As we drifted over a high point on the bank I noticed the angle of the line had come up in the water significantly, so asked Ken how deep it was.

"Just coming up on 22 feet," was his reply.

I shouted back, "All I need now is a Turbot that size," and I remember Ken smiling and laughing. A few minutes later we'd crossed over the bank and I was sat down holding the rod with my eyes closed, thinking it wasn't going to happen... then it did!

The rod was almost pulled from my hands and I was so taken by surprise I instinctively struck and cursed as I shouted out that I'd missed it.

Ken had been watching and said, "No you haven't, you've got a good one on there and you want to get as much line back on that as you can before it gets back to the boat."

I was still reeling but couldn't feel much resistance and was still convinced I'd missed it "Hurry up! It's almost back at the boat. You'd better have your drag set!"

As the leader knot came up through the top few rings I thought that maybe there might be a small one on the end and that Ken was wrong about it being a good one. Then, as it came past the boat, the rod lurched over hard and 20 yards or more of line suddenly got stripped off the reel as the fish tore off down-tide! I got it under control and soon a huge turbot surfaced a good way back from the boat so I carefully teased it back praying the hook would hold as I'd have been devastated if my last memory of that fish was of its huge wide open mouth disappearing beneath the surface.

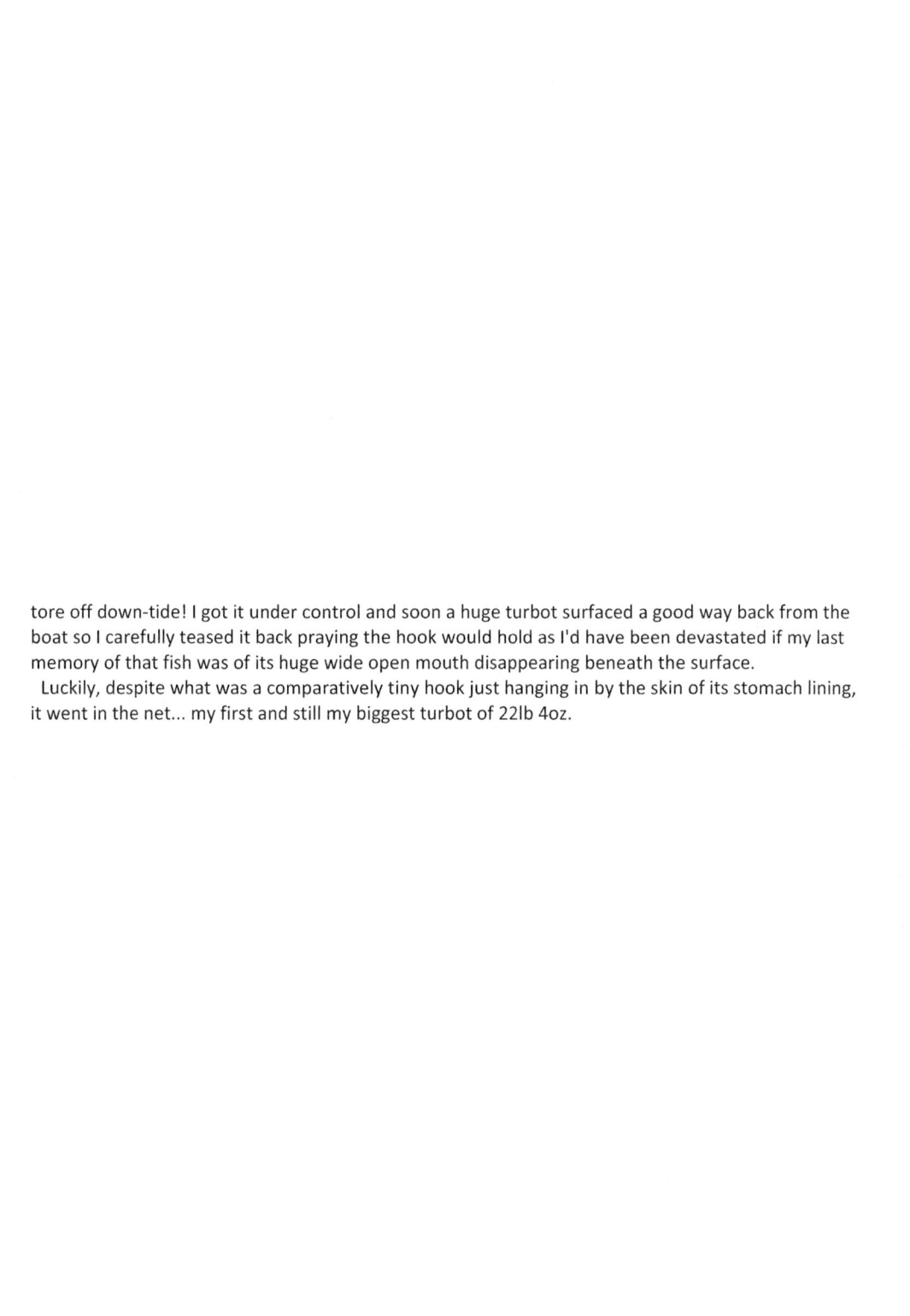

Luckily, despite what was a comparatively tiny hook just hanging in by the skin of its stomach lining, it went in the net... my first and still my biggest turbot of 22lb 4oz.

The Steve Porter Section

Tall Tale 1

Trying to do the Impossible

Ed. Steve Porter. *Entrepreneurial skipper of the very splendid Rodman charter boat True Blue which replaced his very fine South Boat Cat. Steve vision has opened out a whole new range of very exciting projects during the 2020 season showing that even in very grim times, a different approach, backed up by a good deal of previous research, can pay dividends. He's probably just experienced the most exciting season of his life….and provided some absolutely unforgettable sport fishing for a number of very fortunate guests..*

I must confess, I've really enjoyed reading the various posts on this FB group. For a couple of weeks now I've been thinking that perhaps I should put pen to paper to write something myself. Unfortunately, despite successfully avoiding building a new patio at home for the past fifteen years, my latest excuse of needing to write a story here didn't really cut it. Now though with 'Build patio' ticked off on the 'Jobs to do' list, I earned a couple of free tours. Here then is a wee story about a trip that wasn't one of my best days at sea.

WRECKING TRIP; Late March 2004.

There is no doubt about it, being lucky enough to be an angling charter boat skipper is a pretty good way to earn a living. We have some truly amazing days at sea, a few bad ones and most are somewhere in between. Plus we get to meet some really nice anglers, many of whom become long-term friends. Just occasionally though, for all manner of reasons, we have trips that truly put us skippers to the test and days when we would just rather be anywhere else than at sea.
Here is an account of one of my worst ever trips (not the worst) but one from which I learnt so much.
It was late March 2004 and I had been booked for a mid-channel wrecking trip by an angling club from the East coast. They were new customers to me so I ensured there was a good passage of information between us, leading up to the trip. The forecast was for force 4 westerly winds and with a fairly large tide, not ideal conditions but do-able. The go-ahead was given the day before and we agreed to meet for a 7am start.
On arriving at the boat it appeared that the winds were perhaps a bit stronger than forecast. I moved the boat from her mooring to the quayside where I was met by ten very excited anglers who had already been on the road for four hours just to get to Poole. More wind than forecast was just not within their comprehension. They were here now and they intended to fish.
On loading the boat I had to keep reminding myself that I wasn't about to depart for a month long adventure to a far off distant land. Boxes and boxes of tackle kept being handed down from the quayside. 50lb class rods with huge reels and buckets and buckets of lead weights and perks. The anglers though were certainly not dressed for a month long adventure. With most wearing just trainers, jeans and a jacket, I doubt that they were even prepared for a cruise around the harbour. I hadn't seen any flotation suits passed down to the boat so I feared there must be yet more equipment still in one of their cars, somehow

forgotten. Despite the boat already being loaded to the gunwales, I did feel a sense of duty so reluctantly asked the question, "Have you all got your foul weather gear guys?"

To which I received a strange look from all on board and an almost collective reply, "We're wearing it skip".

So, following the safety brief we departed for a mid-channel wrecking trip in potentially marginal conditions in March. I was carrying ill-equipped anglers and their tackle was far from being ideal for English Channel wrecking. (I did say that I learnt a lot from this trip and I think you can already see some of the lessons that I am about to learn.)

Leaving Poole Harbour in a westerly wind can be very pleasant, even in fresh conditions. The sea is sheltered for the first eight miles or so, right up until you pass Durlston Head to the South of Swanage. On this particular day the sun was shining and for a moment I lost myself in my thoughts. We rounded Old Harry Rocks and as we transited across Swanage Bay on a flat sea, I remember thinking, wow! How lucky am I. It's at this point that my doorway was filled with the very large figure of a man. In quite an aggressive tone, he shouted those words. Those words that I'm sure fill most charter skippers with dread; the ones that make the hairs on the back of your neck stand up.

"Skipper, there is something wrong with your toilet".

On investigating, the toilet was indeed blocked. Now I'm not sure if whilst I had been lost in my thoughts rounding Old Harry Rocks, whether we had been visited by Dumbo the Flying elephant wearing some sort of cloaking device, or if this was some kind of man made world record attempt. What I did know was that I wasn't about to deal with it at the time.

"No worries, Lads," I calmly said (Honest), "let's get you all fishing and I'll sort it then".

So we pushed on but within two miles we were leaving the sheltered waters behind as we headed south passing Durlston Head. The sea began to grow. I gauged the wind to be about a force 5 but still we pushed on. The swell buffeted our port beam and as we pushed further south, the wave height increased. By now it was surely a force 5 to 6. I made the decision, but without telling my anglers, to stop about eighteen miles off the coast to fish a bank that is usually fairly reliable for small to medium pollack. This mark was twelve miles short of my intended wreck but in the conditions was a sensible alternative.

I gave the usual five minute warning as I approached the mark and then positioned uptide for the drift. To my horror, not one angler had set up his tackle. There was frantic action on the deck as the anglers hunted for their own tackle boxes. It was a big rolling sea and the wind and tide together was giving us a drift speed of over four knots. It seemed like forever, but eventually the anglers declared that they were ready, albeit with multi hook rigs of muppets and a pirk. We had drifted over a mile from the mark and so now began the long slow punch back uptide.

We must have done about two or three drifts, although I realised after just one that this wasn't going to produce any fish. The strong tide and wind combined, caused the lines to scream away from the boat, we were fishing with incorrect gear and the anglers were losing their tackle almost every drop, despite this being a bank, not a wreck.

It was during these initial drifts that I got chatting to one elderly gentleman, Dave. He was clearly unwell and I witnessed him throwing up over the side. On asking if he was okay, he informed me that he had never been seasick before. It is a strange fact that when any new angler on the boat is unfortunate enough to be seasick, they always say this, as if to divert the blame to either the boat or me as skipper. Although in his defence, we were on True Blue 2 at the time, which was my 33' Islandic Cleopatra. This was a mono-hull and I learnt sometime after selling the vessel that she had been given the nickname locally of Vomit

Comet. Anyway, in telling me of his current seasickness, Dave informed that he had undergone an operation on his stomach a just few months earlier and that could be the cause of his current sickness.

So, three drifts into our fishing, nothing on the deck and by now with several moaning anglers, it was time for a change and so foolishly I admitted to the lads that I had stopped short of my intended destination because of the conditions. Pushing on another twelve miles might produce some fish I said, but I wondered whether it was the best option, especially as Dave was feeling unwell.

"That's okay, Skip", they said. We are all fine, we would like to press on if Dave is okay".

"Sure lads," came the reply from Dave. "I'll be fine".

I demonstrated to them what might be a better rig for use on the wreck and then off we set, pushing further south. What was I thinking? Sometime later we arrived at what was a very reliable wreck. The tide had eased; the lads were now rigged with simple rigs and using a variety of Roger Bayzand lures between them. I began to feel optimistic. The sea state however was still huge, the wind still blowing force 5 to 6 and Dave was still unwell. In fact, he was so unwell that he was now lying on the deck.

My increased optimism was very short lived. The first drift resulted in everyone hooking the wreck. These anglers had expectations that far exceeded ability. A small amount of seawater was being forced through the scuppers and some of it was reaching Dave, still lying face down on the deck. He was oblivious to it and made no effort to move. Suddenly it hit me; I needed to get out of this situation. I explained to the lads that I thought the conditions were too much for them and I was particularly concerned about Dave whose condition had worsened. "Did you know," I said, "he had a stomach operation only a couple of months ago?"

"Yes," replied an angler, "and a heart by-pass op".

Well, there are few things on a boat that are worse than a blocked toilet but learning that an elderly customer has just had a heart by-pass as you watch him in a semi-unconscious state, lying on your deck with seawater and vomit all over him is one of those things. Thank goodness we were not 35 miles from home in a rough sea. Oh!

Dave's condition saved my day. I explained to the anglers that as Skipper I was responsible for their welfare and safety whilst on board my boat. Allowing me to bring someone out to sea without informing me of his current serious medical condition had put me in a very awkward position. As a result, I now had no choice but to return to port. To my surprise, this statement was met with unanimous apologies and full agreement that returning to Poole was the only option.

This story doesn't end here however. About ten miles from the coast with Dave still totally out of it, I became aware of a dull sound. My eyes were drawn to the gauges to check temperatures and pressures but all appeared normal. The sound grew louder, almost deafening. An angler grabbed at my jacket, Skip, he shouted and pointed skywards. I glanced up from the wheelhouse door and there overhead was the Coastguard helicopter. The port side cabin door had been slid back and the crewman was holding a large board with the numbers 67 on it. I gave a 'thumbs-up' and went back into my wheelhouse to select channel 67. As I did so, I wondered if he had been trying to call me on channel 16 and if so, for how long? For some reason, I hadn't been monitoring channel 16 on this trip.

With channel 67 selected, I established coms with the helicopter.

"Good morning, Captain", came a very jolly sounding reply. "We are out doing a bit of training today and we wondered if you would allow us to carry out a practice boarding drill to your boat?"

Now I don't know why, but on glancing down at Dave, I replied, "I can do better than that, I can get you to take an unwell man off."

As I said this, it suddenly occurred to me that Mr Helicopter Pilot probably wouldn't have the authorisation to do this but at the same time, if I had an unwell passenger, he couldn't really refuse to either. There then followed a quite lengthy three-way conversation on the VHF between the helicopter, Portland Coastguard and myself. The result was that authorisation was given by the Coastguard to the helicopter for the casevac to go ahead.

I had been fortunate enough to have experience in helicopter evacuation so the experience on this particular day wasn't at all daunting. It was quite a relief in fact to have my main concern, Dave, removed from the boat. The funny thing though, is that while all this was going on, the VHF chat, the noise from overhead, the winch man strapping himself to Dave, our casualty had remained totally out of it. It wasn't until he was airborne, about halfway between us and the aircraft that he appeared to open his eyes for the first time. I've often wondered if on coming round, he thought he had died and was on his way to heaven.

It was now close to midday and we were heading home with about fifteen miles to run. The anglers were happy and I could hear them talking about the helicopter experience. At this point I started to think about money. This is not unusual for a charter skipper to be doing around March. At this point we are usually at the end of a three month period of high boat refit expense and very little, if any, income. Paydays at this time of the year are very much needed. However, we were going in from this expensive wrecking trip early. Surely I should consider refunding some of what was an expensive charter for the lads. I gave it some thought. The issue here was that I had done the distance regardless of going in early. Loads of fuel burnt, the boat had received a hammering and these lads were unlikely to ever come again regardless of getting a discount. These facts were all in my thought process. The overwhelming deciding factor though had to be my blocked toilet, which I still had to deal with. No discount.

So, confident in my mind that I was justified to keep the full charter fee and with our miles steadily decreasing, I began to relax. Home was only an hour away. At this point an angler came into the wheelhouse.

"Skip, now that Dave is off the boat, can we go back out?"

" No," I said. "You have seen the conditions yourself. It's not ideal and by the time we get there, it will be time to come home."

"What about fishing inshore then?" he asked.

Clearly to say "no" at this point would have gone against all my previous thoughts about the cost of the trip. We were now inshore and conditions were very do-able. If the anglers wanted to complete their day, then they had every right to or to expect a refund. The problem was we had no bait and back then fishing wasn't particularly good inshore during March.

I told the anglers that there was a small chance that we might be able to see a very early bream. Of course this information was given during a momentary lapse. A moment when I had totally forgotten that the angler's lightest rods were 50lb class and that their smallest weights were 1lb.

So, after a detour into Poole to purchase ragworm and squid, we spent the afternoon in the very sheltered waters of Poole Bay. Lots of ground bait type stuff made its way into the water as I tackled the toilet issue and the trip ended up being a full day.

Did we discover an early bream mark? Sadly the 50lb class gear denied us the opportunity to really find out, but I doubt it. Although we did catch one there on the 18th March this year.

Lee Larry Lazarus. *Great story thanks for sharing.*

Roger Bayzand. *Thank you. I am sure most skippers reading this will relate to "One of those days!" You have also reminded me of a couple of stories to tell.*

Paul Whittall. *Ahhh...the pleasures of trying to achieve the impossible!! Well that story certainly 'struck home'.*

Jez Chalong. *I'm getting fed up with this group now....I'm not getting any work done....or fishing*

Tall Tale 2

Tomatoes

During May 2005, I was crossing the English Channel from Poole to Alderney on route to the island for a five day fishing charter. On board were one of my regular crews although this year their numbers were down slightly. I was led to believe this was because a new angler was on board. It seemed this invited guest had not been approved by all and a few of the regular crew had decided not to join this year's Alderney charter as a result.

The new angler was certainly a larger than life character. An ex-submariner who was very rough around the edges. He was tall with huge hands, and an appearance that reminded me of the old Hollywood actor, Jack Palance. I'm struggling to remember his name, so for this story I'm going to call him Dave. Dave was loud, very loud and with a deep rough infectious laugh which was easily heard over the drone of the engine.

This was to be a direct crossing to Alderney with no fishing due to the forecast of strengthening winds in the afternoon. I was joined in the wheelhouse by three of the anglers where we were generally putting the World to right. Out on deck, the rest of the crew were being entertained by new angler Dave and we were frequently subjected to his raucous laughter at the end of his various tales of Navy life.

At about twenty miles out of Poole, the sea was beginning to build. Nothing to be concerned about, just a slight westerly chop on our beam; conditions that were expected from today's weather forecast. Very little cloud meant that we had mainly blue skies and sunshine. All was well on the good ship True Blue.

Suddenly I was aware of a shadow being cast over the helm. On turning around I was confronted by the image of Dave, a giant of a man filling the cabin door opening. He was leaning against the door frame. He didn't look good and was as white as a sheet. All of us in the wheelhouse were looking at him as I asked, "Are you alright?" to which his reply was, "I ain't had me fuckin tomartus" (Tomatoes).

With puzzled expressions, it seemed all four of us in the wheelhouse, replied in unison "What?"

Dave said again, "I ain't had me fuckin tomartus."

Dave was clearly stressed by the tomatoes thing, so in a calm voice I explained that I didn't understand what he was going on about. Could he explain his problem?

I'll never forget what he then said, "I've had bacon, I've had eggs, I've had mushrooms, I've had beans, but I ain't had me f***in' tomartus."

"Okay, "I said, " but I'm still unsure as to why this is causing you a problem now."

"They're still under the fuckin grill," came his reply.

To cut a long story short, prior to leaving his flat in the morning, Dave had cooked himself a hearty breakfast. He had put tomatoes under the grill while cooking the remainder of his breakfast on the hob. He was now telling me that he had forgotten about his tomatoes and that even though he was now twenty miles out to sea, his tomatoes were still cooking away in his empty flat. He was concerned about his elderly neighbour in an adjoining flat. We were out of phone range to call the neighbour, although that didn't really matter as Dave didn't know his telephone number. Apart from making the long return trip to Poole, there was only one other solution. Contact the Coastguard on the VHF and get them to call the police. Ask the police to visit the neighbour to obtain a spare key and ,if Dave's flat was still standing, to go in and turn off the grill. Easy!

We charter skippers are frequently calling the Coastguard for various reasons. We instinctively know what to say and our voice procedure is usually professional with the right tone for the situation but this was different. I pondered how I was going to word this unusual request without causing the Coastguard operator, or indeed all the control room staff to collapse to the floor with laughter.

I picked up the handset and initiated a call to Portland Coastguard. (Yes we had a Portland Coastguard back then). "Portland Coastguard, Portland Coastguard, this is *True Blue, True Blue* over."

"*True Blue*, this is Portland Coastguard. Channel 73 and standby," came the reply.

The instruction to move across to channel 73 was a relief as it meant the whole world wouldn't be listening to my unusual request. Several seconds passed before the radio came to life again. Time enough to gather my thoughts and to mentally prepare my request.

"True Blue, this is Portland Coastguard."

"Portland Coastguard, this is *True Blue*. Good Morning. Eerrrr, an unusual request this one." And so the conversation began.

What followed was a long conversation over the airwaves, but as we pushed further away from land, communications became difficult and eventually unreadable. We pushed on towards Alderney, confident that enough information had been passed to allow police on the mainland to investigate the situation in Dave's flat. All we could do now, was to wait for the outcome.

On approaching Alderney a couple of hours later, I made the VHF call to the Harbour Office, informing them of our imminent arrival and passenger numbers. Alderney acknowledged my call and then added, "We have a message for you from Portland Coastguard."

"*True Blue*, Roger, Send over."

There followed what seemed like an eternity of silence over the radio before we heard the words, "THE GRILL WASN'T ON."

Wow, such mixed feelings filled my mind. Relief that Dave's flat hadn't been burned to the ground, concern that the name True Blue would be forever associated with the tomatoes incident, and a real desire to throttle Dave. The latter obviously ruled out because of his size.

I telephoned Portland Coastguard to apologise for the incident and to thank them for their assistance. To my surprise, I was talking to a very jolly operator who was completely understanding of the whole situation. He explained that it was good to prove the system and to know that in the event of a real incident, it would work. The police had indeed been summoned to attend Dave's flat and had gone there with blue lights and sirens. Above all though, the operator informed me, we had made the Control Room's otherwise routine day, a fun one.

This affair does highlight the value of the Coastguard Service who are always there to offer assistance, no matter how serious or trivial. They give us charter skippers a warm feeling and confidence when tasked with crossing that large expanse of water with fare paying passengers in what, let's be honest, are not always ideal conditions.

As for Dave, I discovered that his unfavourable reputation was misplaced. During the following few days, I found him to be a fine fellow. Well, apart from the night in the Bell View Hotel when he entertained the whole establishment with his Navy songs. I can still remember some of the chorus lines and the look of embarrassment on the faces of the young waitresses.

But that, as they say, is another story.

Tall Tale 3
A Series of Unfortunate Events

It was the 30th December 2003 and we were fishing on the original True Blue for the penultimate time before she was handed over to her new owner, local skipper Malcolm Collins.

Back in those days, I seem to remember we used to get plenty of those cold frosty mornings, which gave way to warm, calm conditions as the sun rose above the horizon. Perhaps my memory is distorted and days like that were only as frequent as they are now. In any event, this tale was definitely on one of those days.

We were anchored in 100 foot of water, about half a mile south of the western measured mile posts off the Purbeck Coast. The tide was flooding and we were catching a steady stream of conger eels. With every bite there came a brief period of excitement as anglers thought they may be about to hook the first cod of the day. Winter cod were bigger and much more prolific back then and the mark we were fishing had produced several fine specimens during the previous couple of days.

As skipper I like to fish whenever I can so I dropped my line in from my usual place on the starboard side and well forward so that I could lean on the wheelhouse bulkhead. From this position I could also see everything that was happening on deck and so react quickly to assist anglers when needed.

With rod in hand I was momentarily lost in my thoughts when suddenly I became aware of a rubbing on my line. I looked up and could see an angler fishing at the port stern quarter reeling in. His line was clearly running to the starboard side of the boat so I said that I think he may have hooked my line. I placed my rod in a rod holder, reduced the drag slightly and then went over to assist the angler. The tangle was a simple one; in fact, not really a tangle at all. His hook had just picked up my main line and had ridden up it. With his hook lifted clear and holding my line, I walked it across the stern from port to starboard so as to drop it clear of other lines in the water.

As I was amidships my line appeared to snag on the boarding ladder but, when I peered over the stern, I could see that it was in fact caught on two hooks that were attached to a lower rung. At this point another angler owned up to snagging the boarding ladder earlier in the day with his trace. In attempting to free it, his trace had parted leaving behind two 6/0 Mustad Viking hooks on a short snood. These hung loosely in the air but were submerged every few seconds as the slight swell lapped over the ladder rung. These hooks had lain in wait for an unsuspecting angler. That angler was me and now both hooks had caught my mainline. It didn't appear too difficult to sort out. I manoeuvred my line this way and that from above, but each time I freed it from one hook, the other hook would get it. Okay, time for a change of tactic. The boat hook, that'll do it. Wrong! No matter how hard I tried those two dangling hooks conspired together to keep a hold of my line.

It was time for another change of tactic, one that in hindsight was a foolish thing to attempt. I decided to climb over the back of the boat, descend the boarding ladder and unhook my line with my hand. What could possibly go wrong? Well, not what you're thinking, Dear Reader.

I successfully found myself standing on the bottom rung of the ladder, while I held onto the transom rail with my left hand. I say the bottom rail but in reality there were a further three rungs but these made up the part of the ladder that folded up when not in use. Even so, water lapped around my boots. I bent my knees and still holding on with my left hand, I followed my line down with my right hand to the two dangling hooks. Aha, near success. I could feel the hooks and began an attempt to free my line.

You may recall that the angler that originally caught my line had only done so with his hook which had ridden up my line. This meant that virtually all my line was still in the water and my terminal tackle somewhere handy to the seabed. As I grappled with the dangling 6/0 Mustad Viking hooks, I felt a mighty tug on my line. It was so sudden and strong that it pulled my hand onto the hooks and one of them went straight into my thumb. Whatever it was that had decided to make my two excellently presented calamari squid on a pennel rig its lunch was not going to let go. It continued to pull, causing the hook to dig deeper into my thumb.

Imagine the situation if you will. I'm stood on a boarding ladder on the back of a boat, my right hand impaled on a hook that is level with my feet, while I hold on with my left hand to a rail that is level with my head. And if this isn't bad enough, a fish is pulling at my impaled hand.

Keeping calm, I quietly asked someone to cut my line. Okay, so maybe I wasn't calm. And maybe I wasn't that quiet either. Actually, I let go with both barrels, screaming at someone to cut the F*****g line. Thankfully this was done quite quickly and I immediately had relief from the pain of being pulled onto a hook. Unfortunately, the relief I felt was short lived. I was still attached to the hook, which by now felt quite deep in my thumb. I was still stuck in the ridiculous position, one hand up and one hand down on the back of a boat.

My thumb began to throb but the discomfort was very short lived as it was at this point that my left arm began to complain at having held my weight for so long. The reality of the situation I was in suddenly hit home. I could not hold on for much longer. As the pain in my left arm intensified, I attempted to rip the hook from my right thumb by, well, just pulling like crazy. I felt nothing from the hook during this normally painful procedure. By now, my left arm had become the most painful part of my body, supporting my weight as I tried to free myself. No matter how hard I pulled, I could not free myself from the hook. I knew that at any moment, I would have to let go my grip on the rail. I was destined to go for a swim in a cold December sea and to hang there in the tide, still attached by my thumb to a Mustad Viking 6/0 hook.

I'm going, I shouted. Get a rope. Instantly a rope was thrown over my head and secured under my arms. Forward thinking by my good friend, Keith Humphreys, who I was lucky to have on board that day meant that he had pre-empted my instruction and was there with rope in hand. Keith and another angler took my weight, enabling me to let go with my left hand. I just held my position for a short while, leaning back against the rope, supported by the guys. It wasn't long before I had feeling in my left arm again. As I no longer needed to hold onto the rail, I was able to hold a knife and reach down to the hooks and cut the short snood. I was free at last, albeit with a Mustad Viking 6/0 hook deep in my thumb.

It took me quite a while to get the hook out, cutting away gradually at the flesh around it with a knife and all the time fending off offers of help from the anglers. All were unanimous in their solution to my problem. I should look the other way while one of them gave it a big yank. Yeah, right!

The culprit fish turned out to be a conger. It was hooked on another line a little while later, still with my trace and line attached. I don't think we caught any cod that day.

It is strange how one little incident, initially my line just getting hooked by another angler and then a series of other incidents, each on their own pretty insignificant, can lead to a near catastrophic event. Going overboard in December could have had serious consequences. It serves as a reminder of how quickly danger can creep up on us when least expected.

I'd like to say that I learnt a big lesson that day. Never step outside the boat. They are wise words and a good rule to have. Unfortunately, I've had to break the rule many times since then usually to free discarded commercial fishing gear from a propeller.

You would think an angler might volunteer to go over instead, at least once!

Steve Woodwood

Seawolf Adventure

The Fraught Delivery Voyage of Seawolf

Ed. *Steve from Southampton tells an attention retaining tale of his first trip aboard his newly purchased vessel, Seawolf. Against many unforeseen difficulties, Steve manages to coax his Aquabell 27 to safety through a combination of mechanical skills and outstandingly determined seamanship. Many boat owners will identify with this tale.*

We had been to see our potentially new boat Seawolf, an Aquabell 27, on a couple of occasions and really fallen in love with her. She was everything we needed and wanted. She was an old girl and needed a bit of love but that being said, she would do for now in her current state.

We got a lift to Hullbridge in Essex on the 8th April and had our last good look around her and checked her over for the journey back to Ashlett Creek at the lower western end of Southampton Water, close to the Fawley Power Station. I felt a little bit out of my depth at this journey and was a little bit "should I really be doing this?" state of mind but with my mechanical knowledge and my experience of boating I knew I could cope with pretty much anything that came my way, within reason!

The weather forecast was very good and it was a lovely sunny day with very light winds. We had to wait for the high tide to be lifted into the water and there was a boat waiting in front of us but we eventually got lifted in around 3pm. The engines sprang into life and as the guy who sold her to us warned me to be aware that the port engine airlocks the cooling system and what to do if it did that. And so we set off.

The river Crouch is quite a long river but the small villages and marinas made it a pleasant journey, even seeing the odd seal near the river mouth into the Thames Estuary. We headed out into open water and is it ever shallow in places!!! The GPS that came with the boat was showing a charted depth of three but the sounder was indicating just two under us!!!! I went through the menus on the GPS and was shocked at my error, all the measurements was set to feet!!! I corrected this to metres as that's what I am in the habit of using and got on with threading our way across the estuary seeing more seals and wind farms en-route. During this time the port engine was refusing to play the game with me and I really couldn't get this airlock in the cooling system to go and she ran hot all the way so we just kept our speed and revs down as I didn't want to kill it.

We made it into Ramsgate around 9.30pm in total darkness and tied up at the first pontoon that I saw. Hungry, tired and wanting a break we went ashore and found a nice little place that welcomed us. After our replenishment, we ventured back to the boat and spent our first night on our new boat. It was really nice and cosy.

The morning was a real shock, windy, overcast and totally NOT what the forecasters had predicted. The waves was coming through the harbour entrance and smashing our boat up and down against the pontoon that we was moored up against. The lanyards were being pulled to the max and Tracey really didn't feel safe, not even just walking along the pontoons to get out of the marina. In the end I knew that I had to move our boat from where she currently was as a matter of urgency into a more sheltered birth and that this was going to be a huge task as now I was on my own. I managed and got away with it and once on a quieter birth we sat and played the waiting game with the weather. Even the marina staff told us that the weather, although it had changed, was a lot worse than was predicted.

The winds eased and the forecast looked a bit better for us to continue our voyage. The time was getting on late into the afternoon. I asked Tracey if she would be worried about running through the night and she was ok with that so that was the plan. Still running on both engines, we set off at a slow but steady speed on to Dover.

As we approached Dover and in fading light, it became clear that the weather had not given up on us and the wind freshened back up, easily to a Force 6 south-easterly and the sea just got bigger and bigger. I was hoping that this was just because of it being a headland but as we punched through it we realised that this was not the case and after having this five ton boat launched into the air while only doing six knots and Tracey almost wearing our cold box and contents we patiently waited for the opportunity to turn around and run inside the safety and shelter of the Dover port. I know I should have had an Almanac but I didn't and we were then faced with the guesswork of trying to find a Marina. We ended up tailing a yacht and it paid off as he was going to one much to our relief.

We got a pontoon allocated to us for the night and as it was really starting to blow by now we really had made the right choice. In the morning it was a lovely sunny day but the wind was really going for it so I went to the marina office and asked for a mooring for a month as the following weekend we were going on holiday for two weeks. We ended up in a marina basin behind a single lock gate and had to wait for the tide to come up to enter it. We phoned our friend to come and pick us up and that's where Seawolf stayed for the next four weeks.

The Saturday after the first May Bank Holiday and all refreshed from our own holiday, we travelled back to Dover armed with a head gasket set and a few other bits to try and get our boat home to Ashlett. Tracey had to work that night so I was going to be doing this alone. I changed the head gasket on the port engine and run her up. It was still getting hot. I had the idea of removing the thermostat which was almost seized in the closed position. I decided I would rather have a cool engine than a cooked one after all. I was shocked to see that the state that the thermostat was in and decided it was definitely coming out!! Tracey stayed there with me as long as she could but had to leave in the end and I had to wait for the tide to get out of the marina. This was around 3pm. I got out of the marina and on both engines and set off again in a beautiful sunny calm afternoon. I cleared Dover breakwater into open sea and it really was lovely, the engine keeping cool and all running sweet; what could stop me now!!!! I spoke too soon as a bearing behind the Jabsco raw water pump gave way!!!!!

This was terminal for the port engine running this time. I had spare impellers but nothing that would fix this. Ok, so now I am having to do this trip on one engine.......

I patiently pushed on, into dusk and then the total dark. I had phone calls offering moral support and even found myself rehearsing my call to the Coastguard should I need to call them on the VHF. I kept the speed and revs down and listened for any change in the engine tone or anything that would get my attention but she kept on going and going. I had made my mind up that I would stop at Brighton marina to get a bit of a rest and got there around 3.30am. What a place to get in to!!! All I can say is thank goodness for GPS plotters. I had a couple of hours kip and went and paid for my brief stay over. The guy in the marina office informed me about the way the marina had silted up and said I wouldn't be able to get out until around 0900. I waited and had a walk about and got some food and drink for the next leg of my voyage. The charter fishing boats started exiting the marina at about 0830 so I thought if they could, so could I. After all, every second counted for me. I set off again.

The weather was once again really lovely with a light breeze and sunny. I pressed on and had no more issues. I phoned a mate who was on his boat in Ashlett as I was motoring past Hill Head and asked him what the tide was doing. He told me that the quay in the creek was under water and I thought I had a chance of making it into Ashlett after all. I phoned him again and he said it was still ok but we all know how fast the creek empties when the tide goes out. I approached the entrance to the creek and oops, not enough water! Thirty minutes; that's all I would have needed!!! I backed up and set off to the waiting buoy in the deep water at the southern end of the Esso marine terminal. Tracey called me up and asked me where I could pick her up so she could keep me company until the next high tide. I told her I would pick her up at the RNLI jetty at Calshot.......... my troubles weren't over!!!

I pulled up close to the jetty to prepare my manoeuvre. The wind had freshened and the tide was hammering out; yep, wind against tide and it was right where I was going. I had never seen it so rough in that area before. I pulled up to the jetty, starboard side on and put her into reverse to pull the stern in. Oh no...... I couldn't get her out of gear!!!!! On one engine and fighting the effects of the tide I was fighting a losing battle and the boat run stern first into the shingle and the slipway. I eventually got her into forward gear and had to punish the engine to get any steerage or response. I got away and came in for a second attempt from the other direction thinking it might have been a one off but just in case, at least I would have open water I could pull into. No, it wasn't a one off and she stuck in reverse again. I had to reverse in a quite choppy sea and tide up to one of the moorings off of the slipway to see if there was anything that could be done. Luckily I did it and although I moored up stern first it gave me a chance to sort this new issue out.

There was no way it was going to come out of gear so I took the good Jabsco water pump off of my good engine and put it on the problem engine that had a good gearbox. This took about half an hour and sorted my predicament out and enabled me to pick Tracey up. The engine behaved and we went up the river Hamble to get some fish 'n chips and a bit of a blood pressure reduction. I dropped Tracey back off at the RNLI jetty later on and had no more issues with anything else. I sat again at the waiting buoy for a couple more hours and once the tide was high enough, I came into Ashlett and moored up on our pontoon. It was now around 1 am.

I don't think I have ever been so tired in my life. It was a mixture of excitement, anxiety, worry and doubt but at the end of it all I came through and have a lovely old boat to show for it.

Thank you for taking the time to read this epic of Biblical proportion. I hope you found it helpful if you ever think about getting a boat from so far away. Oh.. and by the way, the boat would not come out of gear because the clamp that holds the outer cable in place came loose and allowed the whole lot to move; a really easy fix !!!

EIGHT WAVE

Tom Bettle

The Dangers of Bananas On-board

I'm not superstitious but...what is this thing about bananas and fishing boats? What a load of tosh!

I think it was our very own Roger Bayzand that first mentioned this ridiculous belief to me during a rather impromptu conversation on the quay in Alderney and briefly aboard *Sundance II* during a surreal meeting that involved Dave Lewis from *Sea Angler*, Roddy Hays and the late John Wilson.

I had taken Dave and John to Alderney to do a spot of small boat fishing and had gone with the view that John could get something for his book *Another Fishing Year* and Dave could get several features on one of three different small(ish) private boats and some fishing but the weather wasn't playing ball and we were stuck ashore for the day.

We all wandered from our B 'n B up in St Annes down to the harbour where we found this chap, Roddy Hays, loitering with intent and Roger Bayzand tidying *Sundance II*.

I'd heard of Rodd but couldn't remember why. Apparently he'd driven a boat or two and caught a couple of fish but was interested to see both Dave and John's eyes light up wide when they saw him and they all went scurrying off to look at his lure collection or some such.

Apparently he'd made a couple of lures after being a bit lucky on some Marlin once; who knows? He also had some plastic boat called *MacAttack* that he wanted to show Dave. That sounded more interesting. Either way, I lost the two for the day.

I was far more interested in the legendary Roger Bayzand who I'd never had the pleasure of meeting or fishing with but his ability and knowledge was very VERY known to me.

I needed help and I saw Roger as being my saving grace.

I had Dave Lewis and John Wilson with me and I had to show them how to 'fish' Alderney. I'd only ever been with Chris Caines in charge and now I was supposed to be the expert on my own boat. Oh Crap!

I struck up a conversation with Roger by commenting on how smart the boat looked or something similar, hoping I wouldn't be barked at for foolishly bringing my own boat across.

Roger immediately put the mop and bucket down and invited me down the ladder to look around *Sundance II* and welcomed me into the wheelhouse. I explained my predicament with Dave and John and Roger veritably took me under his wing pointing out several marks on his plotter and even scribbling a few numbers down along with some tips.

As a result of that chat with Roger, which I still believe is the one and only time we have met, I turned what could have been a tough trip and egg on my face into several articles in *Sea Angler* for Dave and a piece in John's new book plus some smiles, laughs and new friendships.

But this post is nothing to do with Alderney trips.

I think at some point during my conversation with Roger, and I really can't recall how, the issue with bananas on boats came up.

Perhaps the bad weather was being blamed on someone eating a banana, who knows. The point being apparently the superstition goes that bananas are very bad luck on an angling boat.

Now I hate the little yellow devil fruit with a vengeance but what utter rubbish! Who ever heard of such a thing!?

About three years later I found myself fishing with Captain Ezequiel Conde and his then mate, Marty Bates. I'd saved my pennies and was in Cape Verde for five days of Marlin fishing with good friends from the Sport Fishing Club of the British Isles.

I'd been warned not to expect too much. Marlin fishing was tough and if we saw, let alone caught one in our five days, we should consider ourselves very lucky.

We had a few lures with us from that bloke Roddy I mentioned earlier which by all accounts were quite good so we decided to drag those around for a while.

That week of fishing will stay with me for the rest of my life. The Marlin were found every day and absolutely everywhere. Strike after strike, release after release with fish from an estimated 250lb to a fish going 750lb taken by yours truly whilst demonstrating a most refined stand-up technique that looked like I was fishing for mid-Channel conger with a slipped disc.

We finished our week with 27 Atlantic blue marlin released and on one day we released a total of 15 fish which I am led to believe is rather good.

But on one day during our trip the bite was really hot, we experienced strike after strike but absolutely nothing was connecting. It was as if we weren't using hooks. We were on zero fish for 12 strikes at about lunchtime when one of my co-anglers opened his lunch box. In there was one of the *yellow perils* that had been discussed a few years previous in Alderney.

Jokingly, I shouted, "That's bad luck" and I tossed it overboard.

"THWACK, zinnnnnnnnnnnnnnnnnnnnnng" went the left rigger and Shimano reel together as the first marlin of the day was hooked and finally came to the boat.

We finished that day on four marlin for 16 strikes which was a truly great day afloat.

Bananas?? Surely not?

I became known for commenting about bananas over the coming seasons to the point that at one small boat fishing week in Weymouth held by members of the Online Forum *World Sea Fishing,* I found I was to be jokingly presented with a giant inflatable banana.

One of the guys had the disgusting effigy in the cuddy of his boat and reached in to get it, knocking himself clean out on the deckhead as he stood up prematurely.

Bananas?? Nahhh!

Out of Poole, some 25 miles out of the harbour lies a patch of ground affectionately known as the *Brittle Star Grounds*.

At certain times of the year these offshore banks can be stuffed full of brittle starfish which I guess visit in great numbers for a bit of starfish happy time. Who would have guessed that these skinny little starfish are a culinary delight for cod which have been known to mass on the banks in numbers that are a struggle to believe. This year was one of those years.

My mates and I had a enjoyed a few good trips out and so, as a salesman of the brand of boat I owned and never one to miss a publicity opportunity, I invited the one and only Henry Gilbey to join us for the "best day's cod fishing he would ever have."

Henry is an absolutely delightful chap and to my surprise he said yes, meeting us on a good tide a week or so later.

He bought his camera paraphernalia in a large bag but I hadn't realised that the bag also included one of those dreaded bent yellow fruit which I caught him munching on as we steamed out past Peveril Ledge.

Within a few minutes of dropping lines we were into fish. Dozens of fish, hundreds of fish. It really was the best day's cod fishing of any of our lives. Nothing big, the best was just over 10lb, but in 2 hours and 45 minutes we managed 245 cod between four anglers plus Henry having a go in-between pictures.

The vast majority went straight back but we all had plenty to take home too.

So what with the bananas?

I have (had) a favourite little rod. Made by Stan Massey of Alba Rods, it's a rod for playing silly buggers just for fun. Based around a five or six weight fly rod blank but ringed and with a reel seat for a fixed spool, this rod had always proved a giggle on some improbably good fish. I stupidly lent it to my fishing mate Chris to hope for some cod and on hooking a little one he decided to high stick it and 'BANG' my favourite little one piece was now a two piece still with a codling attached.

Bananas? I'm still not superstitious.

All was quiet on the 'nana front for some time.

The boat was running well and we'd had some great trips and that favourite rod had been replaced as a gift by a very good angling friend.

We were heading offshore on one of our regular trips as a small group of owners.
We were incidentally fishing the same general area as when we had Henry with us but this time we were fishing the wrecks.
Fishing was OK but not great and so the consensus was that we should point south and head another 12 miles or so just into the French side where we wanted to try some new marks.
After just a few moments there was a loud bang and the engines stalled. Opening the engine bay the smell of hot oil hit us followed by the sight of pools of oil in the bilge. Once again, twice in our boat's history, we were dead in the water so down went the anchor as we were sat only about 3/4 mile from the main West-bound shipping lane.
I picked up the VHF and gingerly called a 'Pan Pan'.
We were heard back at the marina office but with no other friends available to come and tow us in we were once again at the mercy of the wonderful boys and girls of the RNLI and their big orange boat, *Earnest & Mable*.
As the lifeboat drew near, friend and co-owner Malcolm started tucking into his sandwiches. They were followed by crisps, a yogurt and then, yes, you guessed it, a bloody banana!
Later the engineer's report discovered that we had hit something solid like a lump of wood or a pallet and this had jarred the propeller sufficiently whilst it was under full load. The usual fail safe would have been the shaft coupling giving way but instead our crankshaft had snapped clean in two caused, apparently, by a main bearing bolt never having been torqued up properly at the factory, working loose and sitting in the bottom of the sump giving just enough play in the crankshaft that it suffered fatigue which showed itself when it was instantly stopped under massive load.

Bananas? What is it actually about bananas?

You? Any superstitions or superstitious stories?

I'm not superstitious but...

Rich Rickman. *I'm with you in the bananas bad Ju Ju belief. Whilst fishing the Lymington Cod Open with George Phillips who arrived late we steamed out to the Shingles. After three hours fishing we had caught nothing. George opened his lunchbox and, yep, a banana ffs. I threw it overboard and 'boom' a 21lb cod was on immediately and he won the competition*

Roger Bayzand. *Nope I was never superstitious about bananas or anything else, in fact I regularly had one with my lunch. It supposedly started on sailing ships when on long passages carried fruit to stave off scurvy. Bananas as they ripen give off ethylene gas which speeds up the ripening of the other fruit causing it to prematurely spoil, with on a long passage would be considered bad luck.*

James Hands. *Great read Tom, I remember getting bellowed at by a skipper for taking bananas on board. It stuck with me and though not superstitious, I have become superstitious of bananas on board!*

Roddy Hays. *There are some very strange superstitions about - there's one from the NE, maybe Sunderland, which states that if one is to meet a pig wearing a clergyman's collar on the way to harbour, you should return home.*

Trevor Small

Boating is Not for Everyone

Ed. *Trevor is the skipper/owner of a fabulous dive charter boat out of Poole named Rocket. Trevor also does a few angling charters. Master of the Pun, Trevor's write-ups on his various trips are hysterical and there is no doubt that his wacky sense of humour finds an appreciative and returning audience. Again, one to see an opportunity, Trevor opened Uber Scuba this year to try and overcome some of the difficulties for his business through Covid-19. His idea worked extremely well and he has enjoyed a successful season with an entertaining variety of charters.*

I recall a two boat trip to Alderney accompanying fellow skipper John Bell and his vessel *Mia Jay*. John is a great friend whose interest in charter angling grew from crewing for Chris Tett. John was a great tutor and if the Olympics had a ' being thrifty' John would've easily won gold. Sometimes I would benefit from his customer overspill, especially when John advertised a trip to Alderney. Back then we both owned Bullet 38's, powered by 11ltr Scania lorry engines that we'd marinised in our back gardens.

My excitement about the trip was heightened by a fantastic forecast and some top secret information had been handed to John consisting of a wreck full of cod but which was halfway to France. It was marked PA (Position Approximate) on the chart so inevitably some searching was required. Roger Bayzand had been fishing this particular wreck and stories of his catches had filtered through to Poole. Every skipper will agree having paying guys aboard limits the time we can spend looking for new wrecks. Most anglers just want fish in the box. But on this particular day the fishing was easy, so the lads agreed to go looking for something a bit special. Well, unfortunately the information proved poor quality and the wrecks position remained a mystery that day. We decided to ice what we'd caught and head
for Alderney.

On scanning the horizon I spotted a boat drifting. I remember looking at the chart thinking PA on the chart and he's in the parish. I will do a flypast and see what's occurring. As we closed in on the vessel, it remained drifting. Surely if this boat had found good fishing he would have long gone. The strange thing was I couldn't see anyone aboard. We shouted over and sounded the horn but nobody acknowledged. This was a true Mary Celeste. It was flat calm and sunny so I decided to come alongside her. Peering through the window I could see a lady sat in the wheelhouse.

"Are you ok?" I asked.

"Not really; we've got something around our propeller," she replied.

At this point I stepped aboard their boat. Firstly I noticed how tender the boat was with water covering the deck and halfway up the engine box. I looked around and could not believe what I saw. A big fella stood up soaking wet with blood running down both arms. I remember thinking, "Oh sh*t. What have I got myself into here?"

It turned out to be husband and wife aboard their own boat, a beautiful Aquastar 28 from Poole named *Locking Bar*. They were on passage to Cherbourg when their prop picked up a nasty length of trawl warp. The gentleman man explained that only weeks before this trip, the boatyard had fitted a prop inspection tube to assist in such a scenario. The problem came when this poor chap didn't have anything aboard sharp enough to cut the butter and sadly not as sharp as his wife's tongue. The boat builder hadn't gelled the inside of the tube but instead left it in bare grp. The strands of glass had cut his arms to ribbons and sea water was gushing up the tube and onto the deck. His wife had divorced him 25 times in as many hours and was now languishing in denial of the bilge pumps.

Anyway the warp was thick but not a challenge for my bread saw. Soon clear and off we went on our separate ways. Fast forward 20 years and I'm stood in *Pavers Shoe Shop* on Poole Quay waiting to be served. There was an old couple in front of me buying half the shop, so the shop assistant leans over and says sorry for the delay this won't take long

I said, "That's fine".

With that the husband and wife turn round and both said, " Ahhh, Trevor."
I asked, "Do you still have your boat?"
The gentleman firstly looked at his wife then replied, "No. We decided to sell our boat as soon as we returned to Poole".

Boating is not for everyone I suppose.

Ed.   So...they would have sunk if you hadn't gone alongside?

Trevor Small. *Not too sure how things would have developed. They had been adrift for a while because the wife mentioned a large ship passing them and as she explained she looked up. I got the impression the ship was very big and very close.*

Ed Taylor.   *Great story Trev, it must be the first time I've seen you write something without a pun in it.*

Chris Ponsford. *Terrific story. You certainly saved their bacon .They were very lucky you turned up!*

Tall Tale 2
Heroes

I would like to pay tribute to the wonderful characters that have shared their hard fought climb to the pinnacle of their profession. Coming from a fishing family, I grew up not following footballers or pop stars but the local fishermen with salt water in their veins. My bedroom walls were adorned with posters from *Angling Times* not *Smash Hits*. My reading started and ended with fishing papers and magazines. I spent hour upon hour reading articles written by legends like Geordie Dickson and Trevor Housby.

Over the years I've been lucky enough to meet many of my heroes. Of course Geordie of *Artilleryman* fame, Paul , Pat, Chris and Tetty from Weymouth plus Anton Proctor and Roger Bayzand from Lymington. You are all role models that following generations of skippers admire and look up to. Maintain the great work and keep the memories coming.

Comments:
Roger Bayzand.   *Well that is very nice to hear, Trevor. Geordie and Ted Cooke were the people who got me interested in wrecking and long range trips. I never got to fish with Geordie but had a few really good trips with Ted. Anton was the first one to go wrecking in our area (one of the few with Decca) and proved the fish were there. The Weymouth skippers have been really good mates over the years, as we met up in Alderney on many occasions.*

Ed: *We pulled into Guernsey and moored up. Geordie Dickson arrived much later and was trying to find somewhere to tie up for the night. Having spent years in silent admiration of the Great Man, I was nervous about inviting him to moor alongside us. As he did so, I noticed he did not have a crewman aboard so I sent my crewman, the infamous Troy, to board* Artillery Man *and give it a scrub down whilst I got the kettle on.*
Geordie looked at the pair of us and growled, "What do you two want?"

"Nothing," I replied. "Tea or Coffee?"

Geordie looked at us both with growing suspicion.

After his boat was scrubbed and he'd had a cuppa or two, Troy and I decided it was time to head into St Peter Port and purchased some Fish 'n Chips. I asked Geordie if he'd like us to get him some.

Geordie gave us an intensely interrogative stare. "What DO you two buggers want?"

"Nothing, Sir," says I as Troy and I cleared off for the evening.

Next morning as we struggled out of our comfy bunks, Geordie was already up and ready to leave. He told me to, "Come aboard".

"You two really don't want anything, do you?" he asked in a manner that indicated both surprise and genuine amusement.

"No," says I.

Geordie handed me a piece of paper with a handwritten list of 'unknown' wrecks to the west and northwest of Guernsey he used.

"Well," said my Hero, "Take this. But don't you dare tell anyone I gave you it. I have my reputation to consider!"

A great man, indeed. A man with a fearsome reputation but with a generosity towards those that he felt might deserve it.

"I promise I won't tell anyone," says I.....now declaring it to the world some 35 years later!!!

Zac Cairns

2020 Shark Encounter

Ed. *Zac Cairns is the talented skipper of Hayling Island based charter boat Valkyrie 6. As the son of the very well known Glen Cairns, Zac has grown up on boats and already has many Cross Channel and Commercial Charters to his credit. Like his fellow 'young' skippers further west, Zac has been finding a few sharks in the IOW area.*

We experienced an unforgettable day yesterday anchored up on some deep banks. It was a little bit quiet with a few tope coming to the boat but then, without any warning at all, customer Geoff Marfell from West London's reel starts screaming off. This was a big fish and it was moving fast. There was no way we were going to stop it in the tide. I called for 'lines up' and pulled the anchor. Now we were ready, I span the boat. Jeff followed his line round to the bow and we were gaining line and catching up with the fish. I positioned the boat so that Jeff could get back on the stern.

After all of this I'm convinced we've got a good hook hold and a realistic chance at landing this fish. The fight was on! Geoff's 20/30lb class rod was bent over double and pulling him all round the boat it. Then it went slack. It was swimming up and Geoff was winding like mad trying to catch up. Before we knew it, the fish was there on the surface...and it's a thresher shark. I couldn't believe it! She was swimming around the boat taking Jeff with her and with a flick of the tail back to the bottom she dived. This repeated itself a couple of times with big powerful runs.

Geoff was exhausted and so too was the fish. Everyone was very excited. I mean, why wouldn't they be? We were just about to land a thresher shark! The fight was almost over and she was coming up for the last time, gracefully swimming side to side just under the boat. After 45 heart stopping minutes there she was laying alongside. Colin and I gently landed her through the side door and then got some water running through the gills to keep her oxygenated. Without a moment to rest, Geoff was called in for photo's so we could get this magnificent fish back into the water as soon as possible. After few pictures were taken, we released her through the side door. She rested alongside for a few seconds then shot off.

Massive congratulations to Geoff for landing this fish of a life time which we estimated around 100lb.

Well Done, that man!

Editor......**And Well Done to All of You for your Sea-dog Tall Tales Contributions**…..

Printed in Great Britain
by Amazon